# The Citizen Audience

In *The Citizen Audience,* Richard Butsch explores the cultural and political history of audiences in the United States from the nineteenth century to the present. He demonstrates that, while attitudes toward audiences have shifted over time, Americans have always judged audiences against standards of good citizenship.

From descriptions of tightly packed crowds in early American theaters to the contemporary reports of distant, anonymous internet audiences, Butsch examines how audiences were represented in contemporary discourse. He explores a broad range of sources on theater, movies, propaganda, advertising, broadcast journalism, and much more. Butsch discovers that audiences were characterized according to three recurrent motifs: as crowds and as isolated individuals in a mass, both of which were considered bad, and as publics which were considered ideal audiences. These images were based on and reinforced class and other social hierarchies. At times though, subordinate groups challenged their negative characterization in these images, and countered with their own interpretations.

A remarkable work of cultural criticism and media history, this book is essential reading for anyone seeking an historical understanding of how audiences, media and entertainment function in the American cultural and political imagination.

**Richard Butsch** is Professor of Sociology, American Studies, and Film and Media Studies at Rider University. His *Making of American Audiences* (2000) was awarded the International Communication Association Best Book Award and the American Culture Association Cawelti Book Prize.

# The Citizen Audience

## Crowds, Publics, and Individuals

Richard Butsch

NEW YORK AND LONDON

First published 2008
by Routledge
270 Madison Ave, New York, NY 10016

Simultaneously published in the UK
by Routledge
2 Park Square, Milton Park, Abingdon, Oxon OX14 4RN

*Routledge is an imprint of the Taylor & Francis Group, an informa business*



Typeset in Perpetua and Gill Sans by
Keystroke, 28 High Street, Tettenhall, Wolverhampton
Printed and bound in the United States of America on acid-free paper by
Walsworth Publishing Company, Marceline, MO



*Library of Congress Cataloging in Publication Data*
Butsch, Richard, 1943–
The citizen audience : crowds, publics, and individuals / Richard Butsch.
p. cm.
Includes bibliographical references and index.
ISBN 978-0-415-97789-0 (hardback) – ISBN 978-0-415-94258-4 (pbk.)
1. Mass media–United States–Audiences. I. Title.
P96.A832U63 2008
302.3′3–dc22 2007028257

ISBN10: 0–415–97789–4 (hbk)
ISBN10: 0–415–97790–8 (pbk)
ISBN10: 0–203–92903–9 (ebk)

ISBN13: 978–0–415–97789–0 (hbk)
ISBN13: 978–0–415–97790–6 (pbk)
ISBN13: 978–0–203–92903–2 (ebk)

For Noah

# Contents

# Acknowledgments

No scholar is an island, entire unto himself. Each of us depends upon generous colleagues. I am most grateful to others from whom I have learned a great deal and who have stimulated my own thinking immensely, often without their knowing; and for the generosity of friends who have taken time to listen to and read my thoughts as I struggled toward the makings of a book. Among the numerous others to whom I owe a debt, I especially wish to thank Martin Barker, Kathryn Fuller, Lee Grieveson, Michele Hilmes, Alison Kibler, Anna McCarthy, Bruce McConachie, Virginia Nightingale, Peter Lunt, and Ellen Wartella. I also wish to acknowledge the support from Rider University in the form of leaves and fellowships, and of the Rider library staff, especially Diane Hunter, Mary Ellen Eckman, and Rose Hilgar. Ava Baron has carefully read multiple drafts of chapters and, as always, has been an incredible font of ideas and invaluable criticism. Whatever richness this book holds is, in large part, due to her.

# Introduction

## The politics of audiences in America

Americans spend a remarkable amount of time as audiences: adults spent over nine hours per day using media in 2004, more than half of all waking hours; and this does not include unmediated live performances and spectator sports, let alone church and school where people act largely as audiences.[1] It is important therefore what is said about these audiences. Today, as in the past, people have been criticized for how they play their role as entertainment audiences. Audiences have been depicted variously as good or bad, threatening public order or politically disengaged, cultivated or cultural dupes, ideal citizens or pathological, and so on. This book seeks to make sense out of the profusion of representations of audiences in the historical record and the political implications of those representations.

We have talked a lot about audiences. This talk most often has occurred when others considered them problematic. To governing classes, audiences, especially of people of subordinate status, often have been a subject of concern and objects of regulation. Before the spread of mass-mediated entertainment in the twentieth century, audiences of live entertainment were the most common large gatherings of persons, aside from church-going and the street. Entertainment venues were unlike churches, where they were under the secure control of a reputable leader, and more like the streets where they were less controlled or predictable. Depicted as volatile crowds and a danger to social order, audiences became targets of government discipline. More recently, the spread of radio, television, and other home media expanded considerably the size of audiences and the time spent as audiences, and this development alarmed many and generated much discussion. In this instance, audiences were seen as a mass of isolated individuals who were vulnerable to manipulation or distracted from their responsibilities as citizens. The preferred audience to both crowds and isolated individuals was a public, people who used their leisure responsibly to fulfill their civic duties.

Audiences have long been conceived as crowds, publics or mass, even before these terms were specifically used to describe them. I do not mean that audiences have always and only been depicted in these terms, but that these are recurring themes. I use these terms as metaphors capturing the imagery of audiences of the times, to show how we talked about audiences as if they were politically significant actors. Representations of bad audiences, while not directly invoking the language of citizenship, use characterizations that are opposites to those of good citizens.

Since the emergence of commercial entertainment in late sixteenth-century England, government officials reacted to audiences at live entertainments as crowds that were incipient mobs and threats to social order. Interrupting this tendency to depict audiences as problems were occasional highly political periods when a counter-discourse gained ascendancy, and self-consciously political theater or media defined audiences, or audiences defined themselves, as political actors in a public sphere. More often, however, the image of publics has been associated with news media and distinguished from entertainment audiences, which have been characterized as bad citizens for not using their time to inform themselves. Entertainment audiences have also been contrasted to arts audiences, and chastised for not cultivating themselves, a pre-requisite to preparing oneself for citizenship, especially in older conceptions of the good citizen. Thus there has been a second criticism of entertainment audiences as lackluster citizens who fail to cultivate and inform themselves. The concept of mass—as distinct from "masses," which I will discuss later—is a term of the twentieth century, when social critics gradually but increasingly became less concerned with crowds and more with an inert mass and isolated individuals. By mid-century, television arrived when there was already a heightened concern about the isolating effects of media, stunting individual development, distracting adults from their responsibilities and brainwashing both adults and children, threatening civilization and democracy. These images reflect concerns by governments or by some citizens who petition government to rein in audiences as crowds, or to protect and arouse them as vulnerable, passive members of the mass; or alternately to applaud and encourage them as publics. They advocate regulation to realize the good possibilities, while preventing the bad aspects of audience practices.[2]

The images were always evaluative and normative, and the standard of evaluation was the conscientious, cultivated, and informed citizen. Crowds were bad citizens; mass and isolated individuals were weak and vulnerable citizens; publics were good citizens. Moreover, the evaluation was class-based and reinforced class and other social hierarchies.[3] To behave as a crowd or mass was an expression of lower or working-class culture and poor citizenship; to behave as a public was an expression of bourgeois or upper-middle-class culture and good citizenship.

## Whose discourse?

Both participants and observers have depicted audiences. Participants have always represented themselves through their performances as audiences. The noun "audiences" makes it appear—and often makes us think—that audience is an identity that people carry into every situation and interaction. But audience is a situated role that people temporarily perform, and in their performance people produce representations of audiences.[4] Also, the role is situated in institutions of entertainment, news, and media that construct subject positions for audiences and, in so doing, represent audiences. Governments, moral entrepreneurs, and others outside this relationship too have represented audiences through their discourse and response to audiences.

At times, I will discuss how audiences have constructed themselves, mostly to indicate the presence and influence of counter-discourses. These representations often are alternative definitions of appropriate citizen behavior that dispute dominant discourses that characterize them as ill-mannered or ill-informed, failed citizens. Alternative discourses, however, expressed as they were through ephemeral enactments, seldom took the form of enduring records available directly to historical researchers. The record of self-representations by subordinate peoples was mostly compiled by and filtered through bystanders.[5]

This study focuses mostly on representations of audiences as "other," that refer to audiences as "they" rather than "we," arising as entertainment, news and media productions construct their audiences, and as discourses originating outside production characterize and critique the audiences produced. The historical sources I have used are durable excerpts from mass media—primarily print media. These record mostly the dominant discourses that exercised more influence upon institutional action toward audiences. By this I mean discourses that are what literary critic Mikhail Bakhtin called "authoritative" and what social theorist Michel Foucault conceived as knowledge/power. Such discourse is dominant in the sense that it is backed by the power of the largest institutions of the society. Part of this power comes from the reach of the speaker; and part comes from the acceptance of the voices, their cultural authority, their political legitimacy. Dominant discourses appear in media with greater amplification power, and echo in the offices of government and other organizations with the power to regulate and shape audiences.

Dominant representations of audiences in the nineteenth and twentieth centuries were bourgeois, made by flaneurs who had the time to observe and to write and publish; by gatekeepers such as journalists, critics and commentators, academic researchers and intellectuals, educational and health professionals who wrote about the worth of things such as entertainment, media and audiences; by theater and media owners and managers who set the rules of engagement and marketing for audiences; and by government officials who held hearings and established regulations. Given that this study focuses on dominant bourgeois discourse, it should come as no surprise that such discourse contained a hierarchical message, praising some statuses and debasing others. The discourses tended to equate good audiences with the middle and upper classes, Euro-Americans and males; bad audiences typically were identified with the working and lower classes, women and subordinate races.[6]

## Citizen

Discourses on audiences can be understood as judgments of fitness for citizenship.[7] Representing audiences as publics draws explicitly on this idea of responsibilities of citizenship. Representing audiences as crowds and as isolated individuals paints pictures of audience attributes that are diametrically opposite to those prescribed for citizens. What pervades these discourses on audiences is a citizenship in the sense of civic republicanism in which people are expected to have rights as citizens and a duty to participate actively in their own governance. This was a citizenship with characteristics that were defined as decidedly masculine, white, and bourgeois.[8]

Within this sort of citizenship, scholars distinguish between ancient Greek and Roman concepts of citizenship in which civic virtue is central and a modern liberal concept in which civil rights are central. Inherent in the ancient concept is an idea that only a select group who has the capacity for civic virtue can act as citizens. Aristotle considered citizenship to be the means through which men attain their full civilized potential. Civic virtue required a strong moral character and the time, ability, and commitment to devote to the community interest. Such a citizen could set aside self-interest and act in the interest of the whole.[9] This concept of citizenship as a privilege for a select group of qualified individuals was revived in modern times. A select few, the propertied classes, were presumed to have the independence and the will to pursue knowledge and the character to transcend their narrow self-interest for the sake of the common good.

Countervailing this exclusive citizenship was the liberalism that arose in eighteenth- and nineteenth-century Europe. Reason and individualism defined its ideal relations of people in public spaces and of people to the state. John Locke argued for a social contract *among men* as the basis of government, in place of fealty between king and subject, implying equal and universal rights and allowing independent individuals to pursue their own interests, so long as they did not infringe on others. John Stuart Mill's nineteenth-century liberalism continued the premise of universal natural rights that led logically to universal suffrage.[10]

Liberalism in practice, however, incorporated the older idea of citizenship as a privilege of the qualified. Locke argued for citizenry restricted to a propertied class; Mill worried about the civic virtue of the mass. For Mill in the 1860s, citizenship was "the grand cultivator of mankind." He believed that, more than self-interest or natural right, citizenship was about self-improvement as a patriotic endeavor. Instead of differentiating people in terms of inherent character, liberalism emphasized achievement of knowledge and culture by self-improvement as the qualification for citizens. But Mill believed that not all individuals were capable of sufficient cultivation; one had to be educated and civilized. He favored educational and property criteria for suffrage.[11] Advocates of liberalism were not different than many of their peers of the time in differentiating among citizens, whether by nature or nurture, as to their capability to fulfill the duties of citizenship. They argued that property signified a commitment to the community and a level of cultivation and education necessary to sound civic decision making. Women, subordinate races and classes, and children were defined as inferior in rationality and therefore excluded from certain rights.[12]

The history of American citizenship incorporates both the ancient republican and modern liberal traditions.[13] Sociologist Michael Schudson's sequence of four citizenship eras is a convenient framework for organizing this brief discussion. During the Revolution, Americans adopted the ideas that men are equal in natural rights and that governments served these men and their rights. The American Declaration of Independence stated it boldly that governments derive "their just powers from the consent of the governed." A decade later, during the debate over the new Constitution, Federalist James Madison repeated almost the identical words, "[government] derives all its powers directly or indirectly from the body of the people." They placed at the center of their argument the "self-evident" fact of the natural rights of all men to "life, liberty and the pursuit of happiness," rejecting the hierarchical relation of king and subject, and shifting the ground of citizenship from privilege to rights. Historian Joyce Appleby characterized liberalism as unexamined assumptions that were so embedded in the culture that they seemed simply reality. The core of this liberalism was rational self-interest enacted through free choice, free inquiry, and freedom of religion.[14]

However, on the issue of who qualified for citizenship, the American founders adopted the ancient republican belief in a citizenship of civic virtue, restricted to those whose property and economic self-reliance assured they were free from coercion and understood and promoted the public interest. Property also freed one from labor and allowed time necessary to develop knowledge and cultivation.

These were the foundation of the culture of deference. They excluded artisans and laborers who had little or no property and depended upon laboring, and slaves, servants, wives and children who were subservient to their masters, husbands, and fathers.[15] This active, virtuous citizenship, a republicanism based in ancient notions of civic virtue but including modern liberalism, was the first definition of citizenship at the beginning of the new nation. While elites naturally favored this definition, common folk did as well, to the degree that they had to defer to gentlemen upon whom they depended as patrons for their livelihood.[16]

But the Revolution also stirred beliefs that (at least white male) common folk were in ways equals to gentlefolk, the culture of deference began to fade, and a new "democratic moment" emerged in the Jacksonian era. At the same time, artisans were becoming proletarianized and class differences sharpened. This new proletariat believed that their interests were not those of the gentlemen of virtue, but were conflicting interests, and that people should form parties to compete with others to advance their interests. This partisan citizenship rejected the idea that only gentlemen possessed the civic virtue for full citizenship, relabeling gentle leisure as idleness and professing that it was labor that was virtuous. States lowered the requirements of property and added as alternative qualifiers taxpaying, military service, labor on public projects, or simply residency, broadening the electorate to include almost all white males. The grassroots influence of political parties would remain politically potent, although changed by Progressivism, into the 1960s.[17]

Schudson's third era of informed citizenship, that encompasses most of the history of this book, might be thought of as the era of the middle class. With the growth of enterprises owned by capitalist investors, opportunities for clerks to found their own businesses narrowed. A new class of accounting and supervising employees and of retainers to such companies grew into a new *middle* class. Through the nineteenth century they increasingly distanced themselves from the working class and then from the rapacious reputation of the new industrial upper class. They rejected the proletarian spectacle of political parties; their ideal of the informed citizen was one who educated himself, deliberated on the issues of the day, and voted individually and privately. In practice, much of this deliberation took place through local private associations of peers, such as the fraternal organizations popular in this era.[18]

Progressive and philosopher John Dewey defined the informed citizen as a category that included people's relationship to the state and governance as well as membership in the community governed by that state, be it a village, city or nation. This accent on community replaced the earlier emphasis on privacy with a new emphasis on citizens as members of publics. Dewey conceived citizens acting cooperatively and in concert to solve community problems and establish public institutions (such as schools) as remedies, charging governments to sustain them. His citizens did not simply pursue their private interests (as consumers, property owners, investors, parents), but were cognizant of their community membership and civic obligations, as Mill imagined. This ideal of the informed citizen remained dominant through the mid-twentieth century, continuing to be influential through the 1970s when the media infrastructure that regularly paid it homage through the voices of professional journalism, began to transform.[19]

Beyond republicanism and liberalism is a broader, cultural sense of citizenship that extends and underlies specifically political citizenship. The good citizen was conceived as an exemplar of his national culture. A citizen in this sense not only performed his civic duty, but exemplified the central values, beliefs and norms of the dominant culture. In the United States, the good citizen represented what it meant to be an American. This included much more than political values and civic virtue narrowly construed; at times, it included civic virtue, cultivation, respectability, and other cultural standards that tended to be those of the middle class.

Cultural citizenship was exclusionary. As political scientist Rogers Smith phrased it, through most of American history lawmakers drew the boundaries of citizenship in terms of "illiberal and undemocratic racial, ethnic and gender hierarchies," based upon simple beliefs in essential differences rather than the universal rights of liberalism. Throughout these citizenship eras, many groups were excluded from citizenship for their ascribed qualities: Native Americans were excluded as "savages," lacking the basic prerequisite of civilization; free African Americans lost their legal right to vote in 1857, regained it during Reconstruction, lost it again in the Jim Crow era, and regained it again only in 1965. All European Americans were citizens if born in a U.S. territory; and they were admitted freely as immigrants with rights to seek citizenship until national quotas were introduced in 1924. Wives lost their independent citizenship in 1855, and from 1907 to 1931 American women who married foreigners could lose their citizenship. The egalitarianism of the liberal tradition was confined mostly to white men, and was, as Smith explained, "surrounded by an array of fixed ascriptive hierarchies" that excluded groups subordinate to them. This attitude of advocating informed citizenship while holding reservations about the inclusion of some groups is well illustrated by a Progressive, John Wheelwright, arguing in 1889 for the Americanization of immigrants as informed citizens, but noting "the problem here is complicated by the presence of the African race [and] the Chinaman," both of whom he wished to exclude. These distinctions reveal that citizenship consistently has been limited by race, class, and gender; and we will see that the same distinctions attended the application of citizenship standards to audiences. Schudson proposes a most recent form of citizenship that emphasizes civil rights and the dismantling of these citizenship hierarchies, which gained ascendancy in the 1960s, but this postdates the period covered by this study.[20]

Smith emphasized the simultaneity rather than sequencing of these different types of citizenship, delineating a history in which liberal, republican, and ascriptive ideologies co-existed and competed, even though one type may predominate in any given era, as the result of political contests and compromises rather than a steady progression.[21] According to Smith, "by 1912 all the main reformulations of American civic ideologies that would compete in the rest of the twentieth century were already visible."[22] It is the definition of informed citizenship, with its ideal of including all but distinguishing between ideal and inadequate citizens, that often inspired media criticism and the shaping of the Citizen Audience.

Criticisms of audiences and of media implicitly represent audiences as citizens or presumptive citizens whose experience as audiences could or should prepare them to better perform their citizenship. When critics described audiences failing in this civic duty, whether as the fault of media institutions, technology, or audience members themselves, media and audiences have been condemned. Crowd psychology condemned audiences because they allegedly acted irrationally or in an uncultivated manner, when rational deliberation and cultivation were presumed fundamental to informed citizenship. When reformers worried about immigrant nickelodeon audiences, they were defining the audiences as presumptive citizens, and the movies as having a duty to Americanize them. When critics lambasted television for aesthetic degradation of the populace or impairing the education of children by displacing reading and other healthier activities, they were presuming a civic role of television and of its audiences.

Audiences were differentiated not only in terms of their performance of citizenship, but also in term of their status. Audiences of subordinate groups were unsatisfactory citizens. This confirmed and reinforced the hierarchies of citizenship, differentiating propertied white males from subordinate groups, a parallel between discourses on audiences and on citizenship, as Smith has shown, with the addition of class to his argument. This discursive subordination buttressed an in-egalitarian system.[23]

## Crowd

Audiences are one example of temporary gatherings. Sociologist Herbert Blumer defined three terms to triangulate and distinguish people in such settings: crowds, publics, and mass. The relation of audiences to these concepts may at first appear obscure, but actually is quite intimate. On the one hand, audiences have long been characterized in these terms. On the other hand, one aspect of defining the nature and operations of these categories of gatherings has been to conceive them as audiences.

Sociologically, crowds are defined as gatherings of people physically together and sharing a common activity. They are contrasted to a mass that is a dispersed population. Both of these are distinguished from publics that exhibit a dimension of debate or discussion absent in a crowd or mass. Conventional crowds are those that have been sponsored and orchestrated by established organizations. Their behavior is routinized. Other gatherings, however, occur outside the bounds of established conventions, and tend to be seen as a danger to the social order. Through history the sensitivity of authorities to the danger of conventional crowds becoming unconventional ones has varied.[24] Audiences are an example of conventional crowds who become problematic when they overstep the bounds and challenge authority. It is concern about these unconventional crowds that has generated fear as well as explanations of how this happens. These explanations have tended to presume that crowds are homogenous and monolithic, irrational and violent, and composed primarily of people of low social status and little education.

Etymologically, today "crowd" is a relatively neutral term, implying nothing more than the ubiquitous aggregations of miscellaneous people in public spaces; "mob," an active crowd not under secure control by authorities and disrupting social order, is seldom used. Crowds and the common people had been synonymous in the minds of elites as far back as ancient Rome. In England, at least as early as the Elizabethan era, crowds in urban settings, while not feared and suppressed, were nevertheless the subject of official concern and even surveillance, as a source of disorder and violence. "Mob" appeared in English in the seventeenth century after the Restoration as an abbreviation of *mobile vulgus*, or "fickle populace," the lower orders of society presumed to be mercurial about whom and what they favored. In the nineteenth century, crowd and mob were commonly linked in print, both suggestive of violence. The fear was based on the presumption that the crowd was composed of lower-class people who were believed to have little invested in the established order and little to lose in disrupting that order.[25]

Elite ideas of crowds have undergone two major shifts over the past two centuries. Authorities of the seventeenth and eighteenth centuries were more tolerant of what we would call riots than would be accepted in the late nineteenth or twentieth centuries in the United States. Elites tolerated crowds as nuisances necessary for defusing discontent, as long as they did not threaten existing class relations or genteel property and privileges. Scholars have documented two types of crowd action, riots and carnival. Several prominent historians demonstrated that when lower sorts in England and elsewhere from the early modern period into the beginnings of industrialization resorted to protests and riots, these actions were not irrational, nor spontaneous, nor violent against persons; more often they were planned to right what was perceived as a detrimental change in traditional arrangements, evidenced a grievance, a culprit and a goal, and directed violence against property more than persons. Crowds exercised what British historian Edward P. Thompson called a moral economy, the right of lower sorts to enforce traditional terms of exchange and mutual obligation. For common folk, as subjects without the rights and obligations of citizenship, crowd action was their only avenue of political expression, a means to gain attention of the crown and his officials whose obligation it was to right injustices, as measured by custom. At the same time, elites and authorities recognized such rights, as long as these actions remained within traditional bounds.[26]

Crowds also were part of the long-standing tradition of carnival. Across early modern Europe carnival was integral to the liturgical calendar through the winter after Christmas, culminating the week before Lent as a festival before the fast. In England, carnival encompassed a wide range of rituals and ceremonies that punctuated the year. The ruling principle of carnival was disorder, a "world turned upside down." Drunkenness and sexual promiscuity were more tolerated. Commoners dressed as kings, men as women. Inferiors were allowed to mimic and show disrespect of their superiors. Commoners even might use this opportunity to exercise a moral economy and chastise their superiors who they believed had violated custom or morals over the past year.[27]

Protests as well as festive crowds of these times were constrained by familiarity. In small, rooted communities, everyone knew who was behind the mask and who did what during carnival. People could be held accountable because others knew them. Disorder was more likely to be within the bounds of traditional acceptance, even if that boundary allowed a good deal by modern standards.[28]

This constraint would weaken as cities grew, leading to greater concern about crowds that were now larger and more anonymous. In the nineteenth century, crowds came to be defined in more negative terms, politically, socially, and aesthetically. Crowds continued to be equated with lower classes. But such classes now were seen as unconstrained and dangerous. The crowd was redefined as a fearful mob, an irrational and destructive beast, spurred by emotion and reckless in its actions. A major turning point was the French Revolution, when Edmund Burke in England decried the *sans culottes* in the streets. Through the nineteenth century, according to historian Robert Nye, there remained strong sentiments among the educated of France against the crowds of the Revolution. These ideas percolated through the nineteenth century, appearing in such popular science as

Charles McKay's 1841 book, *Popular Delusions*, becoming the basis for a new field of crowd psychology toward the end of the century.[29]

This new, scientistic rendering of crowds received its most widely read expression in Gustave Le Bon's 1895 book, *The Crowd*. Le Bon conceived crowds as people who had lost their individuality, reason and will—and he conceived audiences as types of crowd. According to him, witnessing an event or listening to a speaker amidst a crowd, people become caught up in the crowd emotions and act with one mind. Clearly, crowds were antithetical to ideas of rational and independent citizenship. This concept of the irrational crowd driven by a crowd mind, predominated through the nineteenth century, and continued to be important, even in the social sciences, for much of the twentieth century. Robert Park, a central figure in shaping American sociology, wrote that the effect of crowds "is always more or less disruptive and revolutionary," casting them as a danger to social order.[30]

Crowd psychology also incorporated racial theory, claiming that some groups were inherently more susceptible to this crowd phenomenon. When individuals in crowds lost their reason they acted according to a racial "soul," baring the "sentiments" of the race of the nation. Implicit in this formulation was the conception of individuals in a crowd driven by racial instincts, that is, lower mental faculties, and their relation to the crowd as a common race or "tribe." Those perceived to be more primitive and less mentally developed would be more likely to participate in a crowd. Le Bon described a hierarchy with lower classes, women, and certain races and nationalities as more primitive and more likely to make up the bulk of crowds. Le Bon and others who advocated crowd psychology expressed the concern that the responsibilities of citizenship should be restricted to groups less susceptible to crowds, another example of what Rogers Smith called ascriptive citizenship.[31]

## Public

Sociologists have long defined publics as the categorical opposite of crowds, diffuse rather than assembled. Political theories have characterized publics as discussion rather than action-oriented, deliberative rather than impulsive, rational rather than emotional.[32] It is a term with many meanings, etymologically and conceptually. Political theorist Jeffrey Weintraub identifies four distinct usages of the term: public as in the political sphere; public in the economic sense of state ownership versus private ownership, public as sociability and as public space where it may occur, and public as contrasted to the private domestic sphere of family. The first sense of public is the primary focus here, the idea of publics, public opinion, public sphere and their relation to the state. The second plays a part in the story insofar as media and entertainments are products and enterprises of private corporations who influence the representations of audiences. The third is intertwined with the concept of community and its opposite, with public places as sites of community, the mass and the consequences for forming political publics. The last is part of the story insofar as middle-class withdrawal or confinement to the domestic sphere has been implicated in the vitality of publics and the exclusions of women from publics.[33]

Publics in the political sense have been conceptualized as bound up with media. Unlike crowds, publics are dispersed and therefore necessitate means of communication. In one of the first formulations of the concept at the turn of the twentieth century, French theorist Gabriel Tarde linked publics to newspapers. More than a half century later, projecting his concept of public sphere onto eighteenth-century London and Paris, Jurgen Habermas also described print media playing an important role in the conversation of public houses and other public places.[34] The second characteristic feature of publics in both Tarde's and Habermas' concepts, was conversation. This reflects the consistent conceptualizing of publics in terms of discussion and the conceptual neglect of its relation to action. Indeed, most theorists have discussed public discussion as leading to "public opinion," not public action, with the presumption that elected officials of a democratic state would be influenced by opinion.

Tarde said that his was the era of the public, not the era of the crowd, as Le Bon had claimed. He argued that crowds are monolithic since one can be part of only one crowd at a time, since we can be in only one place at a time; while publics, being dispersed, are not monolithic, since one can simultaneously participate in several publics, thus acting as counterweights to each other so that, participating in each, we are likely to be more tolerant of all. The implication was that publics would therefore be less bound by emotional attachment to the group, its members more independent and individual, discussion more rational and deliberative, more civilized and tolerant than crowds. In each aspect of his definition he mentioned reasoned thought, in contrast to Le Bon's impulsive, emotional crowd.[35]

Tarde argued that dispersed publics required coordination through some means of common communication. His choice of newspapers as the medium of publics reflects the fundamental conception of publics as concerned with politics and with the state. At the time, newspapers provided the common object of attention equivalent to that providing coherence for a crowd. Between 1869 and 1912 in Paris the number of newspapers per person rose dramatically. Witnessing people's reactions to reading the papers during the Dreyfus affair, Tarde observed the public become a unit not through assembly and suggestion as crowds were believed to, but through simultaneously reading the news and discussing it. By defining newspapers as a necessary pre-condition for a public, he effectively defined publics as audiences. An audience of readers, however, was considered rational, in contrast to a theater audience crowd that was considered emotional. Reading would trigger discussion rather than riot.

Tarde also claimed that the newspaper by itself did not create a public or public opinion. To constitute a public, readers had to converse with each other about what they read in newspapers. He defined conversation as casual social interaction for its own sake, linking the sociable concept of public to the political. Through conversation, information spread from person to person, producing public opinion. Tarde called conversation, "the strongest agent of imitation, of the propagation of sentiments, ideas, and modes of action," because it produces the greatest intensity of attention.[36]

Tarde defined public opinion as "a more or less logical cluster of judgments which, responding to current [social] problems, is reproduced many times over in people. . . ." By placing reading at the center of his public, he emphasized rationality in opinion formation. By placing conversation centrally he emphasized that a public builds upon individual will rather than a collective mind. For him, opinion formation was primarily an individual process, an act of independent will, in contrast to the crowd's loss of individuality. There could be disagreement in a public. Each individual, in conversing with others, plays an independent part in shaping the public opinion. Tarde's conclusion that publics were tolerant of more than one point of view implied that it would therefore also be more rational, critical and deliberative through conversation.[37]

Robert Park, an important pioneer in American sociology, shared Tarde's view on publics. Like Tarde, he contrasted homogeneity of mind in the crowd to the individual differences retained in publics. He indicated no concern whether publics were assembled or dispersed. Instead, he contrasts crowd and public in terms of emotion versus reason, action versus deliberation. Himself a former journalist, he saw journalism as the mediator of public opinion and, reacting to the yellow journalism of his day, emphasized newspapers' duty "to instruct and direct public opinion." He insisted that newspapers should provide the facts that must be the basis of discussion among members of a public. Park asserted that differences of viewpoint are critical to publics. Differences produce "prudence and rational reflection" before action. Without difference, publics dissolve into crowds whose drives are not contained by critical thought. The difference between Park and Tarde perhaps reflects differences in a journalism (and citizenship) that emphasized the wisdom of an intellectual class expressed through newspapers based in essay form (for example, in France and colonial America), and one that emphasized facts (in the United States) with the democratic assumption that all citizens would compose their own conclusions.[38]

Reiterating this same view late in his career, and seeing the same dialectic between the news press and publics as Tarde did, Park wrote,

> The first typical reaction of an individual to the news is likely to be a desire to repeat it to someone. This makes conversation, arouses further comment, and perhaps starts a discussion . . . discussion turns from the news to the issues it raises. The clash of opinions and sentiments which discussion inevitably evokes usually terminates in some sort of consensus or collective opinion—what we call public opinion. [. . .] [Public opinion] emerges from the discussions of individuals attempting to formulate and rationalize their individual interpretations of the news. Public opinion in this limited sense, is political opinion.[39]

Park's formulations of publics and crowds became the foundation of the field of collective behavior in American sociology. As we will see, it was the American newspaper establishment's own view of their public role and was a view shared by other elites beyond academia. Walter Lippmann similarly claimed the centrality of the news and newspapers in the public sphere, emphasized their role as delivering information, and caustically criticized the tendencies of yellow journalism. He wrote,

> The most destructive form of untruth is sophistry and propaganda by those whose profession is to report the news. The news columns are common carriers. When those who control them arrogate to themselves the right to determine, by their own consciences, what shall be reported and for what purpose, democracy is unworkable. Public opinion is blockaded. For, when a people can no longer confidently repair "to the best fountains for their information," then anyone's guess and anyone's rumor, each man's hopes and each man's whim becomes the basis of government.[40]

John Dewey's concept of publics differed from these others in its emphasis on community rather than communication, and action rather than discussion. Dewey defined a public as a spontaneous group of people that arises as a result of the community being confronted by an issue, and who engage in discussion to reach a collective decision about the issue. He went beyond the formation of public opinion, to say that through such discussion, people arrive at a collective decision and act. Dewey's emphasis on community as the basis of publics was incorporated into the mainstream of sociological thought.[41]

The issue of action has made the distinction between crowds and publics more controversial and political. Ideas of crowds and of publics have focused on two different practices valued differently by two different class cultures. The idea of publics is based on the dominant bourgeois norms of individualism and rationality of classic liberalism, with a nation of citizens each pursuing their own self-interest, conversing, debating and deciding independently without regard to loyalties or obligations. The central concepts of debate imply individual independence from the group. The idea of crowds is associated with working-class and other subordinate cultures, which, historically, have valued loyalty and solidarity above individuality. Debate is inimical to such solidarity; it may question leadership, create dissent, and paralyze or undermine group action. Thus the two concepts, publics and crowds, are interpretations from the point of view of two different class cultures.[42]

Action is likewise judged by these criteria. Debate is an exercise of the mind; action is one of the body. From the point of view of the dominant culture, action must be controlled by the mind and based on individual, rational decisions. The idea of publics is part of a dominant discourse that contains collective action by labeling it the disorder of bad crowds and contrasting it to good publics. Crowds were deemed irrational and thus antithetical to the Enlightenment project of democracy.[43] Secondly, the discourse associated crowd irrationality with uncontrolled emotions and violence.

Effectively, however, the objection is to force. The rowdiness of crowds constitutes forcible action rather than reasoned agreement. Publics presume a society of equals where various parties can reason with each other and achieve a consensus or settlement without resort to force. A public sphere is premised on the existence of a common ground not only physically but also socially and politically.

This has created a conundrum for scholars using these two concepts. Once scholars began to accept crowds as rational and publics as acting, the distinctions between these two categories began to blur. In the 1970s, sociologists and historians began to reject crowd psychology and argue that crowds act rationally, and to merge crowds and the public protests and demonstrations of social movements into a broader category of collective action.[44] Nevertheless, the scholarly work on crowds and on publics have remained separate, depending upon whether scholars emphasize the class and social issues of crowds or the political issues of publics. Scholars still disagree on whether the label of publics should be reserved for quiet deliberation or include raucous crowds as well. The result is that today some scholars describe an event as crowd action, while others call the same event a public in action. In cases of audiences, some see them as crowds, while others see them as vigorous publics. Rather than attempting an essentialist categorizing, we will treat these as competing discourses of contemporaries revealing contrary representations.[45]

## Mass man

Sociologist Herbert Blumer's distinction of crowds, public and mass, separates mass from crowds through its diffuseness, and from publics through its lack of discussion. Media are a necessary component of mass as well as publics, the coordinating focus. But unlike publics, discussion and debate does not ensue among mass audiences as a response to the media. Instead of this intermediate step of gestation and deliberation, this concept presumed that media directly influence the mass to act or to remain inert, a kind of hypodermic theory of communication.

Mass as a twentieth-century concept grew out of the term, "the masses." Raymond Williams traces a long history of English pejorative terms applied by elites to common folk, and notes that "the masses" was a term of contempt among elites. It replaced the eighteenth-century usage of mob [*mobile vulgus*] to refer to the lower classes, reserving mob for a particularly unruly crowd. This transition reveals the underlying long-standing relation between ideas of mass and crowd as well as between both and the lower orders.[46] The idea, sometimes phrased as mass rather than masses, is first evident in the United States in the late eighteenth century. Alexander Hamilton wrote, "All communities divide themselves into the few and the many. The first are the rich and well born, the other are the mass of the people." The masses continued to be used as a term into the twentieth century and applied to working-class movie audiences.[47]

The modern concept of mass is revealed in the proliferation of the term as an adjective in mid-twentieth-century phrases such as mass market, mass media, mass communication, mass culture, mass society, mass man. While still alluding to the masses, it increasingly included the middle class as well as working and lower classes. But more centrally, it came to refer to a population of *indistinguishable* individuals, whose lives, action, and thinking are the same, who work at the same jobs in large corporations, and consume the same mass-produced products from the same national retailers and the same ideas from the same mass media.[48] While the twentieth-century mass was dispersed, in other ways it resembled the crowd of crowd psychology, acting as one mind. Critics claimed that the mass media provided the demagogic stimulus to form this "one mind": mass individuals consumed the same products and media messages and thus thought and acted the same. This mass acted as individuals rather than as a crowd, but individuals shorn of individuality. The negative evaluation of the mass focused not on the propensity for violence as with the crowd, but on the weakness of the individual will, the foundation of the market's *homo economicus* and democracy's informed citizenship. It was the difference in individuals that also distinguished the mass from publics. The concept of publics presumed strong and vital individuals: knowledgeable, civic-minded, and with a strong moral sense. In mid-twentieth century discourse, the mass individual was believed to exhibit none of these.[49]

The sociological reason that the mass was presumed to be vulnerable to media began with the idea that mass individuals were not only indistinguishable, they were believed to be unmoored by community. The community that Dewey envisioned for publics was presumed absent in this mass society. Community was defined in terms of relationships, a network of relations among people who know and interact with each other face to face without mediation. Mass society critics feared the disappearance of such relationships. They expressed concern that places of public sociability, such as the neighborhood bar, hair salon and general store, were disappearing due to suburbanization, home media and shopping malls. They claimed mass marketing and mass media had replaced community relationships with anonymous ones. These ideas were the modern expression of the foundational concern of social sciences since the late nineteenth century, a concern about the loss of community in the transition from traditional agricultural to modern industrial society in the United States and Europe.[50]

Underlying this analysis was a presumption of the disappearance of the public conversation or discussion that was the basis of publics. The traditional public places were imagined as sites of community, important not only for sociability but also for the conversation of publics, that is, for civic participation. Before the twentieth century and the rise of opinion polling, the term public opinion meant a group consensus, implicitly derived from discussion. A good many articles appeared in American magazines in the late nineteenth century on the power of public opinion, formulated as consensus arising from public discussion. This appears to have been part of the Progressive reaction against party politics. An 1889 article in the *Harvard Monthly* stated it succinctly, "We are ever exposed to two dangers: to a grasping plutocracy, wielding huge corporate powers . . . and on the other hand, to the ignorant voters—the unfit kings—led by shameless political adventurers." It emphasized that public opinion was a powerful political force influencing government policy and action, yet it was fickle, changing and not particularly rational or well considered. The editor of *The Nation*, E. L. Godkin's definition of public opinion was a "consensus of opinion, among large bodies of persons, which acts as a political force, imposing on those in authority certain enactments, or certain lines of policy." It is expressed through elections and through journalism. These articles consistently described a distinction between the ideal of public opinion based upon rational discussion leading to consensus, and actual public opinion exhibited by the mass and based more on sentiment and prejudice, but nevertheless influencing policy.[51]

With the arrival and growth of polling an individualized concept of public opinion arose, defined as the sum of individual opinions without the element of discussion. The older ideal of opinion based on rational discussion faded from the discourse, and the opinion of the mass was now encapsulated in statistical summaries. Herbert Blumer's was perhaps the first in a tradition of critiques of such opinion polling. As John Durham Peters, phrased it, "What we call public opinion today is thus actually non-public opinion."[52]

The psychological mechanism proposed for direct influence on the mass was suggestion, adopted from crowd psychology. The substitute for community was mass media, defining mass man as an audience of dispersed, isolated individuals, vulnerable to suggestion from media messages. Even after these theories of mass society began to fade, the image of the solitary, isolated individual, vulnerable to media, remained through the twentieth century.

## The chapters

The organization of the book is framed around the historical progression of the three concepts of crowd, public, and mass of isolated individuals, in concert with ideas of citizenship and audiences. Chapter 1 examines the changes in conception of nineteenth-century theater audiences from acceptable rowdiness into dangerous mobs, the latter theorized in late nineteenth-century crowd psychology. At times, working-class auditors represented themselves in terms of publics, while others characterized them as unruly and undesirable crowds. Chapter 2 continues the story in early twentieth-century movie houses, as crowd psychology was adapted to discussions of mass vulnerability. Audiences were reconceived as suggestible masses under the influence of powerful media, first movies and then radio. The experience of propaganda in World War I and the growth of national advertising in the 1920s contributed to this conception of the masses as suggestible audiences.

Chapter 3 returns to the nineteenth century and the development of the conception of publics. In mid-century the new middle class withdrew from the public sphere typified by working-class roughness and partisan politics, concentrating instead on liberal individualism, self-cultivation, and the private sphere. Late in the century, Progressivism reinvigorated the idea of civic participation. Middle-class reformers proselytized among working-class immigrants to Americanize them. Civic pageantry and political theater treated performance as political communication and audiences as citizens. Chapter 4 follows the transfer of the idea of publics from the press to broadcasting. Debate among government, educators and reformers, and commercial broadcasters produced a discursive field that framed the airwaves as a public sphere, with each party advocating their own versions of broadcasting as a public sphere. Even advertisers positioned themselves and their audiences as citizens.

Chapter 5 explores mid-century intellectuals' preoccupation with mass culture, mass society, and mass media. Aesthetic and social criticism targeted the post-war middle class as a mass of identical, isolated individuals and blamed television as the medium that programmed their lives. Chapter 6 examines the rise of a communication research paradigm that paralleled this public debate and similarly constructed audiences as solitary individuals. Chapter 7 continues with more recent, popular characterizations of audiences as pathological individuals, incapable of fulfilling their role as citizen. The Epilogue takes a brief look at recent discourses on audiences for live entertainments and for the internet.

# Part I

# Crowds

Chapter 1

# Theater audiences, crowds, and publics

Much of the written record about theater audiences in the nineteenth century revolved around depictions of artisan and working-class auditors as raucous, rambunctious, rowdy, and sometimes riotous crowds, much like descriptions of disorderly urban street crowds of the times.[1] It was in relation to these unruly crowds that other classes were advised to avoid sections of the theater or the theater altogether.

Before the nineteenth century, such audiences were not an issue, due to the late development of theater and the late arrival within theaters of a substantial artisan audience. Professional theater did not arrive in the English colonies until the 1750s, when the largest American city was smaller than a second-class port city of England and could not support a permanent theater. Even then, it was banned on religious grounds in Massachusetts and opposed by the influential Quakers in Pennsylvania. Where theater was performed, mostly in the population centers of New York and Virginia, it was more a novelty than a regular practice, and almost exclusively a genteel amusement without the large and raucous crowds of the English pit and the French parterre. Artisans were absent, since they could not afford these events and were out of place in this genteel milieu. Slaves, who sometimes attended to serve their masters, were under strict control. Class conflict was involved, but it was between the genteel audiences inside the theater and the artisans and others outside protesting. Artisans characterized theater a symbol of the English aristocracy they opposed, and the protests were part of the growing spirit of revolution.[2]

The crowded pit of artisans appeared after the American Revolution. The pit was a mixture of plebeian classes, journeymen and master artisans, small merchants, and lawyers. These audiences made theaters places for expression of the turbulent politics of the era, with Jeffersonian Republicans in the pit contending with Federalists in the boxes to control the choice of plays and music favorable to their political views. The gentry and wealthy merchant class began to consider theater an institution naturally inclined to cause disruption, and therefore a matter of concern to the commonwealth (the state and its property-owning citizens). Consequently, around the turn of the century, gentlemen took upon themselves the tasks of criticism and censure by establishing and contributing their observations to the first theatrical publications in the United States, the *Theatrical Censor* (1806–7) and the *Mirror of Taste and Dramatic Censor*. Stephen Cullen Carpenter wrote in 1810 as editor of the *Mirror*, "Since it is the young, the idle, the thoughtless, and the ignorant, on whom the drama can be supposed to operate as a lesson for conduct, an aid to experience and a guide through life . . . it becomes a matter of great importance to the commonwealth that this very powerful engine . . . should be kept under the control of a systematic, a vigilant and a severe, but a just criticism."[3]

Carpenter's statement looks both backward to an old English concern about theater audiences as disorderly crowds and unruly subjects, but also forward to the new Early Republic era of citizenship. Behind his comments was a republican concept of citizenship that entailed both rights and obligations. In a later column, he acknowledged that censorship must be done "without violating the rights of the people."[4] On the other hand, his quote above emphasized that it is not simply a private matter but one "of great importance to the commonwealth" to assure that theater offer "the young, the idle, the thoughtless and the ignorant" of its audience the right lessons. A republic required citizens who had the knowledge and character to fulfill their duties as citizens. Carpenter's columns suggested that theater contributes to creating such citizens.

Dueling visions of audiences as crowds and publics wove themselves through the discourses of the time about theater audiences.[5] Revolutionary discourse framed audiences as engaging in legitimate actions in their roles as citizens, both exercising rights and participating in political debate. Elite discourse however would increasingly frame working-class audiences as crowds that threatened social order and needed to be contained, rejecting any traditional justifications on the grounds that, as citizens rather than subjects, they now had other avenues to express their concerns and interests. In this chapter I will trace this development.

## Early American theater: politics, crowds, and publics

The spirit of revolution in the United States created theater as a sphere for political discourse, but one much more robust and raucous than the rational deliberation envisioned by Habermas. The audience was both a crowd and a public, or a hybrid of the two. Federalists tended to equate the pit with Republican artisans and their lawyer leaders, and their actions as typical of crowds. A parody in the Federalist *Boston Gazette* in 1801 characterized the professional men in the pit as demagogues manipulating the working men to support Republicans and causing a riot, a classic stereotype of a lower-class crowd incited by a speaker.[6]

Through the late eighteenth century and into the nineteenth, the pit audience drew legitimacy for its actions from the traditions of crowd action imported from England. But audience rights were buttressed by a much more powerful justification: the discourse of liberty and elite revolutionary leaders' need for crowd action to succeed in the events leading up to the Revolution. As historian Edward Countryman wrote, "The Revolution gave rioting a new legitimation by identifying it directly with the American cause." The crowd had its purpose. It was enshrined in the language of the Declaration of Independence, which declared the rights of men, the purpose of government to protect such rights, and the right and duty of the people to overthrow such government that abused these rights. While elites were, at best, of mixed opinions about these rights extending to the common man, they resonated powerfully among artisans and the emerging working class. Fixed in Revolutionary language and iconography, the legitimacy of crowd action was not easily dislodged by elites. It was sustained beyond the Revolution by the success of the Jeffersonian Republicans, and then into the Jacksonian era of the common man with its heroic imagery as varied as *Mose, the Bowery B'hoy*, and Whitman's celebrations of the masses. In the Jacksonian era, the idea that work brought civic virtue as much or more than property had gained ascendancy, combined with the idea that all had rights and therefore the right to oversee the government's protection of those rights led to a democratic formulation of citizenship.[7]

Certainly, early Americans conceived themselves engaged in intense and widespread political participation and defined theaters specifically as a politicized public space. Indeed, this era is often described as a high point of public sphere vitality. After the Revolution, Americans from aristocrat to common man exerted themselves to express their new-found rights as citizens. Newspapers flourished as partisan broadsheets intended to rouse their supporters, exercising a new freedom of public expression. There was almost a celebratory aspect to these civic performances during the early republic.[8]

Theaters were actively used for these political performances and they flourished as never before. Formerly condemned as an aristocratic pastime, theater gained newfound legitimacy as one of few indoor gathering spaces for republican political participation.[9] In the feverish political atmosphere of the

Federalist era, theaters experienced a building boom, lowered admission prices, and extended their market to the working classes. Theater was redefined as a republican activity accessible to common men—some English visitors were surprised at mechanics able to afford theater in this era—where all could gather as the body politic and where the entertainment itself had political import. Even ownership of theaters was democratized by shifting from the colonial reliance upon aristocratic patrons to stockholding, offering shares in exchange for the labor of mechanics to build the theater.

Theater-going was not mere entertainment, but an opportunity to celebrate the new republic. American plays appeared on the stage for the first time. Music as well was parsed for its expression of political sentiment. Theater managers were careful what political import might be given to plays and music. English actors, by their nationality alone, were seen as representing a politics favoring England and aristocracy and had to take care of how they spoke off stage as well as on. American actors performing American plays were hailed as heroes. Especially in the early years of this time, both the affluent in the boxes as well as those in the pit treated the theater as a place where they might express their political views. It was thus that discourse reconstructed theater as part of the public sphere.

But one man's public was another's crowd. While theaters were acknowledged places of public discourse, contemporary descriptions sometimes make it appear more as a quarrel between two mobs.[10] The Federalist Theater in Boston in the 1790s made its politics obvious in its name and in its policies. The Haymarket Theater was built as the Republican response to the Federalist. Divided audiences in other theaters shouted each other down, each singing their own songs. Where theater managers tried to steer a course satisfactory to both parties, they were assailed from both sides, as at the Chestnut Street Theater in Philadelphia. Theater managers censored plays to avoid anything that might incite a demonstration and damage their pocketbooks.[11] Neither side held sway.

American plays that were popular at the time were typically hot-blooded, patriotic spectacles and melodrama, featuring obvious and stark contrasts between heroes and villains, good and bad. William Dunlap's *Glory of Columbia* (1803), a play about the heroics of the Revolution and the victory at Yorktown, became a fixture of national holidays. Likewise John Daly Burk's *Bunker Hill* (1797) became a favorite for its glorification of the battle near Boston and its treatment of the British. The anonymous *The Politician Outwitted* (published in 1789) presented a Federalist argument for the proposed Constitution. Selected scenes in many other dramas suggested similarly patriotic themes and evoked similar sentiments. The effect was to appeal more to the crowd's passions than the public's reason.[12]

At the same time, news of the French Revolution reaching American shores alarmed patricians, as they feared crowds out of control in ways they did not before the American Revolution. Federalists used the Sedition Act to suppress just such crowd action, while Republicans considered crowd action the bulwark against tyranny and their rightful inheritance from the Revolution.[13] Many of the pre-industrial elites considered this rowdy political expression by artisans and the lower sorts presumptuous and lacking in deference to their genteel superiors.

As industrialization began and cities grew rapidly, the chasm between these discourses would grow wider. The Jacksonian era, dubbed the age of the common man, ushered in a transformation of class structure. Ownership of production was passing from master artisans to businessmen and investors, while journeymen artisans were being reduced to permanent proletarian employees. At the same time, expanding businesses required increased numbers of clerks and managers to run, and lawyers and other professionals to service, such enterprises. The consequence was a new class structure of capitalist owners, served by middle-class managers and professionals, and employing a working class of permanent journeymen, apprentices, and laborers.[14]

Each class began to establish its distinctive culture. In their leisure, single journeymen and apprentices made themselves noticeable by their rough manners and outspoken public expression. Concentrated in urban boardinghouse neighborhoods, they spent much of their time and money frequenting public places. In the theaters of major East Coast cities, this newly forming working class was uninhibited in vocalizing their opinions, particularly against alleged insults to America by English actors, or cheering their own kind, and in their manner and dress rejecting middle-class respectability—and they did so collectively.[15]

At first, some gentlemen and a few literati like Walt Whitman praised the common man. With the growth of the penny press and the appearance of theaters catering to mechanics in the major cities in the 1830s and 1840s, the working classes found themselves positively represented in print and performance. The epitome of this image of the good, fun-loving workingman's crowd was the Bowery b'hoy, a characterization of young, working-class men who worked and lived in the Bowery of New York City.[16] Even the *Spirit of the Times*, a newspaper of leisure for affluent sporting men, emphasized the gregarious nature of the b'hoys at the Bowery Theater,

> the pit is a vast sea of upturned faces and [b'hoys'] red flannel shirts, extending its roaring and turbid waves close up to the footlights on either side, clipping in the orchestra and dashing furiously against the boxes—while

> a row of luckier and stronger shouldered amateurs have pushed, pulled and trampled their way far in advance of the rest, and actually stand with their chins resting on the lamp-board, chanking peanuts and squirting tobacco juice upon the stage. And now Mr. [Jack] Scott makes his appearance in one of his favorite characters and is greeted with a pandemoniac yell as he rushes with gigantic strides down to the front. . . . At length, after executing a series of the most diabolical grimaces, during which the sympathies of the audience have been working themselves up to a pitch of intense excitement. . . . At this thrilling spectacle the enthusiasm of the audience finds vent in a perfect tornado and maelstrom united of "hi hi's!", cat-calls, screamings, whistlings and stampings. "That's it Jack!", "Give him thunder, you old buster!", "hurrah for Scott!", "Oh, get off my toes!", "Put your toes in your hat!", "I say you Jo Jackson up in the third tier! Come down here and I'll kick yer into fits!"[17]

One thing distinguished the b'hoy from the other icons of the American common man, the riverboatman and the frontiersman: the b'hoy was always part of a crowd and he always acted collectively. In positive representations such as *Mose*, this was depicted as good-hearted, working-class camaraderie.[18]

Then disapproval of crowds began to gain ascendancy, motivated at first by a desire to contain this population, avoid contact with them, and suppress their antics. The emerging capitalist elite and their new middle-class retainers wished to contain their proletarian brothers in forging industrialization. Historian Paul Boyer terms this era "a time of almost continuous disorder and turbulence among the poor." The era spawned publication of numerous representations of cities as dangerous places in a range of genre, from literary magazines to sensational newspapers and books. By the 1840s the increasing effrontery of this working class and its disorder was wearing thin among the upper classes; the divide between the two classes' views was widening and hardening.[19]

The words of these patricians were almost hysterical with fear and filled with disgust of crowds of lower classes in the streets, equating them with dirt and impurity. George Templeton Strong described them as insects, the streets "absolutely swarming, alive and crawling with the unwashed Democracy." Philip Hone, one-time mayor of New York, blamed the "vulgar and uneducated masses" as a source of "vile disorganizing spirit which overspreads the land" and "gangs of young ruffians who prowl the streets insulting females, breaking into houses." Among other things, Hone feared the loss of control of the polity, saying "the heterogeneous mass of vile humanity [produced] unrestrained power in the hands of a mob of political desperados."[20]

The language describes subhuman working-class crowds taking over the city from embattled middle and upper classes. They were "unwashed," "vile," and "uneducated." The fact that they were "unrestrained" and "disorganizing" "ruffians" and thieves who prowled and insulted women called out for suppression. The descriptions stand in stark contrast to images of the respectable classes and citizens who are depicted as clean, polite, educated, law-abiding individuals. Increasingly, concern turned to controlling crowds of these common men. At first, physical restraint was the recommended solution, as the respectable and cultivated increasingly called for cities to use force. Full-time municipal police departments were established as much to control crowds as to stop crime. In both, they functioned to contain and control the working class.[21]

The Astor Place Opera House riot of 1849 in New York City and its representations in most metropolitan newspapers constituted an end to favorable consideration of the b'hoys among the middle and upper classes. In this moment, two groups with divergent views confronted each other and clashed: one which hewed to the traditional view of audiences exercising their traditional rights to discipline the stage; the other depicting the audience, in the Opera House and out in the streets, as a mob led by demagogues. The b'hoys lost. It was a watershed, marking the end of civil authority tolerance of crowd actions that had typified the eighteenth century, and a definitive change of attitude by municipal authorities regarding the need to control crowds. It was a clear statement in favor of suppression.[22]

The immediate issue of the riot was support of the American actor Edwin Forrest by the b'hoys and of the English actor William Macready by the cultural elite. Forrest and Macready had had a trans-Atlantic argument for some time, when Macready arrived for an American tour. In New York, they were scheduled for competing performances of Macbeth in different theaters just a few blocks apart. Such "contests" were not uncommon and spurred ticket sales. Macready was at the fashionable and exclusive Astor Place Opera House. But on the first night, working-class supporters of Forrest attended and succeeded in stopping the performance. They returned the second night when Macready who, following custom, had decided to cancel his performance in the face of this opposition, was persuaded by several prominent cultural elites to change his mind and perform despite the threats of riot. On this second night, the city leaders marshaled a considerable armed force to control the theater inside and out. This only inflamed the crowd more. To make a long story short, there was much breaking of theater windows (not uncommon) and throwing paving stones at the armed forces. Eventually, militiamen were ordered to fire into the crowd in the street, killing twenty-two and wounding over one hundred.[23]

Metropolitan newspapers generally supported the actions of the recently formed police force and the militia. William Cullen Bryant's New York *Evening Post* headlined the May 7 action stopping the performance, "Disgraceful." On May 9, the letter from prominent New Yorkers urging Macready to perform was published in the papers. The *Evening Post* commented, "Those who desire to witness the performances of Mr. Macready, have a right to do so without interruption from any class of men whatever, and we hope to see this right insisted upon and enforced." This statement replaced the long custom of rights of audiences collectively to stop performances, rights traditionally associated with lower classes, with the rights of audiences as individuals to hear the performance for which they paid, customers who in this case were specifically middle and upper class. The language of rights, moreover, cast this as a political discourse about which rights and which citizens the state should defend, and which to attack, thereby revoking their citizenship. This statement implemented classic liberalism's elevation of individual rights as the foundation of citizenship.

On May 10, after people in the crowd outside the theater protesting the performance were killed by the militia, the *Evening Post* repeated its defense of Macready's right to perform in such circumstance, contradicting custom. On May 11, it referred to the "masterly" management by the chief of police, dismissing any criticism of the killings as forced upon the military who had "no other recourse" than to fire on the crowd. On May 12, it declared that "the supremacy of the law has been maintained . . . a source of unmixed gratification and pride . . . we trust a profitable lesson has been taught to that infatuated class who have supposed that they might with impunity violate the rights of private citizens." The paper had jettisoned any past tolerance of crowd actions and cast those in the crowd outside the category of citizens. Again, the newspaper defended the rights of contract in the ticket purchase for performance. In ensuing days, the *Evening Post* instead blamed the killings on demagogues who "instigated and led on the riot, who inflamed the prejudices and passions of the mob, who countenanced and encouraged the stoning of the Opera House." A third time, it repudiated the right of audience sovereignty in favor of private contract rights, "There is, we take it, little doubt that a conspiracy to hiss down an actor, or otherwise interrupt any public entertainment by noise and disorder is a breach of the peace, as well as a breach of morals, and is punishable by law."[24]

On May 16, the *Evening Post* published a letter from an anonymous but obviously capable writer who condemned those who urged Macready to perform, on the ground they had known the dangers and yet insisted on what was "best calculated to exasperate and inflame" those threatening to stop Macready. The letter claimed the press generally sided with these men and condemned the riot leaders. The *Evening Post*'s response was to equate the right to attend the play in a commercial theater to the rights of abolitionists to meet, or of people to attend a house of worship.[25] Like the *Evening Post*, the businessman's *Courier and Enquirer* on May 9 called the pit audience actions "outrages," and on May 15, bluntly stating events in class terms, it hailed the suppression of the protest as "an excellent advertisement to the Capitalists of the old world that they might send their property to New York and rely upon the certainty that it would be safe from the clutches of red republicanism, or chartists or communists of any description."[26]

Before the tragic night of May 10, James Gordon Bennett's Democratic-leaning New York *Herald* was more sympathetic to those opposed to Macready. The *Herald* wrote lightheartedly about the demonstrations at Macready's first night, May 7, confirming the traditional rights of audiences to demonstrate, even the hurling of rotten eggs and potatoes, a shoe and a chair on stage, saying that there was no intent to hit the actor and that it halted as soon as Macready left the stage. Nor did the *Herald* express concern at the poster calling opponents of Macready to the Opera House on the second night of performance. Adhering to the language of publics and citizens, the poster itself called "Working Men" to "dare to express their opinions this night, at the English Aristocratic Opera House! We advocate no violence, but a free expression of opinion to all public men. Workingmen! Freemen! Stand by your lawful rights!" But after the killings, it too sided with the authorities against the crowd. [27]

In parceling blame for the dead, few newspapers blamed the military or police or city authorities. Many blamed the rioters, distinguishing them from innocent bystanders and curious observers, insistently using the phrases "the mob" and "ruffians" in contrast to the "respectable" supporters of Macready. Several blamed the literati who urged Macready to appear a second time in defiance of opposition. Some blamed Forrest for stirring up his fans against Macready. Only artisan papers faulted the authorities or blamed Macready.[28]

Historian Peter Buckley charts this moment as a watershed. The *Tribune*, *Herald*, and the Philadelphia *Public Ledger*, as well as private accounts, described the events as creating a new gulf between the upper class and "the great popular masses" of New York City. Through the remainder of the nineteenth century, histories of New York used the riot to represent the working class as a dangerous, "insensate" mob or to prove why police were needed to control such mobs. Buckley described the Jacksonian era in New York City as one in which the classes of working "b'hoys" and the fashionable grew apart and opposed, creating as Buckley phrased it, "two audiences and two versions of what constituted the 'public' sphere of communication and culture."[29]

When seen in the longer history of theater audiences and class issues, the Astor Place riot is simply an extreme of these class tensions that lay within theater, wherever lower classes gained entry. In 1849 New York, working-class theater-going had reached an unusually high level of participation. The consequence was class segregation of drama performance. The Bowery and Chatham theaters catered more to the working class. The elite of the city withdrew even from the venerable Park Theater, built the Opera House for their personal use in their own fashionable neighborhood around Astor Place, and excluded others by virtue of an upper-class dress code that required men to wear white gloves. The riot was simply the culmination of a growing elite intolerance of the lower classes and lower-class resentment of their treatment.

In the Astor Place riot, authorities definitively replaced placation with suppression. Thereafter, theater audiences seldom rioted. But it did not end trouble in the streets. Artisans were losing control of their craft and becoming proletarianized permanent employees. The Astor Place riot occurred as city artisans were beginning to organize trade unions for the first time since the 1830s. During the spring of 1850, outdoor mass meetings and strikes demonstrated union strength to their adversaries and the public. When tailors struck, the newly formed municipal police force waded into the crowd with nightsticks. This provoked a general strike. When thousands rallied before the City Hall the police again clashed with workers, killing at least two workers and wounding dozens. Even while the labor press and some metropolitan dailies expressed sympathy for workers, many newspapers blamed the workers for the disorders and excused the police protecting strikebreakers.[30] Such battles in the streets and justifications in the newspapers, echoed the recent events and news of the Astor Place riot, to cement an image of this new proletariat as troublemakers and whetted elite desires to quell the working class and to separate themselves from that class.

This hardened attitude to crowds and riots became permanent. Joel Tyler Headley in his influential 1873 book, *The Great Riots of New York*, railed at the barbarity of the lower classes in these crowd actions. The very successful light-and-shadow author, James Dabney McCabe, presented lurid accounts and illustrations of the labor strikes and riots of 1877 in *The History of the Great Riots*. Even sympathetic newspapers that painted the plight of the individual workers condemned their efforts to right conditions collectively through crowds, strikes, and violence.[31] Depicting manual workers as violent mobs disconnected them from their claims to Revolutionary heritage and to citizenship. In middle- and upper-class discourse that was redefining public behavior and citizenship in terms of rational individualism, rioters and strikers would forego their citizenship by their disorder.

## Nineteenth-century crowd psychology

These characterizations of the working class were encapsulated and affirmed in the late nineteenth century by the "scientific" discourse of crowd psychology, advanced by intellectual elites in Europe and America. In the United States, this was another era of intense labor strife and violent clashes between strikers and police; and of unprecedented flood of poor immigrants from southern and eastern Europe who seemed alien to Anglo elites. Contemporaries wrote that 1886 witnessed "far more extended agitation among members of organized labor than any previous year"; the 1890s included the Homestead strike, the Pullman strike, and mass demonstrations of unemployed. Although immigrants were used to undercut wages and break strikes, their allegiance to employers was unreliable, as they joined strikes and unions. Crowd psychology both expressed and fueled elite fears about these people who lived by manual labor. Its implied solution was to disperse crowds or to provide them with elite leaders who could propagandize them.[32]

The most influential statement of crowd psychology was Gustave Le Bon's *The Crowd*, first published in French in 1895. The ideas were not new. It synthesized and gave a scientific sheen to views of many late nineteenth-century intellectuals about crowds and the emotionality and suggestibility of subordinate groups. These ideas had been circulating widely among elites of Europe shaken by the revolts and revolutions of the nineteenth century, and elites of the United States shocked by the millions of poor new immigrants. The book influenced the agenda and direction of American sociology and social psychology into the mid-twentieth century. A half century after its first publication, eminent social psychologist Gordon Allport wrote that it was "perhaps the most influential book ever written in social psychology." A characteristic that made it perennially successful, was that it could be read to look backward to the nineteenth-century fear of mobs, as well as forward to the twentieth-century concern about the mass.[33]

Le Bon described crowds as,

> only powerful for destruction. Their rule is always tantamount to a barbarian phase. A civilization involves fixed rules, discipline, a passing from the instinctive to the rational state, forethought for the future, an elevated degree of culture—all of them conditions that crowds, left to themselves, have invariably shown themselves incapable of realizing. In consequence of the purely destructive nature of their power, crowds are like those microbes which hasten the dissolution of enfeebled or dead bodies. When the structure of a civilization is rotten, it is always the masses that bring about its downfall.[34]

Le Bon elides the distinction between crowds and masses, treating the two as one and the same. Like his crowd, his masses are dangerous, a mad beast thrashing about blindly and dumbly. He believed that "the entry of the popular classes into political life" through broadening suffrage meant the end of civilization, and that only an elite could rule successfully. Le Bon was expressing the views of many elites of his generation, except that in the United States elites were inclined to see the masses as less threatening, although "incapable of realizing . . . an elevated degree of culture."[35]

According to Le Bon, the primary characteristic of crowds is that people lose their individuality and reason, and become subsumed in a monolithic, passion-driven "crowd mind." He said individuals lose independent thinking as a suggestion "implants itself immediately by a process of [emotional] contagion in the brains of all assembled." He describes the most effective suggestions as repeated, concise assertions "free of all reasoning and all proof."[36] He claimed that

> an individual immersed for some length of time in a crowd in action soon finds himself—either in consequence of the magnetic influence given out by the crowd, or from some other cause of which we are ignorant—in a special state, which much resembles the state of fascination in which the hypnotized individual finds himself . . . the slave of all the unconscious activities of his spinal cord, which the hypnotizer directs . . . more irresistible in crowds than in that of the hypnotized subject, from the fact that, the suggestion being the same for all the individuals of the crowd, it gains in strength by reciprocity.[37]

Le Bon highlighted suggestibility, a concept rooted in nineteenth-century theory of hypnosis, as a hallmark of crowds.[38] The concept of suggestion was the coordinating stimulus to explain why many people responded the same when reason was rejected as the cause.

But Le Bon emphasized that not everyone is equally susceptible; some people may "possess a personality sufficiently strong to resist the suggestion." He especially emphasized race—at a time when nationalities were defined as races—which, he said, "exerts a paramount influence on the disposition of crowds." According to Le Bon, crowds exhibit characteristics "which are almost always observed in beings belonging to inferior forms of evolution—women, savages and children, for instance" and "the masses," groups that crowd psychologists considered more prone to be impulsive, emotional, and suggestible.[39]

According to Le Bon, crowds require leaders. Leaders start as one of the crowd, "possessed" by an idea and no more rational than the crowd. They wield "despotic authority"; they implant suggestions through the emotional intensity of their words and stir the crowd to action. Without a leader, "the crowd returns to its original state of a collectivity without cohesion or force of resistance."[40]

In the United States, similar statements to Le Bon's were published about the same time in the new fields of psychology and sociology. These publications gave academic affirmation and systematic formulations to widespread beliefs among American elites. In 1899, psychologist Boris Sidis published a book on crowds mirroring that of Le Bon. He was a Russian immigrant and Harvard student of William James and Hugo Munsterberg (who later used crowd psychology to analyze the effects of movies). In a foreword, James called the book almost the first discussion in English of crowd psychology, "no more practically important topic to the student of public affairs." Like Le Bon, Sidis singled out women and lower classes as especially suggestible, and lower classes as predisposed to become mobs. Sidis' work was cited by Stanford sociologist Edward A. Ross, a prolific interpreter of American academic discourse on crowds and social control to the middle and upper classes.[41]

An even more important figure in American sociology, Robert Park, used Le Bon's ideas to shape that field's approach to the study of crowds for decades. Park's interest grew from his prior career as a newspaperman. Like Sidis, he studied with Munsterberg at Harvard. For his dissertation in Germany he contrasted crowds to publics, incorporating Le Bon's conception of crowds. His most influential student, Herbert Blumer, in turn extended this influence of Le Bon into the mid-twentieth century. Blumer's formulations were incorporated not only into sociology textbooks, but also into military and police crowd-control manuals. What is remarkable is that both Park and Blumer were renowned for their advocacy of empirical observation and yet neither tested crowd psychology against actual observation, which would have shown that such assumptions as anonymity, collective hypnosis, and crowd mind were invalid. Blumer also applied concepts of crowd psychology to movie audiences.[42]

## Crowd psychology and audiences

Crowd psychology defined crowds as audiences, in making attention to a central object or speaker important to the formation of the crowd mind, and also defined audiences as crowds. Le Bon classified audiences as "heterogeous anonymous crowds," the kind of crowd that was the subject of his book. Sidis described social suggestion in various audiences, from those for a concert pianist to those for religious revivals. Others stated similar ideas in newspapers and magazines. *Current Literature* cited an article from *Progress Magazine* (Chicago) that, adopting Le Bon's theory, stated "The human mind is more susceptible to suggestion in a theater than in any other place" because drama plays upon emotions, heightening audiences' suggestibility. It cited a judge quoted in the *New York Times* saying "Unquestioningly, stage crime has a tendency to inspire crime" due to its effect of "hypnotic suggestion." The judge concluded, "I have frequently referred to this fact from the bench," thus introducing the theory of suggestion and audiences into legal argument.[43]

Conceiving audiences as crowds was widespread among cultural elites of the time. This is illustrated in a turn-of-the-century book, *The Psychology of the Aggregate Mind of an Audience*. The book presented statements from sixty-eight well-known American public speakers, "leading orators, lawyers, lecturers, preachers and psychologists." Many quotes asserted that audiences act as crowd psychologists claimed, revealing how much these assumptions pervaded elite discourse of the time. A prominent judge, the Honorable George Wendling, said "the basis for an oration to be successful must be . . . the instincts, emotions and imagination." An author on rhetoric, William Matthews, said that an orator uses sentiment and emotion and "turns a vast multitude into one man, giving to them one heart, one pulse, and one voice, and that an echo of the speaker's." Respondents agreed that instincts are the bases for their appeal to audiences, that emotions are the cohesive force forming the aggregate mind. Mirroring these claims, they said that reasoning and individual will play no part in the aggregate mind of the audience.[44]

They described the aggregate mind of the audience in terms then associated with children, women, and African Americans, as being "lower than the individual mind," "dependent and passive," weak in will and intellect, "fickle and unstable," "pliable" or open to suggestion. Another referred to the audience as a woman, "full of moods," who must be alternately persuaded, caressed, or bullied; yet another thought of the audience as children. Also like crowd psychologists and most elites of the time, speakers saw audiences of inferiors as more susceptible, saying that the "popular" audience is easiest to fuse since they are "not sufficiently informed to be hypercritical."[45] The general thrust of this discourse was that audiences were susceptible to control through suggestion and appeal to emotions and instincts; and that lower status groups were more suggestible.

There is here a subtle but important shift away from crowds conceived as mobs. Classic crowd psychology was concerned about the crowd as *actor*. The speaker or focus of the crowd was simply the trigger to unify it into one mind, making it more powerful; its emotionality and volatility then made it an agent of chaos and destruction. The concern was not the demagogue who stirred up the crowd, but what the crowd did once it was stirred up. Le Bon and his European contemporary elites were reacting to their experience of large crowds in revolts and revolutions throughout the nineteenth century. Their contemporaries in the United States also could remember the draft riots of the Civil War and more recent violent workers' strikes. They feared the violent mob that destroyed property and threatened the status quo.

In contrast, the statements quoted by Diall and found in other American sources at the turn of the century tended to represent the crowd as dependent upon and under the control of the speaker. The agent now was the speaker to the crowd. The concept of the unitary crowd mind was interpreted in terms of its usefulness to control the crowd. Concern was shifting from the dangers of the crowd to the dangers of the speaker/message. This would become an important shift in defining audiences and crowds in the twentieth century. It would be a first step toward the substitution of the concept of "mass" to replace "mob," and a shift to the effects of the speaker rather than the crowd and its actions. This paved the way for linking crowd psychology to examine the new "speakers" and "messages" of mass media.

## Ivy League crowds

Even while elite depictions of lower-class crowds were turning increasingly hostile, it is instructive to contrast them to depictions of upper-class college students after Thanksgiving Day football games in New York City in the 1880s and 1890s, in the early days of college football fandom. The news articles covered these events in a boys-will-be-boys tone, despite the fact that they caroused in the streets, jostled women, disrupted restaurants, bars, and performances at theaters, and did this each year as part of the post-game "tradition." Reports referred to them as "coltish collegians" and "bright boys" expressing "the froth and foolishness of post-football enthusiasm." The whole tone of these articles was tolerant and cheerful: "[Yale] in theatre and at the bar showed she still could hold her own. . . . Dimpled joy reigned at the Hoffman House, where Princeton proceeded to let herself down the giddy slopes of Avernus."[46]

Even the stuffy *New York Times* was remarkably enthusiastic in its account of violence in a game between Penn and Wesleyan in 1887. The *Times* described with approval how players "pull each other's hair and scratch each other's face . . . punching and slugging," and how "punching was universal [with] bloody noses, blackened eyes, scratched faces, barked shins, and sore ribs." They reported heroically that, "that made no difference. As long as a man could stand up he fought" and ended admiringly with "everybody who saw the game was sorry that both sides could not have won." The only negative was a reference to "hoodlums present" who jeered a costumed student couple, the pejorative apparently indicating some non-collegiate outsiders.[47]

At theaters, the college students disrupted performances with little interference from the police. The *Times* cheerily reported that, in the famous Koster and Bial's vaudeville house, about a thousand collegians without seats, "swarmed all over the house and ran the show to suit themselves. The principal actors were familiarly saluted by their first names and then cheered with the complicated but satisfactory cheers of Yale or Princeton." The manager of the Bijou Theatre regretted that he could not host more often the Yale students who had filled his theater for a performance.[48]

Only after several years of tolerance, did managers and police begin in 1893 to reign in this Thanksgiving carousing. The newspapers however continued to report in tones sympathetic to the boys. A pre-game report that year indicated that patrons of theaters and restaurants were annoyed by the behavior in years past and quoted managers of these places who vowed they would not allow it this year. A *New York Herald* report phrased the tradition, "the good old days when Thanksgiving night following a football game was one long Bacchanalian revel, when the boys owned the town, whether the 'coppers' would have it or no, when theatergoers were driven out of playhouses and players howled off the stage by the wild eyed raucous voiced collegians." The next year the *Herald* wrote, "everybody was more or less disappointed" that the carousing boys of previous years were silenced, commenting "electricity [that is, the carousing] is life," that a "wet blanket" had been thrown upon the affair, and that "the good old times are gone." This did not entirely stifle the boys. The next year some continued the tradition again at Koster and Bial's, where they threw beer mugs at the stage.[49] Calls for crowd control of these upper-class boys were unheeded or answered half-heartedly and without the support of newspapers. Throughout all the reporting, terms such as "mob," "riot," or even "crowd" were absent, even when describing incidents that police came in numbers to quell.

By contrast, in 1888 a New York audience made fun of an incompetent, apparently amateur, actor performing Hamlet. One newspaper chastised the audience for its "sheer and wanton brutality [to] laugh and jeer and hold him up to ridicule." Another paper described the audience as an "assemblage of an inferior class of playgoers" who were "heartless enough or silly enough to find pleasure in guying him." The New York *Tribune* referred to the audience as a "howling mob" at a riot in 1893 at the Yiddish Thalia Theater in the Bowery, a rather unfashionable district, with a working-class Jewish immigrant clientele. The audience was reacting to the manager canceling the last act of the play because it was past midnight and in violation of Sunday closing laws. While the short report was generally neutral in its description, it repeatedly described the audience as a mob and noted that it took a platoon of police "considerable trouble" to drive them away.[50]

Chapter 2

# From crowds to masses

## Movies, radio, and advertising

At the turn of the twentieth century, dominant discourses already were shifting to the faceless masses from the dangerous street crowd. The riots of the nineteenth century were fading from memory. American elites were more concerned about the un-rooted "masses" of immigrants filling the slums of cities, unconnected and uncommitted to the status quo and vulnerable to recruitment for changing it. Novels consistently presented images of cities full of anonymous faces. Reflecting in 1900 on the crowds of cities, Progressive journalist Ray Stannard Baker wrote, "What a different world I knew from that of my ancestors! They had the wilderness; I had crowds. I found teeming, jostling, restless cities . . . I found hugeness and evil."[1]

Baker and these novelists were expressing the experience of native-born Americans after the Civil War. The importance of small towns, in their relatively self-sufficient economies and reputed sense of community, was declining. The Jeffersonian ideal of American localism was disappearing. In its place were arising big cities and national corporations run by distant, unknown, and unreachable elites. Those whose lives had been most comfortable in these towns, the local professionals and small businessmen who had faced little competition or questioning, were most alarmed. At the same time, an enormous population of new immigrants was becoming emblematic of large cities. They also added a dimension of danger as well, with their "un-American" ways. At a time when one in four industrial workers were foreign born, they were associated with labor strife and left political organizations of the time. They became scapegoats for the fears of native-born, middle-class Americans whose influence was slipping away.[2]

Newspapers and magazines provided numerous tales of these immigrants, so visible in their crowded and poor tenement neighborhoods. The fact that some of the largest of these neighborhoods were only blocks away from many publishers, especially in New York City, made them a convenient topic for the press. The concern was not the momentary crowd in the street, but the whole population of lower classes in their daily living. Conservatives and Progressives alike increasingly turned their attention to these masses.[3]

Crowd psychology conceived these masses as easily suggestible. When nickelodeons appeared early in the century, the concept of suggestibility was transposed to this new terrain, so that discussion tread along the same lines that crowd psychology had, the suggestible masses' vulnerability now to media rather than demagogues. Movie audiences represented the masses congregated as crowds in theaters. Radio eliminated the crowd and dispersed the masses, but theories of radio audiences would retain the idea of suggestibility. Concern about the danger of suggestibility supplanted that of the danger of riot. This was heightened by the revelations of the effectiveness of propaganda during World War I, which suggested both the profit of advertising and the specter of propaganda.

## American movie audiences

At the beginning of the century, lower-class immigrants were very visible, with their foreign languages and habits and their numbers concentrated in dense tenement neighborhoods. They also reputedly flocked to nickelodeons near their neighborhoods.[4] These massed foreigners and their alleged attraction to movies worried elites fearing audiences easily influenced by the wrong movie messages. This set the initial terms for how movies and their audiences were constructed in the discourses of the times, drawing audiences again into the nation's political agenda.

Le Bon had anticipated claims of movies' power of suggestion, stating that,

> The figurative imagination of crowds is very powerful, very active and very susceptible. . . . It is only images that terrify and attract them and become motives for action. For this reason theatrical representations . . . always have an enormous influence on crowds. . . . Nothing has a greater effect on the imaginations of crowds of every category than theatrical representations. The entire audience experiences at the same time the same emotion . . ."[5]

Movies too were image-based and effective at evoking emotions and instilling suggestions. Women who, through the second half of the nineteenth century, were defined as unfit to vote due to their alleged emotionality and suggestibility, were believed to be a large and regular part of the nickelodeon audience. Such representations made women appear to be looking at these moving images with desire as consumers rather than as citizens.[6]

Critics of movies soon focused on one aspect of crowd psychology, suggestion, to describe the effects and dangers of movies. Fears (and hopes) about the effects of silent movies were based on claims that movies "implanted" ideas in people's minds. In an address in 1911 in New York at the People's Institute, an organization devoted to helping lower-class immigrants, Reverend H. A. Jump claimed that movies operated through "psychologic suggestion." Jane Addams similarly claimed that her young working-class charges were powerfully influenced by nickelodeons. Progressives like Addams and Jump worried that movies implanted bad ideas, but hoped movies could also be turned to "Americanize" these poor immigrants, teaching them citizenship and its cultural foundations. Psychological suggestion could be a tool for socialization of lower classes into "normal and proper" middle-class manners and morals and good citizenship, or into deviant, lower-class morals and irresponsible citizenship. Reformers and their academic allies were preoccupied at the turn of the century with socialization of the lower-class masses. The movies seemed a particularly prevalent and effective tool of socialization that attracted their concern and their interest. They advocated censorship to be sure that the ideas implanted were good and not corrupt.[7]

Harvard psychologist Hugo Munsterberg was the first academic to publish a book about movies, his 1916 monograph, *The Photoplay*, still remarkable for its analysis of the experience of the film spectator as a perceptual process.[8] It was relatively complimentary to film and some accused him of being paid by the movie industry to write it. More significant is that he gave scholarly legitimacy to the mechanism of implanting thoughts in viewers' minds, an idea that would continue to characterize academic writing about movie audiences through the silent era. At the turn of the century, Munsterberg was an important figure in American psychology. He was a student of the German psychology pioneer, William Wundt, one of the founders of experimental psychology, and was brought to Harvard by William James to establish a psychology laboratory. Munsterberg was a founding member of the American Psychological Association, and a prolific writer of scholarly treatises as well as articles in influential magazines for the literate elite. He also had taught both Boris Sidis, who wrote the first American treatise on suggestion, and sociologist Robert Park, who wrote an early thesis on crowds and publics.[9]

Munsterberg would seem to have had little respect for such concepts as emotional contagion in crowd psychology, since he was a staunch materialist, denied the existence of the subconscious, and disparaged his esteemed colleague and sponsor, William James' interest in studying mystics, a subject categorized with hypnotism and suggestibility. Yet like many other important scholars of the era, he took suggestion quite seriously as a fundamental psychological and social category; and he shared with them the belief in racial, class, and gender differences in will and suggestibility. (Among other things, he repeatedly proclaimed German superiority over Americans, which ruined his reputation after World War I.) Without explicitly saying so, his language implied that he considered unsophisticated classes more suggestible. Like Progressive reformers, he urged use of film for "aesthetic cultivation" of "the masses," writing "the reformer ought to focus his interest still more on the tremendous influences for good which may be exerted by the moving pictures."[10]

Munsterberg placed the concept of suggestion at the center of his explanation of the effects of movies, and replaced the idea of the crowd as mob with the idea of movie audiences as the masses. He already had used the concept of suggestion in his books on forensic psychology and advertising. A suggestion he said, "is *forced on us* [italics added]. The outer perception is not only a starting point but a controlling influence . . . as something to which we have to submit." In *The Photoplay*, he wrote that the moviegoer is "certainly in a state of heightened suggestibility" and "The intensity with which the plays take hold of the audience cannot remain without social effects . . . the mind is so completely given up to the moving pictures." He repeatedly referred to the "spellbinding" power of movies. He claimed that "the sight of crime and of vice may force itself on the consciousness with disastrous results. The normal resistance breaks down and the moral balance which would have kept under the habitual stimuli of the narrow routine of life, may be lost under the pressure of the realistic suggestion." As an example of these "social effects," he recounted how "the sensuality of the nickel audience has been stirred up by suggestive pictures of a girl undressing" and how a sudden jump cut to another scene inflamed the audience's imagination as to what happened. Munsterberg disapprovingly argued that the movie, without showing it, could implant the idea of the naked girl in the spectators' minds.[11]

Another prominent academic of this generation, sociologist Edward A. Ross, seemed to think of the movie audience as a mass under the influence of suggestion. He was a proponent of crowd psychology and made the concept of suggestion central to his famous study of social control. He claimed movies made young people prematurely "sex-wise, sex-excited and sex-absorbed" and blamed movies for "less-concealing fashions, pornographic literature, provocative dances, and briefer bathing suits" of the 1920s. Even an advertising textbook declared the power of movies, "In the field of propagandism there is hardly a more powerful method of arousing and controlling public opinion [than film]."[12]

Through the 1910s and 1920s many influential Progressives continued to crusade against the dangers of movies for children and teenagers, who were believed to be especially suggestible. The focus on children would help shift the concern from marauding mobs to movie messages. Reformers and academics alike that wrote about movie dangers differed notably from the hysterical invective found in Le Bon and others who depicted crowds as incipient violent mobs. Instead, they tended to talk in terms more indicative of the masses than mobs.[13] The operative mechanism of suggestibility located control of effects in the media rather than in the audience. The idea of implanting was the beginnings of an effects approach that would become the dominant paradigm for audience researchers, for government investigation, and for the public for over fifty years. Much of the research would be driven by public concern and moral panics.

The most notable such effort was the ambitious Payne Fund Studies in the mid-1920s that employed several of the most prominent and would-be-prominent psychologists and sociologists in the nation, to demonstrate the effects of movies on children. The Payne Fund was established by a wealthy Cleveland Progressive, Frances Payne Bingham Bolton, for the purpose of developing juvenile reading. Reverend William Short, a crusader against movies, proposed and led a large and ambitious study of the effects of movies on children. Short emphasized the importance of scientific research to prove the dangers of movies and convince opinion leaders to do something about their impact. To give greater credence to the results, Short sought the participation of leading academic scholars.[14] Ultimately, the project produced eight volumes of research reports and a popular summary, published by a commercial publisher and reviewed in newspapers and magazines across the nation.

Short was convinced that commercial interests had captured what was a powerful tool for education and morality and were producing movies that undermined the moral education of youth. His goal, expressed in his title of an early plan for the research, was to shape national policy on the movie industry.[15] Clearly Short considered movies a threat to the nation as well as to individual children. The reports and summary were not explicitly concerned about the impact on citizenship, but the project was part of a larger Progressive discourse linking the cultural and moral education of children and the Americanization of immigrants to the viability of the nation. The popular summary emphasized that the movies had a very powerful and "indelible" influence on the 28 million children who went to the movies every week. It declared the effects of movies to be "of immense national and social importance." The author Henry Forman asserted that movies regularly presented scenes that violated the nation's moral code, and compared the consequent decline of the nation to that of the fall of the Roman Empire. He concluded that, "it is extremely likely to create a haphazard, promiscuous and undesirable national consciousness."[16] He connected movies to national decline through a degraded citizenship, since character and virtue were considered important and integral aspects of good citizenship.

How did movies accomplish this? According to some of the reports, the mechanism of suggestion explained the power of movies. This was most explicit in the reports by Herbert Blumer, who had been trained in crowd psychology. Short had recruited University of Chicago sociologist Robert Park and his former graduate student, Blumer, who began this research shortly after completing his dissertation and would become one of the most important figures in American sociology. Park soon accepted a fellowship that took him to Japan and China, and left the work to Blumer. Blumer wrote two of the thirteen reports published by the Payne Fund on the effects of movies.[17] He had studied crowd psychology with Park and soon shaped the sociological field of collective behavior that grew out of crowd psychology. In this work, he used the term "circular reaction" in place of Le Bon's "contagion" to indicate a mechanism of mutual reinforcement of excitement among members of the crowd. He also accepted the ideas that the crowd focused on a common object, that action arose as excitement built, and that an act by one easily led to others joining in.[18]

Blumer employed these aspects of crowd psychology, especially the idea of suggestion, to explain the influence of movies in both his reports for the Payne Fund, *Movies and Conduct* and *Movies, Delinquency and Crime*, co-authored with his graduate student, Philip Hauser. From the outset, Blumer held very negative views about the influences of the movies. In both books, Blumer used a concept he called "emotional possession" to describe the grip movies held on viewers, so strong that, "even his efforts to rid himself of it by reasoning with himself may prove of little avail."[19] The concept incorporated a version of the idea of "implanting" popular in the 1910s, and echoed Le Bon's idea of "emotional contagion." Emotional possession, implanting, and emotional contagion all were presumed to operate through suggestion—the readiness to believe and respond without critically and rationally examining the message.

Blumer did not equate movie audiences with Le Bon's crowd, however. He noted that they rarely engaged in any form of concerted, collective action, beyond a few jeers at the screen or foot stamping if projection problems arose. Instead, he formulated his analysis of audiences as a mass in modern society. He defined the mass as composed of "alienated individuals in a new area of life not covered by local group tradition . . . essentially alike, individually indistinguishable," anticipating language of later theories of mass society but rooted in the sociological tradition of distinctions between *gemeinschaft* and *gesellschaft*, or folk society and modern society. He contrasted these alienated audiences to idealized "folk communities where the forms and scope of life are ordered."[20]

Blumer saw movie audiences as a symptom of the breakdown of traditional folk mores and the rise of modern mass society. He expressed this in *Movie, Delinquency and Crime*, where he concluded that the effects of movies were determined by "the social milieu [of the movie-goer]." He also emphasized that the effects were stronger in "socially disorganized areas," a phrase used by his University of Chicago colleagues to indicate working-class and immigrant neighborhoods.[21]

While Blumer characterized movie audiences as alienated, this was not corroborated by contemporary accounts of actual nickelodeon audiences which described gatherings that had a strong community feeling to them, the audience composed of people of similar backgrounds from the immediate neighborhood readily socializing with each other.[22] Film scholar Miriam Hansen identifies these gatherings as alternative publics rather than crowds. Even though there is little evidence of political deliberation, the audience members clearly defined these places as public spaces for social interaction much like a town square and acted as a community, which for John Dewey was the foundation of any public. In that sense, through their enactment of their role, these audiences constructed themselves as publics—in contrast to the Payne studies' construction of them as suggestible crowd or mass.[23]

Hansen argues that movies, exhibition spaces, and management constructed a subject position of audiences as sociable publics. Prior to the development of the classic narrative film, early films and exhibition practices did not construct a strong spectator subject position that fixed audiences' attention on the story and away from their companions. The shortness of each film, for example, created momentary intermissions for conversation and movement. Simultaneously, other activities, either sponsored or allowed by theater managers, broke the absorption of viewers in the fictive reality of the film. Live and participative entertainment, such as piano players and creative projectionists or sing-alongs, combined with people eating and talking, and entering and exiting at will, would have disrupted any spellbinding effect.[24]

Some of this remained in neighborhood and especially working-class theaters long after the nickelodeon era and the establishment of the classic feature-length narrative film from the late 1910s on. People continued to come and go as it fit their schedule. They ate and talked unless shushed by their peers. Children talked, giggled, screamed, and sometimes ran about, chased by ushers, and teenagers necked in the balcony. Moreover, they went weekly to this familiar place and recognized their neighbors and schoolmates there—including the ushers. It was less than the sociable public of the nickelodeon, but still a community place and practice.[25]

## Radio and mass hysteria

In contrast to movie audiences, radio audiences were dispersed and by definition not a crowd. To constitute the audience as a social unit required some common object of attention delivered to them at their dispersed locations. Thus it required some means of mass communication. Everett Dean Martin, a psychologist, claimed that a dispersed mass was no different than a dense crowd in the formation of a crowd mentality. Hadley Cantril, a professor of psychology at Princeton University and pioneer of radio audience research, similarly described a dispersed mass reacting as one, demonstrating a crowd mind like Le Bon's.[26]

Cantril participated in most major developments of media research in the 1930s and 1940s. He established a radio research project at Princeton University in the late 1930s, which then became Paul Lazarsfeld's base for path-breaking radio research in the 1940s. He also was one of the prominent American researchers who participated in monthly seminars between 1939 and 1940 to shape the future of the field of communication research.[27] Cantril, like Blumer, is particularly revealing of his time, since he was a Progressive who believed that people were culturally unequal but educable and should have equal economic and cultural opportunity. He also offered a rather complex, multi-causal explanation for collective behavior. Yet he used concepts borrowed from crowd psychology and consistently characterized lower classes as more irrational, suggestible, and problematic. This revealed a persisting emphasis more on the masses and their emotionality, despite allusions to the conceptual "mass."[28]

In the mid-1930s, in collaboration with his former professor at Harvard, Gordon Allport, Cantril began to study radio audiences as suggestible masses. In 1935, they co-authored *The Psychology of Radio*, one of the first books of research on radio audiences. The book reviewed existing research and presented the results of a series of controlled experiments on the effects of radio. The experiments compared live speakers to radio speakers and different styles of speaking on radio to determine which were more effective at persuading or arousing audiences. Cantril and Allport used the concepts of suggestibility and a crowd mind. They defined suggestion as the mental mechanism "which brings about the acceptance of a proposition for belief or action without the normal intervention of critical judgment," that is, without using reason. They said "radio, more than any other medium of communication, is capable of forming a crowd mind among individuals who are physically separate from one another." As did Le Bon and Blumer, they conceived suggestion operating on emotion rather than reason, leading to acceptance of a message without critical examination. They considered all people susceptible to suggestion through radio, but said comprehension of auditory presentation, that is, radio, varied with "cultural level," which Cantril later operationalized as the level of education. They defined comprehension based on reason as the opposite of suggestion; those of higher "cultural level" would use reason more and be less suggestible.[29]

Cantril continued to use the concept of suggestibility in his influential 1941 book, *The Psychology of Social Movements*, in which he discussed "mass psychology," or how large numbers of people were persuaded to act collectively. He presented as cases a lynch mob, followers of two religious groups, a pension reform movement, and the Nazi Party in Germany. In each of these cases, he discounted logical reasons for participating in these groups, and attributed it instead to demagoguery and irrational responses. He did not categorize certain classes of people as innately more suggestible, but said it varied with level of education and thus with class. He explained the success of social movements in terms of demagogues using emotion to sway people to follow leaders without thinking.[30]

Cantril used this same analysis in his 1940 book, *The Invasion from Mars*, about the "panic" response to the *War of the Worlds* broadcast, a striking case where suggestion had gone awry. Panic was one of several terms used by early social sciences to describe what was characterized as simultaneous irrational behaviors by large numbers of people in response to a common stimulus. The mechanism proposed to explain the common response was the concept of suggestion, which made emotional contagion effective and a crowd mind the result.[31]

When Orson Welles' radio drama *War of the Worlds* created a national panic on Halloween night, 1938, Cantril saw a rare opportunity to research radio listeners' susceptibility to suggestion. It involved the two topics he was most interested in concerning radio: as a tool for propaganda and a stimulus of crowd behavior. On Halloween night, 1938, CBS broadcasted an adaptation of H. G. Wells' *War of the Worlds*, directed by Orson Welles and performed live for *Mercury Theater of the Air*, a program of original radio dramas. The script was written in the form of an emergency news broadcast interrupting a regular music program. At the beginning of the broadcast it was announced that this was a drama and not an actual news report. However, many listeners tuned in after this announcement and began listening to what sounded to them like a real emergency news broadcast about the landing of a mysterious airship near Princeton, New Jersey. The drama proceeded to describe it as a Martian spaceship and report Martians killing people and moving toward New York City, leaving death and destruction in their path. Some listeners actually thought it was Germans that had invaded. Of approximately six million people who listened to the broadcast, about one million all over the nation reported believing it was real, at least for a time. Some people called others to warn them. Some prayed or cried. A few packed up their families and fled. A few others prepared to defend themselves. Newspapers described the incident as a panic, playing up anecdotes of individuals as if they described millions. *Time* called it "pretty close to national hysteria;" and *The Nation* a "mass hysteria" caused by the masses' ignorance. In ensuing years it has continued to be labeled a "panic."[32]

Cantril was interested in the event because he saw it as a real-world experiment that could provide insight into the "psychology of the common man," his susceptibility to radio and crowd behavior. He confirmed newspaper descriptions of the event as a panic and said it was no coincidence, as "radio is the medium par excellence for informing all segments of a population . . . arousing in them a common sense of fear or joy and for enticing them to similar reactions," that is, creating a crowd mind.[33] He focused on those who mistook the drama for real events and gathered a wide array of data to investigate why they reacted as they did. Running consistently through his explanation is the theme of educational level. In table after table presenting the results of different data, he showed that people of lower class and less education were more likely to believe the event was real. From this, he concluded that lower classes were more suggestible. Cantril explained that those who mistook the drama for news accepted it without checking what they heard against other observable information and often discounting information that contradicted their fears. He contrasted this suggestibility to "critical ability" and, in his conclusion, said that "young people, women and uneducated people," the familiar list of subordinate groups, were less likely to check facts and therefore to panic.[34]

Ironically, Cantril included in his book some information that could support an alternative interpretation of the class differences in panic. He noted the tendency of all people to rely on radio for matters "far removed from one's own immediate everyday experience." He wondered why some less-educated people who believed it was real had not checked with police or other local authorities, not considering that in the 1930s they may have not trusted local authorities who were associated with racial bias, strike-breaking, and other activities antagonistic to working-class interests. He did not consider that lower-class panic could be due not to less education, but to less familiarity with the conventions of drama and/or news. Cantril discussed "deviant cases" of educated people who panicked and uneducated ones who did not. Each of the five uneducated people who did not panic had some familiarity with these conventions, an interest in "serious literature," in current events and news, or familiarity with science fiction.[35] Throughout the study, Cantril was careful to state that the susceptibility of people to the radio program was due to multiple factors. But he repeatedly returned to education and cultivation as central, arguing that formal education made one less vulnerable to mass media, and lack of education made lower classes more vulnerable. He did not recognize the practical knowledge of less-educated people that might serve them well in other circumstances.

Michael Denning, in *The Cultural Front*, critiques Cantril's conclusions and argues that working-class reactions did not warrant labeling them as lacking critical ability. Cantril claimed that people were insecure, based on a Gallup Poll question that indicated they felt economically insecure in the midst of the Depression and concerned about the growing threat of Germany and war in Europe. But Cantril underplayed the degree to which the show was interpretable as a German attack. Moreover, this was only the third broadcast of *Mercury Theater*, so it was understandable that many people were not expecting a drama on radio at that hour and mistook it for a news broadcast.[36]

Others have also pointed out that a closer examination of the surveys indicates that the book's presentation tends to exaggerate the degree and extent of panic. What is remembered is Cantril's estimate that one million "panicked." But, while in the preface he used the term "panicked," in the text he wrote "frightened or disturbed." Further explanation reduced this to momentary fear for many and "panic" only for a few. But these qualifying remarks were overshadowed by what is discussed at great length in several parts of the book and in vivid detail, the reactions of a small number of people who did panic. Most of those who genuinely panicked lived where the events were supposed to be taking place and in the path of the supposed imminent attack, and these are the people that Cantril interviewed.

At the same time, *The Invasion from Mars* rejected wholesale condemnations of lower classes as inherently inferior. Cantril repeatedly emphasized the importance of education as a factor and explicitly discounted what he called "oversimplified" explanations in terms of instincts or "innate racial, sex or class differences." He later stated his own social goal of "a society where maximum economic and cultural opportunity will prevail for everyone." But he was quite clear that there were, in his mind, important existing class differences in suggestibility. In a 1939 article on listener responses to radio news commentators, he said people of less education were more prone to accept what a commentator said "because of their comparative lack of knowledge or initiative in seeking information."[37]

## Mass and propaganda

Hadley Cantril's interest in radio was due to its perceived significance for propaganda and public opinion. Both crowd psychology and propaganda presumed a particular sense of citizenship. Rather than the independent, informed citizen, propaganda presumed someone under the control of others. It also presumed a *medium* to transmit the message to the dispersed masses. Elite concerns about movies and radio centered on how these new media were "directing" the masses. Intellectual elites disagreed on whether propaganda was bad or a necessary evil in a mass society. But both sides tended to see media as powerfully suggestive and condemned the misuse of media in sending the wrong messages.

Propaganda arose as an issue of intellectual concern after World War I. To build support for the war, President Wilson created the Committee on Public Information and appointed journalist George Creel to run it. The Committee was far more effective in persuading Americans than was expected. At the end of the war Creel published a book, *How We Advertised America*, boasting of this. In the opening chapter, he wrote that disagreement about the war and U.S. purpose "were conditions that could not be permitted to endure. What we had to have was no mere surface unity, but a passionate belief in the justice of America's cause that should weld the people of the United States into *one white-hot mass instinct* [italics added] with fraternity, devotion, courage and deathless determination." In other words, he considered vital a citizenry that would believe and follow its leaders without thinking or questioning, not a citizenry assessing information and drawing its own conclusions about what was best for the nation. Creel and his committee had mounted an enormous campaign based on emotional appeals to create that "mass instinct," including 75 million pamphlets, 750,000 speeches by 75,000 speakers, and a newspaper with a daily print run of 100,000, across the United States with one consistent message, that the U.S. war aims were good and the enemy was evil.[38]

Due to the propaganda's effectiveness, the end of the war brought with it a widespread concern about the relationship between mass media and mass manipulation.

Critics feared media able to manipulate the beliefs of entire populations. Borrowing ideas from crowd psychology, Freud, and others that modern mass man was uprooted from community and irrational, critics constructed an image of powerful media and weak suggestible audiences. Following crowd psychology, what came to be known as propaganda analysis treated audiences as a mass and assumed that people differed in their susceptibility to media messages depending on their social status. Even federal laws intended to combat foreign propaganda incorporated these assumptions.[39]

"Democratic realists" characterized the mass as incapable of fulfilling the role of publics described by democratic theory. The most influential realist, Walter Lippmann, as a youth took to socialism and defended the masses. By the time he wrote *Public Opinion* and *The Phantom Public*, however, he was disenchanted with the masses. In *Phantom Public*, he proposed that an intellectual elite govern the masses. He described "the public" in terms consistent with what others called the masses, ". . . it discerns only gross distinctions, is slow to be aroused and quickly diverted . . . personalized whatever it considers and is interested only when events have been melodramatized." In *Public Opinion*, he labeled them "the mass of absolutely illiterate, feeble-minded, grossly neurotic, undernourished and frustrated individuals." He distinguished from this an educated, culturally refined, and cosmopolitan executive class who could staff government and run the country. [40]

Psychologist Everett Dean Martin agreed, claiming it necessary in a mass democracy,

> Our society is becoming a veritable babel of gibbering crowds. . . . The councils of democracy are conducted on about the psychological level of commercial advertising . . . the tendency of crowd-mindedness has greatly increased in recent years . . . we must become a cult, write our philosophy of life in flaming headlines, and sell our cause in the market.

Like so many others in this era, Martin was giving up the faith in rational discussion as the basis of democracy in a mass society. Instead, he argued that the crowd was irrational and only followed "propagandist tongues." Political science pioneer Harold Lasswell, adopting Freud's analysis of humans as irrational, also argued that people were deeply involved in private issues of the unconscious, and therefore only through these could they be drawn into public issues. He thought in terms of how to persuade the masses through emotion.[41]

While Lippmann and Lasswell saw propaganda as a tool, from the beginning Cantril's interest in radio was stimulated by a concern about its potential for propaganda as a danger. In his 1935 book, *The Psychology of Radio*, he defined propaganda negatively, as "the systematic attempt to develop through the use of suggestion certain of the listener's attitudes and beliefs in such a way that some special interest is favored." He opened the book with a reference to "the tenacious grip that radio has so swiftly secured on the mental life of men" and proceeded to described two incidents of demagogues' use of radio. His 1940 book, *The Psychology of Social Movements*, again emphasized cases where demagogues gained influence through radio broadcasts. For Cantril, the lesson to be learned from the panic incited by the *War of the Worlds* broadcast was that education determined vulnerability to suggestion and therefore was the antidote to propaganda.[42] He was keenly interested in propaganda, but disturbed by its effectiveness.

John Dewey, in reviews of both of Lippmann's major books, *Public Opinion* and *The Phantom Public*, rejected his pessimism and what Dewey considered his misplaced emphases. Dewey held onto the prospect of publics making rational decisions and, like Cantril, put his faith in the education of the masses. Dewey answered the realists in his 1927 book, *The Public and Its Problems*. While he agreed that there were problems with mass society, he was more disturbed by the prospect of manipulative propaganda. For him, it was the conditions of public debate that needed improvement. Propaganda thwarted these improvements. Dewey cited sensationalism in news as one problem. The new technologies of communication and transportation, the bases for mass society, were growing faster than the proper use of them, leading to the more profitable sensationalism. Another problem was the commercial promotion of amusement, diverting attention from political interests. Both of these undermined the possibility of distributing information to people so that they could be educated enough to make informed political judgments required for democratic governance.[43]

The decline in the faith in reasoning publics, the visibility of urban masses, and the growth of mass media led to a new conception of America as an irrational mass connected by mass media. Some, like Lippmann, saw media as the solution to mass democracy; others, like John Dewey, blamed the media for failure to educate while also seeing its potential to teach the masses to think. More opportunistic types, like the pioneering public relations man Edward Bernays, saw media as a means to manipulate people for profit. Bernays, like the academic researchers Hadley Cantril and Harold Lasswell, did not distinguish between advertising and propaganda—even while they disagreed about their import. All saw propaganda, advertising, and entertainment as alike in influencing the masses through media. In fact, the first professional admen had worked on American government propaganda during World War I and, after the war, sold their skills as advertisers for American manufacturers of consumer goods. Bernays opposed the distinction made by others between propaganda and advertising, arguing that propaganda had been unfairly defamed.[44] Both the conception of America as a mass society, and the idea of using media to direct the masses, formed the bases of business advertising as well as government propaganda.

## Mass and class: twentieth-century advertising's audience

In 1948, looking back over the previous two decades, sociologists Paul Lazarsfeld and Robert Merton expressed the opinion that the greatest concern about mass media should not be about government propaganda but about corporate publicity. They wrote, "Increasingly the chief power groups, among which organized business occupies the most spectacular place, have come to adopt techniques for manipulating mass publics through propaganda."[45] Advertising and government propaganda relied on and presumed the suggestibility of audiences. Practitioners and theorists also presumed that they were superior to their suggestible audiences, and that their audiences were in need of suggestion from them, for the sake of democracy.

Modern advertising arose in the early twentieth century to serve a new demand from national corporations that began to dominate the American economy and society in the latter part of the nineteenth century. These companies needed and could afford a means to communicate with their national clientele other than by word of mouth. National media magazines also were seeking to expand revenues by increasing sales of space for advertising.[46] America was becoming a mass-market economy.

The business of advertising, or what was called publicity at the time, was to persuade mass media audiences. The new style of advertising emphasized suggestion, fantasy, and emotion rather than information or reasoned argument. Historian Roland Marchand wrote that academic psychologists had emphasized emotion as central to advertising since Walter Dill Scott's 1903 *Theory of Advertising*. By the 1920s, a consensus existed among advertising agencies about the emotional basis of audiences. Suggestion, in the crowd psychology sense, was becoming a systematic practice of advertisers. Ivy Lee, who began public relations practice in 1906, said in 1921 that "publicity is a matter of mass psychology" and on another occasion, ". . . mob psychology is one of the important factors that underlay this whole business."[47] The "mob" and "mass" were labels for various subordinate groups.

Like Le Bon, these PR pioneers distinguished elites who they believed could resist suggestion, from the rest, including the high-school educated middle class of the early twentieth century. The leading figures of the newborn industry of advertising agencies in the 1920s described the mass audience as quite different from the "class" audience, that is, the college-educated, cultured, rational, and rich like themselves, the top five percent or so. Advertising men characterized their audiences as a breed separate from themselves, whom they had to understand in order to sell. Their opinion of the masses was quite unfavorable.[48]

Among the most successful of these pioneers, Edward Bernays, like Lippmann, believed that an elite of intelligent experts should guide the masses. While publicly referring to himself as one of the masses, Bernays clearly considered himself one of the elite. He argued that advertising and propaganda were necessary to democracy, in order to narrow and channel the choices of the mass.

Otherwise there would be chaos. He opened his book, *Propaganda*, which promoted the social benefits of advertising, with the declaration, "The conscious and intelligent manipulation of the organized habits and opinions of the masses is an important element in democratic society."[49]

The advertising elite generally described the masses with the same traits as those attributed at the time to movie audiences, crowds, and subordinate groups generally. Distinguishing elites from the masses, one quipped, "While he is intellectually 12, you are intellectually thirty." Bernays based his psychology of public relations on Le Bon and also W. Trotter, author of a book on the herd instinct, who, Bernays wrote, "approached the subject in a scientific manner." Bernays characterized the masses as acting on impulses, habits, and emotions rather than thinking, having a herd instinct, and tending to follow a leader.[50]

Advertising executives believed that these "masses," the vast bulk of the population, responded more to emotional appeal since they lacked intelligence. They considered their middle- or low-brow tastes another indicator of their stunted minds. In their words, the mass had "incredibly shallow brain pans," was "susceptible to emotional appeal," and was more "guided by its subconscious impulses and instincts than by its reason." They also claimed the masses were "averse to [mental] effort," culturally backward weak-kneed conformists, and an "irresponsible public."[51]

The same stereotypes were applied to women, who were the primary targets of advertising. Gallop declared himself amazed at the low level of taste of women newspaper readers and the "stupidity" of the women he interviewed all over the nation. Home economist Christine Frederick referred to the average woman having the intelligence of a fourteen year old and lacking in civilized habits such as brushing teeth. Frederick added that, just like a mob, these women had ruthless power. They saw the movie-going crowd, especially the female matinee audience, as typifying the masses. Matinee audiences were stereotyped as hysterical female fans. Movies reputedly appealed to the masses and women because they were visual and emotional and required little of the intellectual effort of reading. The lesson advertisers drew from the movies and movie palaces was that the masses felt trapped in a drab life, desired luxury, and valued illusion and escape.[52]

In the 1920s, ad agencies saw daytime radio as a means to sell to the women of the masses, while evening radio was seen as a means to uplift the masses with cultural programming. They saw radio as an intimate means to reach the masses, where the listener would feel the speaker was talking just to them—masking the mass nature of the message. While among themselves they talked of the undifferentiated mass, in their advertising they talked as if addressing each individual personally. This practice continued into the late 1930s, when radio executives still considered their target market for daytime advertising to be the "women of the broom," lower- to middle-class housewives whom they considered uncultured, emotional, and impressionable. They considered college-educated women too rational to be taken in by ads and therefore unimportant to advertisers.[53]

Part II

# Publics

Chapter 3

# From cultivated individual to public citizen

The new middle class of the mid-nineteenth century were insecure in their status and eager to distinguish themselves from manual workers. They equated the lower classes with filth, disease, and crime, each a form of disorder. The conditions of their neighborhoods were attributed not to their poverty but to their depravity and perversity. Their rowdiness and roughness was a behavioral manifestation of their polluted nature.[1] They were talked about in collective stereotypes, as nameless crowds, street gangs, tenement dwellers, and raucous and rioting theater audiences. The middle class identified the public and public space with this class and its disorder.

By contrast, middle-class culture emphasized privatization, respectability, and cultivation. Privatization called for withdrawal from public space to avoid the undisciplined pollution and disorder of the lower classes. Respectability required discipline of the body, a withdrawal into oneself as a safeguard in public. Cultivation mandated discipline of the mind, an orientation to public experience equally controlled but also elevated, a display of cultural capital contrasted to impoverished lower-class minds. The middle-class aspired to avoid the undisciplined, suppress the body, and enhance the mind.

Late in the century, some of this class re-emerged into the public sphere as Progressives, shedding privatization for public duty. They reacted to the crassness and corruptness of robber barons on the one hand and to the living conditions of the immigrant working class on the other. The righteousness of their respectability served to distinguish them from the public immorality of the very rich. They came together to collectively struggle against these wealthy and powerful and to uplift the poor and Americanize immigrants, to cure the pollution and to proselytize middle-class values to the lower classes, to recruit government in this effort, and to bridge the chasm between classes exposed in the Astor Place riot by celebrating shared citizenship and patriotism.

## Privatization

At mid-century, middle-class culture defined its own kind of citizenship that contrasted a reserved and mental conception of masculinity against a bodily and spontaneous working-class masculinity. Politics of the Jacksonian era were marked by unbuttoned rallies and parades in public spaces that attracted noisy crowds. The new middle-class ideals eschewed indiscriminant mingling and participating in raucous spectacles customary among political parties of the day. Their new ideal was a citizen whose participation was based on sober, individual reflection. They redefined their role in politics in terms of private individualism in contrast to public display.[2]

One aspect of this was the middle-class characterization of the "party man" whose job it was to talk to the rank and file, promise them help, and assure their vote. To the middle class he was a confidence man, ready to dupe naïve young men living in urban boarding houses and no longer moored by family, or immigrants disembarking from a ship and similarly unmoored. These men were believed to demand party loyalty and surrender of independence and of principles. Young men were warned against such party representatives in the plentiful ante-bellum advice manuals that urged each man to have "independence of mind," and that expressed hostility to the parties with professional politicians and previously unknown levels of party organization emerging in the Jacksonian era.[3]

Appropriate civic participation for the new middle class emphasized civic duty as an individual act. In 1852, the editor of *Gleason's Drawing Room Companion* wrote that the respectable man "deposited [his vote] in the ballot box *quietly*." Historians Glenn Altschuler and Stuart Blumin summarized two other wide-circulation magazines of the time, *Frank Leslie's Illustrated Magazine* and *Harper's Weekly* as saying that the sober citizen should inform himself, ignore the spectacle, vote, and return to his private affairs. This whiggish outlook displaced the *noblesse oblige* of the pre-industrial elite with a liberalism that focused on the individual.[4]

This middle-class model of civic duty included another aspect that would be integral to the ideal of publics late in the century—the central importance of rational deliberation. This required independence and information rather than unquestioning party loyalty. Rational deliberation would epitomize the ideal public sphere. But at this stage, reasoning was expected to be more private and individual than public and collective. Thus the middle class substituted the rational, private individual as the ideal over the crowd or mob that they equated with public space.

Achieving the ideal of privacy and respectability was difficult in large and rapidly growing cities. Cities were regarded as cesspools and places of dangerous crowds. Alexis de Tocqueville declared that, "the lowest classes of these vast [American] cities are a rabble more dangerous even than that of European towns." By mid-century in larger cities, the middle class and wealthy began to avoid pollution from contact with lower classes by relocating to class-segregated residential neighborhoods away from factories and their workers living nearby. Since middle-class women were living symbols of their class, their reputation risked not only gender but class status, making their comportment highly significant. The rise of a cult of domesticity constrained where middle- and upper-class young women could go and required a male relative for an escort. Pastimes were confined to the private domestic sphere. The central tenet of the sentimentalism that pervaded middle-class life of the 1830s and 1840s was that private experience was morally superior to the public life. *Godey's Lady's Book* and other domestic magazines and books in the 1850s offered instruction on how to mount parlor theater and *tableaux vivant* in the home for close circles of invited guests.[5]

This withdrawal from public spaces simultaneously created separate spheres for men and women. Men were expected to participate in the world of work outside the home, confronting its "dangers" by suppressing fear and other emotions in favor of rational calculation and a reserved exterior, the masculine form of respectability. Middle-class women, stripped of productive roles, became defined as bearers of emotion and culture, and in need of protection from the heartless world outside the home.[6]

Leaving the domestic haven was sometimes necessary even for women. Making one's way through the city required a map to identify disreputable streets or establishments. One needed to know that New York City's Broadway, where fashionable women promenaded in the afternoon, became disreputable by 4pm. A growing middle-class fear of strangers complicated this further. It was becoming commonplace in major cities to experience public spaces as places of strangers and to fear impostors that could endanger one's respectability. Novels and light-and-shadow books became popular guides to cities and city life, simultaneously feeding fears and mapping safe and dangerous places. The new street grid patterns of nineteenth-century American city growth aided individuals who wished to limit intercourse and maintain their bubble of privacy. Broader, straight thoroughfares and fewer squares encouraged movement and were less conducive to crowds.[7]

But contact in the streets and other unsecured public places was unavoidable, requiring a social barrier when crossing paths with polluted persons. Under such circumstances, the middle class sustained respectability and avoided social intercourse by repressing self-expression and presenting instead a shield of ritual. Spontaneous expression, a mark of the Jacksonian working class, was deemed rude; respectability required restraint. Self-denial and self-control were central to mid-century middle-class culture for both men and women, and continued to be so to the end of the century. Willpower and reason supplanted spontaneity, nature, and emotion. Middle-class self-control was juxtaposed to aristocratic dissipation on the one hand and to lower-class disreputability on the other. Every motion of the new middle class declared their respectable status.

Manners aided privacy to achieve this respectability. Etiquette manuals and advice to the young taught self-presentation in private and public, and how to read others as well. They were plentiful, elaborated numerous rules for countless settings and occasions, and were remarkable for their detailed lists of "don'ts." They cautioned against the outburst of positive emotions such as laughter, as well as negative emotions such as petulance. They prohibited involuntary bodily functions such as belching and flatulence. They warned the reader to avoid touching walls and furniture as well as people. Even eye contact was to be controlled. Manners replaced spontaneity.[8]

The same strategies of class segregation and reserve in public display applied to audiences. The middle class was advised to avoid rowdy theaters and display proper manners in safer venues. In the past, theater was condemned on religious grounds as immoral; at mid-century, some continued to disapprove of theater to protect social reputation. But trading on the discourse of respectability, a few entrepreneurs promoted their theaters as domesticated public spaces to attract middle-class clientele. Moses Kimball in Boston and P. T. Barnum in New York City introduced museum theater in the 1840s, adopting the manners of the middle-class parlor and assuring a moral climate on and off stage. They appealed to mothers to come with their children to dramas, such as temperance or abolition dramas, that were promoted as educational or morally uplifting. In the 1850s, theaters that hoped to attract a more lucrative middle-class clientele eliminated traditional masculine features such as prostitutes, drink, and tobacco. They changed the name of the pit to the "*parterre*" and replaced benches with upholstered reserved seats bolted to the floor that increased comfort and reduced crowding. They introduced matinees specifically for female audiences whose husbands and fathers were at the office. They relocated to the newly developing shopping districts of department stores that catered to women. All of these changes proclaimed the theater as a respectable, domesticated feminine space. Rough audiences continued to frequent "cheap theaters," where they formed one large boisterous crowd. But the middle class patronized "legitimate theater," where audiences attended as small private domestic clusters of family and friends and spoke mostly with each other.[9]

By 1870, the change was firmly in place, as evident in a *Harper's Monthly* "Easy Chair" column contrasting the old Park Theater of the early nineteenth century to the fashionable new Wallack's Theater in New York City. The audience was no longer "the noisy crowd of men massed upon hard backless benches" with classes commingled in the same house, but "a luminous cloud of lovely toilets [and] *jeunesse doree* . . . a house in which, so to say, there are no classes . . . the whole house seems to be a family circle." The middle- and upper-class goal of avoidance was explicit in a remark by the director of the New York Metropolitan Museum of Art, "we do not want, nor will we permit a person who has been digging in a filthy sewer or working among grease and oil to come in here, and, by offensive odors emitted from the dirt on their apparel, make the surroundings uncomfortable for others."[10] This expression of disgust at the polluted nature of the lower classes and the contrasting perfumed air of the better classes defined the difference between classes and the necessity of separate theaters.

## Cultivation

For proper audiences, cultivation worked hand in glove with respectability. Etiquette rules presumed that the duty of the audience was to give full attention to the performance, in order to cultivate oneself. Any action that interfered with others' ability to do that was rude. Whereas previously speaking and acting out had been considered a right of audiences, by the 1850s such behavior was limited to working-class theaters. The middle class characterized it as an outrage against both performers and other members of the audience. *Harper's Monthly* Easy Chair caricatured a family, "the H—s", who exhibited all the grossest behaviors at theater, "bustling entrance and loud conversation," "gabble and giggle" during the performance. An 1855 manual warned that at opera, "There can scarcely be a worse piece of manners, or a more palpable injustice than to continue a conversation while the performance is going forward" since ticket-holders had a "right to the uninterrupted enjoyment of the music. The singers have a right to your silence." It prohibited wearing a hat or beating time for music with a cane or one's feet. An 1886 manual warned about "being in your seat before the performance," not eating audibly, nor breaking peanut shells, rattling papers, or rustling about one's chair, nor bringing children, standing up during a performance, or wearing large hats. To talk, whisper, or laugh was "an indignity to both audience and performer." An 1899 publication for school children summed up the whole era's attitudes, "Perhaps nowhere are bad manners more disagreeable than in public places of amusement . . . [where people] are defrauded of the pleasure they have paid for by the conduct of those about them." This was followed with a list of don'ts: it was not polite to performers or audience to arrive late, to stare and look around the assembly, to look at one's watch, to applaud too faintly or too boisterously, to stamp feet or whistle, and to leave early "even though it does not prove very interesting."[11]

Lists of "don'ts" were intended to prevent interference with the rights of other members of the audience to witness the performance. The references to rights in these quotes indicate the completion of the cultural shift from conceptions of collective rights of audiences to *individual* rights of audience members that began in the Astor Place riots of 1849 (see Chapter 1). What had been conceived as audience sovereignty in an earlier era was grounded in collective rights. By the second half of the century, the middle class advocated the right of the individual ticket-holder to undisturbed self-cultivation.[12]

Self-cultivation defined life as a constant duty to improve oneself; it opposed idleness and self-indulgence of the rich or the poor. It focused inward on the self, rather than outward on the community or the public. It emphasized individual improvement rather than public betterment, or nineteenth-century liberalism's public betterment *through* individual improvement. It was the complement to privatization. It replaced leisure with re-creation. Self-cultivation was adopted almost as a religion to guide middle-class life in the latter part of the nineteenth century, when it appeared not only in intellectual treatises but also as the theme of regular articles in magazines. It even became a criterion of citizenship. Exemplifying this trend, Reverend S. H. Emery, Jr. neatly summarized its constituent parts in 1877, "Cultivation and discipline go hand in hand. . . . Culture is education of the intellect. Discipline is education of the will." Emery linked willpower to shape one's self-presentation or "self-conscious personality," with that shaping being cultural rather than economic, mental rather than manual, and by rational choice rather than emotional instinct. Like respectability, cultivation was conceived as the dominance of reason and intellect over emotions. One had to learn to respond with studious thought rather than spontaneous feeling to music, art, and ideas.[13]

In the mid-nineteenth century, managers of "legitimate theaters" redefined theater-going as cultivation. Once they had silenced audiences through new policies, they began to promote drama as art. Soon critic-approved stock companies such as those of Laura Keene (1855–1863) and Lester Wallack (1852–1887), who resisted stage spectacle and the star system, would offer dramas certifying cultural sophistication. Dramatic realism was central to this cultivation movement in theater. William Dean Howells, the editor of *Harper's Monthly*, described the new Wallack's in 1870, presenting a new kind of play to match its new clientele,

> the character of the drama had changed as radically as the arrangement of the house and its associations. The mirror was held up to nature with a precision and firmness that resulted in the most delicate and faithful reproduction . . . no fine speeches, no puns, no extravagance. . . . All the incidents and contrasts were such as life, artistically viewed, constantly furnishes.[14]

Beginning in the 1870s, producer-directors like Augustin Daly and Steele MacKaye began to supplant melodrama with advanced realism as a new form of script, acting, staging, and auditing. Acting gestures and expressions were less exaggerated and more realistic. The changed taste is well captured in two quotes from the time. Criticizing the old style of acting, the *Galaxy* objected, "the old school still seems to our perhaps squeamish modern sense to presuppose in the auditor the absence of anything like quick physical perception, developed imagination, ready wit, or refined taste." A *Spirit of the Times* praised the new, realistic acting by Frank Mayo, ". . . delineation of the backwoodsman never overdone. The light and shade of the character are portrayed very artistically. . . . Every detail was carefully filled out and the great charm of Mayo's acting was in his perfect naturalness; there was nothing stagy, nothing strained. He is always artistic . . .."[15]

Lighting also facilitated realism, de-emphasizing the public, social experience and heightening a private, psychological and aesthetic one. Theaters began to install electricity in the 1880s, illuminating the stage well enough to reduce the need for exaggerated gestures and making realism more successful. It also made it feasible to darken the auditorium to focus audience attention on the stage, to become immersed in that "reality," and shed their obligation to attend to their neighbor.[16] The new policies and etiquette of theater-going complemented the dark to enhance concentrating on the stage.

While this applied to the self-cultivating classes that attended legitimate theater, at other theaters lower classes continued to assert their own definition of the situation, to trespass and violate the imaginary reality on stage, and to contest the definition of the audience as solitary individuals. They continued to hiss and hurrah in unison as a crowd. But among the upper-middle and upper classes, the audience was redefined as a collection of individuals, each singly experiencing the play alone.

## Cultural hierarchy: theater critics, cultivation, and commerce

Cultivation ranked activities and experiences in a cultural hierarchy. It elevated the arts over entertainment as the proper choice for self-cultivation. Dramatic realism was part of the institutionalization of cultural hierarchy in America. Professional drama critics were the primary spokesmen for this view, guiding laymen and women in their search for cultivation at the theater, and elevating art over commercialism and entertainment. Instead of the traditional puff-pieces, they wrote critical reviews, set standards of dramatic taste, and expected audiences to practice cultivation.

William Winter was one of the most influential drama critics of the nineteenth century, writing for the *New York Tribune* from 1865 to 1919, as well as for many other publications. He was one of a group of prominent writers in the 1860s who were disenchanted by the change wrought by the war and industrialization on American culture. They represented what was called "the Genteel Tradition." Winter considered theater a temple of art, "not merely a workshop for shrewd and vulgar speculation in popular credulity," a reference to crass commercialism. Another influential critic, John Ranken Towse, for the *New York Evening Post* from 1874 to 1927, believed theater should "illustrate and enforce the soundest principles of art, morality and social law under the seductive guise of entertainment." He wrote that theater had a responsibility as "an elevator of the public mind and morals" and should be "conducted as an agent of the higher civilization."[17]

These critics considered theater to have a public duty not only to cultivate, but also to socialize people and, by extension, to prevent social disorder. Implicit in their concept of hierarchy was a conception of theater controlled by an intellectual-cultural elite to guide and educate other classes. Consequently they opposed commercialism in theater, explaining the success of melodramas such as *Camille* and *East Lynne* as exploitation of immorality and emotions for the purpose of making money. As Winter expressed it in 1862, "tears may be crystallized into currency." Through their long careers, Winter and Towse continued their criticism of commercialism and argued for a revival of theater as art. They reasoned that art raised the intellectual standard of a society, while entertainment reduced a society to its lowest tastes. They sacralized dramatic performance in the same way that others sacralized Shakespearean text and symphonic music in the same era.[18]

Institutionally, sacralization was a withdrawal from the commercial market, changing the experience from consumption into cultivation, and audience from consumers to art appreciators. Cultivators were most alarmed by the commercial success of the Theatrical Syndicate in 1896. Harrison Fiske, editor of the *New York Dramatic Mirror*, attacked the syndicate upon its inception, calling it "a hateful, corrupt and dangerous institution conceived by men who have no sympathy with the arts of the stage." Editor and critic Norman Hapgood wrote, "nothing does more than the existence of this powerful association to prevent the growth of the American drama." He blamed the six "uncultivated" men who ran the syndicate for "the dearth of repertoires, of great dramas, of American plays." *Harper's Monthly* editor and critic William Dean Howells wrote, "Not merely one industry, but civilization itself is concerned, for the morals and education of the public are directly influenced by the stage. Everyone who takes a pride in the art of his country, must regret a monopoly." John Towse, looking back over his sixty years of theater in 1916, blamed not only the Theatrical Syndicate but also "a public press which, in the interest of commercialism, has not hesitated to accept false standards and help the managerial game. . . ."[19]

Theater critics and other advocates of cultural hierarchy in drama also contrasted their ideal, self-cultivating audience to the self-indulgent unappreciative rich who they complained disrupted performances, and the untutored working class who preferred low-level melodrama and music hall. Both groups, they believed, provided theatrical businessmen profits from low artistic standards and thus degraded drama.

Winter expressed his attitude toward audiences in his memoirs. He made clear his prejudices against the working class: "the Music Hall is the deadly foe of the Theatre . . . the obvious 'want' of the Pee-pul, considering what they accept, in all our great cities, would seem to be Trash." But also he was disgusted by the uncultivated upper classes, saying actors were distracted by "the swish, swish, swish of whispering, indifferent spectators, the slamming of seats, the creaking of doors, the ostentatious parade and noisy bustle of fashionable females, arriving late and divesting themselves of the evening wraps as they throng into the boxes and indolently and often superciliously place themselves on exhibition." He accused the majority of the theater audience of being "vulgarians, who know nothing about art or literature and who care for nothing but the solace of their common tastes and animal appetites." For Winter, audiences were to be quiet appreciators of the actors' art for the sake of their own cultivation.[20]

Like many other observers of late nineteenth-century American theater, he preferred the earnest middle-class audience for whom the cost of a ticket was not a trifle and who took seriously the artistic appreciation of the performance. Similarly, Charlton Andrews wrote in *Theatre Magazine* that, "the only way to elevate the stage is to elevate the audience . . . the mentally incompetent ought to be barred from serious drama," that the theater was held down by "the gloomy dead weight of a vast and hopeless unintelligence," by whom he meant the rich who can afford the highly-priced tickets, and that "Intelligence is usually found in the cut-rate seats." His sarcastic solution was to grade people for admission to theaters of their proper level, with first-class theaters for "intelligent, appreciative and courteous ladies and gentlemen"; middling playhouses for those more limited or who "through education may yet ascent"; "tenth-rate music halls and houses of raw melodrama and slapstick [for] children of adult years"; and movies for "intellectual unfortunates."[21]

## Cultural uplift and Progressives

Not all believers in cultural hierarchy considered the working class to be "children of adult years" or "intellectual unfortunates." While privatization and self-cultivation continued to be the preference of cultural elites and some of the middle class, others considered it their civic duty to return to the public sphere and promote the cultivation of others less fortunate. Progressives were more hopeful about the masses, and rather than avoiding them as polluted and condemning them as dangerous crowds, they hoped to "civilize" them.[22]

The Progressive concept of citizenship revived republican civic virtue. The basic premises of the settlement house movement of England, which inspired the American movement, grew from a revolt against individualistic utilitarianism and a call for organic community. One of its intellectual forebears, Thomas Carlyle, exhorted, "Men cannot live isolated, we are all bound together." Applied to the conditions of poverty, this meant that the privileged could not ignore the poor and should become models of character and cultivation for the poor. Toynbee Hall, the first English settlement house, was based on the idea that privileged young men would live among the working class of East London to give "not money, but themselves."[23]

Not only men, but middle-class women were returning to public life, forming a social movement to help poor families and lobbying government to institutionalize these services. It had long been acceptable for this class of women to care for the physical welfare of the poor and unfortunate, but this was private charity to reduce suffering. Progressives aimed to change their condition, to develop the downtrodden mind, character, and culture, to change who they were and how they behaved. Progressivism also widened the stream of these women, making it respectable for women to engage in civic participation and public service. College-educated women, in particular, began to move beyond their previous circuit of society events, charity, and self-cultivation—and women took the lead in cultural uplift.[24]

Cultural uplift was a founding principle of the settlement movement in working-class neighborhoods. The influential founder of the Chicago settlement, Hull House, Jane Addams argued that refinement and cultivation "must be made universal if they are to be permanent." As historian Mina Carson phrased it, "The premise of the settlement movement had been that people of education had a special gift to offer the poor . . . the individual's personality and character formed the conduit though which the 'sweetness and light' of culture would flow." The co-founder of Hull House, Ellen Gates Starr, insisted on providing art for "the hungry individual soul which, without art, will have passed unsolaced and unfed."[25] Liberal arts-educated women would show their working-class clients how to appreciate the arts, to be cultivated audiences.

For Addams, theater was an important portal to draw working-class people to cultural uplift. At the beginning of Hull House in 1889, she found that the local working-class youth were strongly attracted to the local melodrama theater, lining up for matinee seats on Sundays, and eager to talk about what they saw there. She described it as "the only place where they can satisfy that craving for a conception of life higher than that which the actual world offers them . . . a veritable house of dreams," and prescribed a program of drama at Hull House.[26]

Dramatics were a common part of the programs of many settlement houses across the United States. Settlement workers however went beyond performing *for* their clients. With little funding, they relied on the voluntary labor of their clients. The settlements turned this into an asset, giving clients an opportunity to mount their own productions, from selecting the plays, to creating their own costumes and sets, to the actual performances. They performed some of the usual canon of English drama, such as Shakespeare, but also ancient Greek plays and Yiddish dramas drawn from the cultures of and known by their working-class clients, and freshly written pageants to tell stories past and present. At the same time, these plays and pageants drew working-class audiences from the neighborhoods. Settlement staff hoped to mount productions that appealed to these untutored audiences, "great things, simply told," pleasurable but also with messages and morals.[27]

Hull House incorporated plays into many activities. All the clubs put on performances for the community, including plays, pageants, and pantomime; a Dramatic Association formed in 1897, creating the Hull House Players. The Education Alliance of New York formed a children's orchestra, a music society, a choral society, literary clubs, and held concerts, art exhibitions, and theater performances. The Henry Street House in New York City similarly began with street pageants to celebrate spring and other events, involving not only costumes and acting, but dancing, pantomime, and choral singing. As these productions grew in sophistication, in 1915 they established the Neighborhood Playhouse, which became a prominent part of the Little Theater movement.[28]

The hope was that the moral messages of the plays would help form strong moral character and good American citizens. Many settlement houses in the United States were situated in immigrant neighborhoods, and were concerned with assimilating immigrants to American middle-class values. This was implicit in almost everything that settlement workers did, whether teaching hygiene, English, or art. Some, like the business-sponsored settlement houses of Gary and Indianapolis, Indiana in the 1910s, introduced citizenship classes. Wealthy German Jews of New York founded the Education Alliance in 1889 especially to Americanize Eastern European Jews of the Lower East Side. The Alliance provided classes to prepare children to enter public schools, English classes for adults and even Hebrew teachers, and classes on western music and art.[29]

The settlement house movement was part of a broader Americanization movement concerned about the flood of immigrants around the turn of the twentieth century and the efforts to educate them on the American concept of citizenship. Americanization was conceived as a type of cultural uplift. Progressive Lydia Kingsmill Commander expressed this view: "Altogether the foreign and the ignorant comprise the bulk of the American people. The principal problem that confronts us in our struggle to develop an American democracy is the education and uplifting of this vast mass." The central concern of Americanization was to teach English and civics in order to socialize immigrants into the mainstream. It attempted to create an imagined community of American nationhood out of this flood of immigrants, or what playwright and novelist Israel Zangwill called "a melting pot." It was also about class; the ideal envisioned in the programs of Americanization was to inculcate *middle-class* American values and norms.[30]

Americanization campaigns included a wide array of organizations with a range of motives, including the U.S. Chamber of Commerce Americanization Committee, the Red Cross Foreign Language Information Service, and various organizations formed by successful earlier immigrants, such as the Jewish

Educational Alliance.[31] The pioneering organization devoted to educating immigrants to be good citizens was the North American Civic League for Immigrants, initiated by the YMCA in 1907. Its president, Daniel Chauncey Brewer, stated the purpose of his organization was "nothing less than the conservation of cherished institutions, which it believes will be threatened if means and measures are not taken rightly to guide the incoming hosts of strangers and to familiarize them with constitutional government." Its 1909–1910 Annual Report stated that it "has no more important function to perform than to push the teaching of English and primary civics to the immigrants." It published in ten languages a pamphlet on what it means to be an American citizen, how to become a citizen, and the importance of learning English. It persuaded businessmen, schools, and other public and private social agencies to cooperate with it in providing education, especially nightschool, for immigrant adults. Its parent organization, the YMCA, promoted a middle-class definition of manhood that included hard work, individual acquisitiveness, self-restraint, and civilized morality.[32]

Americanizers looked to use movies to teach immigrants how to behave as American citizens. John Dewey listed movies and other commercial media as undermining the health of publics. But he also wished to use these media to educate audiences to behave as publics rather than as a manipulable mass. Film scholars have long talked about the Americanizing effects of the movies on immigrants, but recently some scholars have documented specific efforts to produce and exhibit commercial films with an Americanizing purpose. In 1907, Jane Addams tried to adopt the alleged power of film by starting a movie theater at Hull House for uplift and acculturation. About the same time, a reaction began against the French film studio, Pathe Freres, which had gained dominance in the U.S. market. Stories in the press, perhaps instigated by American film companies, claimed that foreign films were immoral. American companies then joined the Americanization chorus and began producing westerns as a thoroughly American genre. *Making an American Citizen*, released in 1912, was a commercial film, but with a very strong Americanization message, apparently directed at Eastern European immigrants. In later years, the YMCA, various corporations, and other organizations developed documentary and institutional films with messages about citizenship. In 1920, the State of Connecticut Department of Americanization produced *The Making of an American*.[33]

## Cultivation returns to the public sphere

Ideas of self-cultivation and cultural uplift also were woven into the Little Theater movement, civic pageants, and women's clubs around the turn of the twentieth century. These drew the middle class into civic projects to support and sustain cultivation. Ironically the self-cultivation born in privatization grew into public cultivation, the reinvigoration of the public sphere, and specifically the redefinition of audiences as citizen publics. By the turn of the new century, cultivation was a public service, directed at the civic health of the community rather than private improvement. Settlement work, community theater, and even women's clubs were becoming civic-minded. These movements mirrored Dewey's ideas of communities acting collectively to solve problems, and creating institutions as on-going solutions that become incorporated into government.[34]

Even the seemingly private activity of reading migrated into the public sphere. Through the nineteenth century it was customary for middle-class family circles to read to each other in the privacy of their home for self-cultivation. But affluent women who had been active during the Civil War, after the war joined reading clubs with other women, where they also discussed the political rights of women. By the 1890s, reading by itself seldom characterized these clubs, which were involved in a range of reform activities. Even conservative clubs were critical of the status quo and advocated change concerning women's issues. Perhaps most fundamental, these reading clubs developed women's confidence to speak their minds, a resource most valuable for any sort of participation in public issues, even in talking about them with their husbands and families. They also developed a repertoire of organizational and other skills that would be useful for participation in the public sphere. Local clubs began to federate, forming a national organization, sharing information, book lists, and speakers, and thus creating a public sphere of their own based on reading and speakers. By the end of the century, women's clubs were deeply involved in reform. They cooperated with the Women's Christian Temperance Union, were instrumental in establishing many of the nation's public libraries, passing child labor legislation, creating a separate juvenile justice system, instituting kindergartens, and promoting education for women.[35]

Women's clubs that included a range of interests rather than a focus on reading were an integral part of upper-middle-class white women's culture from the 1890s through the 1920s. Post–Civil War middle-class women were expected to be cultivated enough to appreciate art, but not so as to be professionals. In this context, women's clubs advocating the arts were a part of every town. While generally devoted to the arts, these clubs also afforded women opportunities for civic activism. Like reading clubs, they were interwoven with the Woman's Movement and Progressivism of the era. While some were outright supporters of suffrage and Progressive reforms, others described themselves as extending their domestic skills to their communities through the organized activities of their clubs, exhibiting a "domestic feminism" of "municipal housekeeping."[36] Women's clubs began as exercises in self-cultivation and developed into civic-oriented public activism, mounting community pageants and founding Little Theaters, as well as more direct engagement in settlement and municipal reform movements.

Given the dual threads of cultivation and civic participation that wove through settlement houses and women's clubs of the turn of the century, it should be no surprise that this culminated in the development of dramatic movements that cast performances as public spheres and audiences as citizens. The Little Theater movement was conceived as a civic contribution as much as a contribution to the arts. It arose from both a spirit of artistic anti-commercialism and the general climate of civic participation created by Progressivism. Most participants were not theater professionals, but civic leaders from the professional and managerial class, active in their local communities.[37]

Little Theater companies in the 1910s and 1920s constructed their audiences through instruction in schools and colleges, ushers and programs in the theater, subscription campaigns and other efforts to attract and organize a loyal audience, and through the drama itself. In contrast to commercial theater, they sought a cultivated audience who would read program notes to guide their understanding and appreciation of the performance; who would not expect orchestras and famous actors; who would hold their applause until the end of the play; and who would accept amateur performers and non-theatrical venues since they valued the message of the play more than spectacle, scenery, music, and celebrity. These theaters also sought an audience for whom going to the theater was an act of support for a civic institution that enhanced the city's culture and its people, making them better citizens. Many incorporated John Dewey's rejection of the passive audience in favor of active involvement, and encouraged participation in the production and in support auxiliaries. For example, E. C. Mabie, founder of the University of Iowa theater department, claimed that "community drama and pageantry is a splendid means of democratic, educative, public recreation." Little Theater companies often treated the theater as a public sphere in which they made a statement about current issues faced by its audiences, with the expectation that audiences would recognize the relevance to pressing real-life matters.[38]

The civic dimension of this era's theater was most evident in the pageant movement of the early twentieth century, from about 1905 to about 1925.

Pageants and parades had been a part of American culture from the beginning. But typically they had been celebrations of specific groups. At the turn of the century, local elites wished to promote their city as a whole and to incorporate all groups into this civic pride. Pageants were intently designed for art to serve democracy by fostering identification with the city. They celebrated the community and performed outdoors to a large audience of the whole community. Frequently, rather than presenting a dramatic narrative, they recounted events that fabricated a civic history. Women's clubs, the Little Theater movement, the settlement house movement, and civic boosters all contributed to the growth of civic pageantry.[39]

As with Little Theater, the leaders of this movement were a mix of civic elites, artists, and Progressive reformers. But they varied in their purposes: artists used pageants as a vehicle to develop American styles of art; educators wanted to teach immigrants English, history, and civics; settlement house workers used pageants to acknowledge immigrants' ethnic heritages; suffragists to advance their cause; civic leaders to instill patriotism and loyalty to the city or town. Elites and civic boosters promoted pageants that portrayed the city's history as a progression of a uniform whole, ignoring the diverse ethnic immigrant populations. Philadelphia's 1908 pageant to celebrate the city's founding exemplified this kind of event. A Local historian Ellis Oberholtzer, under the direction of the city government, planned a parade of floats as a city-wide event of civic education. It focused exclusively on identification with the city rather than particular groups or neighborhoods. Oberholtzer hired professionals for much of the artistic work, and reserved leading roles in the procession for members of the city's elite. This form of pageantry emphasized a citizenship of civic pride and social order. It envisioned a well-behaved mass of citizens guided by an enlightened elite.[40]

For others, the goal of pageants was to involve communities not simply as neutral witnesses or passive audiences but as participants, a theatrical form "of the people, by the people, and for the people." One artist advocate of this approach, Percy MacKaye, claimed that participation would mean, "a new self-government [of leisure] in which political self-government must be rooted to have its flowering." The intent was to involve people in the activity from planning to performance in order to demonstrate to them the power of their own united efforts in the realm of art, with the hope of inspiring a sense of citizenship in and civic duty to their city, much as Dewey imagined. Nevertheless, the emphasis still lay on celebrating the city and erasing memories of difference.[41]

Civic activism was to be channeled into the pageant, but not encouraged as independent collective action. A planner of the pageant to celebrate the 150th anniversary of the founding of St. Louis, echoed MacKaye, ". . . if people play together they will work together. . . ." In Boston, the purpose of the pageant planned by the Boston 1915 Committee was to created the right "state of mind" on the grounds that, "To secure a city which is properly planned, decently ordered and economically administered, its citizens have only to get into a 'state of mind' where they not only want these things but also believe them to be possible" and that this would result from democratic participation in planning and completing the pageant. These words reveal desires to avoid class and ethnic conflict in cities and to create consensus built on a common identity with elite visions for the city. The pageant movement was a movement based on ambivalence. Concerns about crowds and riots and worries about the hordes of un-Americanized immigrant masses were still alive among elites. Leaders wished to foster a sense of citizenship in their cities, but were fearful of independent activism. Active participation in pageants and other leisure events was a safe way to encourage a sense of citizenship. Elites wished to unify the population under their orchestration.[42]

In the 1930s another civic theater movement, the Federal Theater Project, would make its agenda that public theater be an exercise in citizenship which encouraged grass-roots activism rather than submerge it under elite direction. The Federal Theater Project was part of Roosevelt's Works Progress Administration to give jobs to the unemployed, in this case writers, directors, and actors. It was one of the largest theatrical enterprises in the world. In less than four years, it employed over 10,000 workers, who mounted over 1,000 separate productions, including almost 200 plays, many of them new. It included many different units and programs, including Living Newspapers, Experimental, Negro, Children's, Puppet, and Classical Repertory theater, a poetic drama unit, a vaudeville unit, a playwriting unit, and a monthly magazine. Despite the fact that they were prohibited from advertising, they performed for the equivalent of a quarter of the U.S. population, an amazing feat for live performances.[43]

The head of the project, Hallie Flanagan, wrote in her history of the project that, "We all believed that the theatre was more than a private enterprise, that it was also a public interest, which, properly fostered, might come to be a social and educative force." She said they were interested in depicting "the conditions back of the conditions" of the Depression, to raise issues about the economic circumstances that their audiences suffered and to suggest what to do about them. It was to be more than an aesthetic or intellectual or pleasurable experience; it was a public sphere to consider issues of the day. Flanagan said about her Congressional opponents: "I could see why certain powers would not want even 10% of the Federal Theater plays to be the sort to make people in our democracy think. Such forces might well be afraid of thinking people." She justified her goals by saying, "Either the arts are not useful to the development of the great numbers of American citizens who cannot afford them—in which case the government has no reason to concern itself with them; or else the arts are useful in making people better citizens—in which case the government may well concern itself increasingly with them."[44]

First and foremost, the Federal Theater Project tried to bring theater to people who were seldom seen in theaters. Even in the heyday of blood-and-thunder circuits in the late nineteenth century, professional dramatic entertainment was an uncommon experience for most working-class people. The Project reached these people by keeping admission prices low, as low as five cents for children, and by mounting plays that resonated with these people's lives. Many Theater Project plays captured the daily lives and struggles of working-class people during the Depression. Even the classics were often revised to fit current events or the local audience. Its Negro theaters tailored their productions to black communities, such as *Macbeth* set in Haiti. It mounted programs in Yiddish in Jewish neighborhoods, including a scene about concentration camps omitted from other productions. The Living Newspapers dramatized current events in short scenes sometimes taken from local newspapers. Sinclair Lewis' *It Can't Happen Here* speculated about fascism in the United States. Paul Green's *Hymn to the Rising Sun* featured a young slave boy who, having been beaten, sings "My Country 'Tis of Thee." *The Revolt of the Beavers* was a children's play about hard-working beavers mistreated by their bosses.[45] Most famous was *The Cradle Will Rock*, produced by John Houseman and directed by Orson Welles, a play about striking steel workers. Congress shut it down before the first performance, but the troupe mounted the play as a private production for over 100 performances.

Flanagan described the audiences as the antithesis of "metropolitan productions attended by the privileged and affluent few." They were mesmerized and delighted. A director in Peoria, Illinois reported audiences who "come from miles around on show nights, sit as near the front as they can get and never want to go home when the play's over." A New Jersey newspaper described Project audiences, "whistling and stamping in a veritable frenzy of delight." In Seattle, longshoremen in the audience were so excited that they jumped upon the stage and joined the actors in the final scene of *Stevedore*. At *Power*, a play about damming rivers for electric power, the audience got into the spirit of the play and hissed the villains and cheered the heroes. Theater historian Barry Witham said the play was integral to "one of the great public debates in the history of the Seattle community." The *New York Sun* wrote in 1938, "The WPA has brought into the legit theater a new, vociferous and rather engaging audience. . . . Its face is not frozen. It is not sitting on its hands. When it hisses it is not self conscious and when it cheers, it means it."[46] The Federal Theater Project brought a whole new working-class audience into theater by making theater a public sphere dealing with issues facing the nation. It had included these people as citizens in the great debates of the time about what could be done about the state of the nation and of their lives. A century before, theater had been a lively public sphere. For a time, it was again.

Chapter 4

# Broadcast publics

Broadcasting has been defined as fundamentally part of the public sphere in ways that theater and movies had not. Its public service obligation and the news and public service programming that arose from it framed broadcasting from the beginning as a technological extension of the newspaper in its role in the public sphere. Newspapers were essential to preparing the ground for this, so a brief history of the press will be helpful as background.

Historians and political theorists have labeled the press since the eighteenth century as central to the public sphere. In the United States, contemporaries as well conceived newspapers in these terms. Thomas Jefferson considered a free press fundamental to a citizenry acting as a rational, deliberative public. In 1787 he wrote:

> The way to prevent these irregular interpositions of the people [referring to Shay's Rebellion] is to give them full information of their affairs thro' the channel of the public papers, and to contrive that those papers should penetrate the whole mass of the people . . . everyman should receive those papers and be capable of reading them.

He argued that it was important to "keep alive their attention" to public affairs. Otherwise governing classes would become wolves preying on the people. Newspapers could "enlighten" the people with the truth if all citizens received them and were educated enough to read and understand them. Newspapers would be the crucial link that would enable citizens to know about their government and "their affairs." Without these papers they would be uninformed and would not act.[1]

Newspapers themselves framed their readers as citizens; even as the definitions of citizenship changed over time, newspapers reflected these changes in their own changed forms. Newspaper historians Kevin Barnhurst and John Nerone identify four periods of American newspaper form: printerly, partisan, Victorian, and modern newspapers. Each of these forms represented readers in ways consistent with the conception of citizenship in the dominant discourse of the time. Throughout this history, commercial and political interests shared newspaper space, written for the market as well as the forum, for the seller and consumer as well as the citizen, one sometimes in ascendance over the other. But politics and the citizen always remained essential.[2]

The printerly phase encompassed most of the eighteenth century. The readership expanded from an exclusive clientele of colonial gentlemen to a broader public during the Revolution and the Federalist era. However, throughout this period, even during the heated debates over ratification of the Constitution, the artisan printers who produced newspapers in small shops claimed to be providing a non-partisan medium of conversation among the gentry who could afford subscriptions. This was consistent with the contemporary idea of republican citizenship and the hierarchical culture of deference. While newspapers also addressed the farmers and artisans upon whom the Revolutionary cause depended, and later the broad male electorate of the new republic, there remained an expectation that commoners would defer to the superior wisdom and civic virtue of gentlemen. The newspaper form itself acknowledged this. Columns were written in the formal style of a letter from one gentlemen to another that presumed the reader had the leisure and sophistication to not only read, but to respond in writing. Readers were subscribers and presumed to follow stories from issue to issue. Through all this, there remained the idea of a citizen as a man with civic virtue who placed the interest of the republic above self-interest.[3]

By the 1820s democracy was replacing deference as the guiding principle, shifting toward a new idea of partisan citizenship, in which the citizen acted out of self-interest, selecting a party that served his interests. Politics had been reconceived as a marketplace in which parties competed for votes. Parties funded newspapers and installed their own editors to run them, creating the partisan paper. At the same time, new technologies of rotary presses and other devices multiplied the size of print runs and were beginning to change the nature of newspapers. These changes created the penny press and reached deeper into the class structure for a market. This increased the need for a new product, the news, and adjusted the style of writing to appeal to this readership.[4]

The Victorian publisher's paper after the Civil War was the culmination of commercialization. It was now a business enterprise, in contrast to the printer's or editor's paper, requiring great capital to employ the newest technologies and mass produce on a scale even greater than the earlier period. Whereas the partisan paper increased appeal by providing political attractions to citizens, the publisher's paper provided visual appeal in the appearance of the page, thanks to typeface innovations and spectacle in the stories themselves?[5]

At the end of the century, newspaper publishers began to declare themselves independent of political parties and promote the idea that they were neutral and objective. This modern newspaper represented itself as providing the facts that informed readers needed. The professional, factual newspaper proposed to cover the whole world in all its facets. It offered a map of the social world from elections to society events, sports, and fashions, to entertain as well as inform. This appealed to the interests of consumers as well as citizens.[6]

A new discourse on professionalization defined journalism as central to the operation of a public sphere and contrasted it to low-brow yellow journalism. Adolph Ochs purchased the *New York Times* in 1896 and announced policies based on professional journalism: to give all the news, give it as early as any other "reliable medium," to give it impartially, and to make the *Times* "a forum for the consideration of all questions of public importance and, to that end, to invite intelligent discussion from all shades of opinion." The *Times*' statement captured the essence of the discourse, placing news at the center of the bourgeois public sphere.[7] In this discourse, newspapers were supposed to serve a vital civic function of providing the information with which publics might debate issues. Echoing the *New York Times*, E. L. Godkin, editor of *The Nation*, wrote in *Atlantic Monthly* in 1898 about the importance of newspapers for expressing public opinion and therefore the need that papers be independent of parties. Similarly, the first issue of the *American Journal of Sociology* in 1895 described education and newspapers as central to democracy, education to provide an intelligent and rational citizenship, and newspapers to provide information that could be the basis of deliberation and decision by citizens. The essay contrasted this ideal to the three-fourths of citizens—'the masses'—whose opinion was based on "a mixture of sense and nonsense, of sentiment, of prejudice."[8]

Yellow journalism played a key role in this discourse by being painted as the news for these masses—the opposite of everything that responsible newspapers should be. The term was coined to refer to Joseph Pulitzer's *New York World* and William Randolph Hearst's *New York Journal* in the 1890s and any other papers that adopted their brand of sensational journalism. Pulitzer bought the *World* in 1883 and quickly turned it into a paper concentrated on crime, scandal, and sensation, that is, news read for entertainment that appealed heavily to emotion. Hearst bought the *Journal* in 1895 and immediately began competing with Pulitzer. The two tried to outdo each other in the outrageousness of their papers. Ervin Wardman, editor of the *New York Press* and purportedly the creator of the term "yellow journalism," repeatedly published scathing insults about both papers.[9]

In early 1897, several libraries and clubs began boycotting the yellow press, on the grounds that such papers were immoral and corrupting. But the boycott had little effect: it constituted few subscriptions, and the heads of these organizations and the members of these clubs were upper class and unrepresentative of yellow journalism's popular market. The discourse about the yellow press was distinctly about class. Yellow journalism positioned itself as identified with the working class by publishing stories that punctured the pompous and encouraged crusades against the powerful and privileged. Its critics tended to be the cultural elite who reiterated the yellow press association with the working class and immigrants. The *New York Times* published a letter characterizing the yellow press as more for "a certain class of ignorant and uncultivated readers than for public enlightenment, and are the result of a morbid craving on the part of the lower order of mankind for sensational reading and illustration." *Bookman* magazine wrote, "The banality and sensationalism of the bad papers are a shade above the banality and coarseness of the people who read them." Their pandering to such debased senses was considered to undermine the exalted role of newspapers to guide and enable citizens to fulfill their duty in a democracy.[10]

The "factual" newspaper coincided with the image of the informed citizenship engaged in non-partisan, rational assessment of facts. This new definition of journalism placed news at the center of the bourgeois public sphere. It was incorporated into Tarde's and Park's concepts of publics of the time. Moreover, it prepared the ground to define twentieth-century broadcasting as an information medium central to the public sphere.

## Radio as public sphere

Radio arrived just as immigration was choked off, first by World War I and then by newly restrictive immigration laws. Immigration plummeted from 8.8 million in the 1900s to 4.1 million in the 1920s to 0.5 million in the 1930s, defusing fears about it. Also, radio listeners, dispersed and invisible as a group, were less threatening than the visual image of people "crowded" together in a movie theater. Radio publicity in the 1920s emphasized it as a domestic activity. Photographs of radio listeners depicted individuals and small groups or families in domestic settings. Radio magazine covers and advertisements consistently placed radios in living rooms with family members gathered round. These developments dissociated radio listeners from the image of crowds and provided an opportunity to define radio as a tool for informing and constituting Americans as a public and affirming a national American identity.[11]

Within this context, the U.S. government took the unusual step of defining the airwaves as public property. Broadcast license owners could rent but not own the airwaves. Moreover the license was a privilege, a *quid pro quo* for which license-holders must serve the public interest. The public's interest took precedent over the private interest of the licensee. Public rights were at the core of law and regulation of radio and television for 60 years, continually contested and often undermined or contradicted, but always framing the debate.

According to historian Louise Benjamin, the idea of the public interest was given two conflicting interpretations: one considered the development of new technologies and industries such as radio inherently in the public interest; the other emphasized radio's duty to present a diversity of political viewpoints to citizens.[12] The former tended to favor commercial license-holders and accepted their claims of free speech to ward off regulation. The latter tended to oppose corporate monopoly of radio and make diversity a central criterion of regulation, as expressed by Representative Luther Johnson in the debate over the Radio Act of 1927,

> It will only be a few years before these broadcasting stations, if operated by chain stations [networks], will simultaneously reach an audience of over half our entire *citizenship* [emphasis added]. . . . American thought and American politics will be largely at the mercy of those who operate these stations . . . then woe to those who differ with them. It will be impossible to compete with them in reaching the ears of the American public.[13]

This legal and regulatory discourse effectively presumed a definition of the audience as a public of citizens. It defined radio as an institution of the public sphere in contrast to commercial entertainment, as movie exhibition was legally constituted. It conceived radio listeners as publics first and consumers second. A 1927 Federal Radio Commission statement of its interpretation of "public interest" declared that, "advertising should be only incidental to some real service rendered to the public, and not the main object of a program." This became the justification for giving licenses to private operators. Of course, commercial radio and advertisers defined audiences as consumers and government ultimately favored commercial enterprises. But the basic legal framework was unusual in its use of the public sphere as a foundational concept and its conceiving radio listeners as a public. This aspect wove its way through much of broadcasting history, often turned on its head and violated, but nevertheless remaining an ideal until the 1980s.[14]

Even before broadcasting, radio was framed as a public good. As wireless telephony, radio was especially valuable for communication at sea. The Radio Act of 1912 limited amateur radio transmitter operators' use of radio on the grounds that unfettered use of the airwaves interfered with sea and military communication, establishing the precedent that public safety preceded private use. Using the public safety argument underlying priority for commercial sea communication, amateur radio operators formed the American Radio Relay League to promote themselves as providing a public service by relaying messages for emergencies. During World War I, the U.S. government seized property and patents of the Marconi Company, an Italian company on U.S. soil. This presented a question about how the government should use or dispose of these properties. The U.S. Navy argued for retaining them, so it could better control communication at sea. The Navy did not prevail, but its argument reinforced the idea that commercial development should be secondary.[15]

When broadcasting began in the early 1920s, another dilemma again led to framing radio in public terms. The Radio Act of 1912, meant for wireless telephony, was inadequate to regulate broadcasting. Regulation was in the hands of Commerce Secretary Herbert Hoover, who attempted to gain voluntary cooperation from broadcasters to solve problems of interference and other issues. Hoover was favorable to private station owners, particularly the larger ones. Nevertheless he expressed the goal of defining the airwaves as public property. In 1924, he wrote:

> We seek to preserve the ownership of the road through the ether as public property that we may maintain initiative by holding it a free field for competition; to keep alive free speech; to avoid censorship; to prevent interference in the traffic.[16]

After several attempts by Hoover to gain voluntary cooperation among broadcasters had failed and court challenges to his authority limited his ability to control development, chaos in broadcasting mounted. Congress passed the Radio Act of 1927 and established the Federal Radio Commission to regulate broadcasting. The new law defined the airwaves as public property and specifically required that broadcasters, to obtain or retain a license, must serve the "public convenience, interest and necessity." This phrase was borrowed from legal terminology applied to railroads, defining them as common carriers and requiring them to offer their services unbiased to the public generally. Despite its commercial origins, in interpreting this phrase the Federal Communication Commission and the courts in the 1930s began to construe it in a political sense, building upon past association of radio with public service and attaching it to the idea of radio functioning to provide citizens the information and means of communication that they needed to fulfill their role in a democracy, that is, as a source of news and public information and a place for public debate, like the press.[17]

This trend began with hearings after the passage of the 1934 Act and the creation of the new FCC. The networks were successful in defeating efforts to reserve a quarter of the radio spectrum for non-profit stations, a defeat of the actualization of radio as public sphere. But, in order to defeat the reform, the networks presented themselves as providing public service programming. They thus committed themselves to something that they would thenceforth be expected to deliver. Radio stations began to appoint "public service directors" as liaison with non-profit groups, who sometimes acted as counterweights against commercialism and supporters of the ideal of radio audiences as citizens. When Congress or the FCC began to raise questions or debate issues concerning radio, commercial broadcasters responded by introducing new public affairs programs.[18]

The concept of broadcasters serving the public interest continued as the core of broadcast regulation and was restated by Congress in 1954:

> . . . the spectrum is a natural resource belonging to the entire national public . . . may be used for private purposes only insofar as such will benefit the public interest . . . the right of the public to service is superior to the right of any licensee to make use of any frequency or channel for his own private purposes.[19]

It was dramatically affirmed again in Newton Minow's famous 1961 "vast wasteland" speech to the National Association of Broadcasters. Only in the deregulation era of the 1980s, after a half century, was this basic principal of broadcast regulation abandoned.

This is not to say that the conception of radio as a public sphere was uncontested, or even dominant. Broadcast historian Erik Barnouw wrote that the FCC gave lip service to the idea of public interest while actually benefiting commercial broadcasters. Media historian Robert McChesney notes that public interest was interpreted in some rather peculiar ways. After the passage of the 1927 Act, for example, the Federal Radio Commission interpreted public convenience in such a way as to prefer commercial over non-profit stations, which they called "propaganda stations." Thus, while the ideal of publics remained part of the discourse about radio audiences, institutions that might have been a force for realizing the ideal of a radio public sphere were being systematically neutered. Non-profit stations had contributed the voices of subordinate groups to the public sphere. For example, labor unions used radio to present their views as a counterpoint to the voices of business in commercially-sponsored radio, such as CBS's *Forum of Liberty*, which provided a pulpit for major corporations. The term "propaganda stations" characterized non-profit stations as demagogues turning mass audiences into collective actors who were bad citizens, while networks and their sponsors, with the cooperation of the FCC, presented themselves as disinterested and offering programming that constructed audiences as good publics. In the face of these efforts, what is remarkable is the duration of the framing of radio in legal discourse as a public sphere, a result of a variety of coincidences and opportunities, against which broadcast corporations found they had to persistently work, even if successfully and with the help of a cooperative commission.[20]

In the early days of broadcasting, other discourses *on* radio and in magazines *about* radio also were framing broadcasting as a public sphere and a tool for democratic participation. This was evident in rural areas, where half of the population still lived in 1920. Since radio constituted a valuable and dramatic means to overcome rural isolation, it caught on more rapidly there than did other communication technologies. The National Weather Bureau had been seeking means to inform farmers in time to protect their crops and animals. Similarly, the U.S. Department of Agriculture sought to bring to farmers current market prices for their crops so that they could better decide when to sell and what price was reasonable to expect. By 1923, over 100 stations reported weather and crop prices. Also, radio reduced the isolation that many farm families experienced in winter, bringing music, entertainment from the outside world, and reducing the psychological and familial costs of isolation. State agriculture extension services across the nation established many pioneering broadcast radio stations and, in some cases, even provided community radio receivers to poor rural communities. For farmers and their government agencies, radio broadcasting in its early days was first and foremost a public service.[21]

Radio magazine articles also explicitly emphasized radio's potential as a medium of public information and debate that might foster a vibrant and broadened public sphere. From the beginning of broadcasting in 1922, *Wireless Age* published many articles touting the blessings of radio: classical music and other cultural and educational possibilities for the masses, and its contributions to making the public into better citizens. The magazine canvassed stations in 1922, during the first national election to involve the use of radio, and declared radio "an absolutely unbiased and impartial medium through which public expression may be given to subjects that have public interest."[22]

The October 1924 issue of *Wireless Age* devoted several articles on the political significance of radio, including one by Herbert Hoover. For the first time, radio provided live coverage of the national conventions of both political parties and apparently drew large audiences who listened for long hours. Introducing the special issue, editor William Hurd raised the question of how much radio might broaden interest in politics among citizens, concluding, "It is by radio that he can be aroused to wide apprehensions . . . and through this means come by example to know and by good education to acquire, the scientific habit of mind of wanting to know why." Assistant Secretary of War Dwight Davis affirmed, "Speeches over the ether will be shorter . . . less of exaggeration and more of fact. . . ." Senator James Wadworth claimed that, "in the truth-attaining home circle where facts are faced willingly . . . these people are not carried away by the group influence so prevalent in crowded meetings."[23] These writers were apparently thinking of radio listeners dispersed in their homes as being inoculated against the effects of crowd psychology and therefore more "reasonable." They believed that radio created the classic informed citizen and enabled more of the population to participate in this manner.

## Town meetings of the air: forging audiences into publics

To fulfill the FCC requirement of serving the public interest and to enhance the public-spirited image of radio, network programming of the 1930s and 1940s included much news and many public forum programs. Such programming was successful commercially as well. Radio had the advantage over newspapers of being able to present news events live, making them more dramatic. Moreover, in the 1930s the Depression and the rise of fascism in Europe stimulated a greater interest in news. Inherent in news programming focused on government actions, as much of network news did from the 1930s on, was the presumption that listeners were fulfilling their roles as publics, ingesting information they then would discuss with friends and neighbors to voice their opinion to government.[24]

Programs discussing public issues were quite widespread during these decades: over 50 programs were aired on network radio from 1926 to 1956 in the category of "public affairs talks and forums," a category separate from "news and commentary." Several lasted more than a decade: *National [Radio] Forum* (CBS, 1929–43), *University of Chicago Round Table* (NBC, 1933–55), *America's Town Meeting of the Air* (NBC Blue, 1935–41; ABC, 1942–56), *Northwestern Reviewing Stand* (MBS, 1937–56), *American Forum* (MBS, NBC, 1928–56), and *People's Platform* (CBS, 1938–52). With a few exceptions, these were all sustaining programs, aired by networks without commercial funding as part of the public service obligation of broadcasters. The FCC "Blue Book" of 1946 even recommended that such programs were better kept as sustained rather than sponsored.[25]

*American Forum* was typical of these long-running programs. It was founded by Theodore Granik, a prominent lawyer promoting free speech, and began broadcasting in January 1928 from radio station WOL in Washington DC, with two panelists in debate before a live audience that submitted written questions to the speakers. It was picked up by the Mutual Broadcasting System (MBS) radio network and then NBC until 1956. It appeared on NBCTV from 1949 to 1957. At the end of each broadcast the announcer stated that the program was "presented as a public service," that is, fulfilling the FCC requirement. To encourage listeners to think about and discuss what they had heard, they distributed a weekly pamphlet transcribing the speeches and debate, beginning in 1939. Similarly, on the NBC radio forum program, *University of Chicago Round Table*, referred to as "the oldest educational program" on radio, prominent experts spoke and then responded to each other. It too published weekly pamphlets for its programs, which made clear that *Round Table* was conceived and intended as a civic education program. The pamphlets encouraged continued reading, thinking, and discussion, suggesting questions and further readings to consider. In the 1950s it also advertised "*Round Table* home study courses."[26]

Public forum shows were run according to the traditional public debate form, with positions presented by knowledgeable or notable people, responses made, then a question and answer period. Beyond this a good bit of variation existed. Some shows featured live studio audiences who also could ask questions or respond to panelists. Some also encouraged people to write in and express their views.

To a greater or lesser degree, these shows took as their mission creating a public out of radio audiences. They conceived their audiences as citizens rather than consumers, and strove to inform them. But the programs varied in what kind of public they aspired to produce. Most were not fully committed to a Deweyan public that would assemble, collectively discuss, and act to petition their government. Rather, the educational emphasis seems to suggest a kind of Lippmannesque public who would listen to the broadcast debate among the elite experts who represented public debate for them and to them, or at least an individualized public who, once informed, would act individually rather than collectively. Certainly, the broadcast of debates complemented with pamphlets lent themselves to some listeners discussing and acting collectively. People listened as groups to *Chicago Roundtable* and *People's Platform*, even though the shows did not actively organize groups. But there seems to have been limited instrumental efforts by most public forum programs to realize this potential. This limitation may well have been due to costs: networks and sponsors were unwilling to pay for such "extension services" for their programs.

Something of an exception to this was the most well-known public forum program, which initially placed much emphasis on audience participation in the public sphere: *America's Town Meeting of the Air*, which aired for 21 years, 1935–1956.[27] Each program focused on a particular public issue and included a panel of guests experienced with the issue. Panelists spoke for an allotted time, then the studio audience responded with questions and comments. In the 1930s many topics concerned New Deal programs, such as "Is government competition retarding business recovery?", "Should we plan for social security?", "The state and our civil liberties," and "How can labor and industry solve their problem?"

The creator of the program was George Denny, Jr., director of Town Hall, Inc. Town Hall was part of the League of Political Education, an organization of the suffrage movement that, after the passage of the 19th amendment, continued to work for wider political participation. They had built a large auditorium in the New York City theater district at which they presented public lectures, debates, and other events to promote their cause. Denny wanted to put on the air the kind of programming the League had promoted at Town Hall. He envisioned his program as a means of recreating the popular democracy of the old town meeting. NBC accepted his proposal in 1935 and its Blue network broadcast the program on a sustaining basis without advertisers.[28]

*America's Town Meeting* explicitly conceived its audience as a public, and made considerable efforts to encourage audiences to discuss issues and register their opinion with government and politicians. According to its fifteenth anniversary booklet, the show was the first forum to include audience participation. The booklet characterized the show as allowing "all without fear or favor [to] enjoy the privilege of free and orderly discussion." Denny allowed lively participation by the studio audience; some described it as rowdy. He made a point of distinguishing the format from debate. To him, debate was about winning. His program was intended instead as an airing of both sides of an issue and then discussing them to achieve understanding and hopefully come to consensus, just as in the ideal New England town meeting. He sought "honest discussion, with integrity of purpose and mutual respect." He and the program's publicity used the term "discussion" rather than "debate" in describing the show's format.[29]

*America's Town Meeting* stood out as the show that most actively organized listening groups. Town Hall Inc. initiated and funded these efforts, while NBC paid for producing and broadcasting the show. In fall 1937 *Town Meeting* began encouraging the formation of discussion groups by offering printed "listening aids" to them. It urged groups around the country to listen to the show collectively and then engage in their own discussions after it concluded, to create town meetings all across the nation, linked to each broadcast. Town Hall obtained the cooperation of YMCA, the Chautauqua Literary and Scientific Circles, the American Library Association, and the WPA Adult Education division to mail their members information promoting the formation of discussion groups. They solicited the Rockefeller Foundation for funds to study their fan mail, and the services of Paul Lazarsfeld and the Princeton Office of Radio Research to study the reactions of working-class listeners.

To support these groups, Town Hall prepared and mailed out, at nominal costs, a wide range of printed material to aide in organizing groups and leading and participating in discussions. They provided a book, *Town Meeting Comes to Town*, a handbook for discussion leaders and a guide for each member on how to discuss. To prepare listening groups for each upcoming broadcast, they sent a weekly announcement providing background on the speakers, a summary of pros and cons on the issue for debate, and a reading list and topics for discussion. For use after the broadcast, they published a weekly bulletin with the complete transcript of speeches, responses by speakers, and even the questions and comments from the studio audiences; and they provided an advisor service by mail to answer any questions on organizing, and so on. To further encourage participation, they sponsored essay contests for adults and for children to write about an issue that would be the subject of a future broadcast in which the winners would participate.

Town Hall, Inc. planned an extension division staff for 1938–39 to deliver such services. It was to include five supervisors, ten corresponding secretaries, and three to five field agents, with an annual budget of $30,000. Indicating the extent of work that went into this effort was an inch-thick bound report of alternate proposals for services, including detailed plans for terms of membership, group charters, and subscriptions. The proposals were based upon thorough analysis of listeners' letters. A staff read the mail and prepared weekly reports summarizing how many wrote, who wrote, and what they wrote.[30]

A survey in 1940 found almost 2000 organized listening groups in the United States that formed in the 1930s and participated in this exercise in publics. More groups listened to *America's Town Meeting* than to any other program reported by those surveyed. The groups were predominantly men, suggesting the program's public-oriented agenda. By contrast, the next most widely attended programs dealt with family problems and women predominated in these groups. About half of formal groups met in homes. Organizations provided meeting places for the rest. Groups ranged from as few as five to ten in homes to hundreds in public halls. About two-fifths of group members were not high school graduates. Members were earnest in their participation: they "believe in the social importance of discussion. They feel they are assisting to make democracy work."[31]

Reverend Phillip Steinmetz described being in one of these listening groups:

> In about 1938, when I was serving a church in New Milford, Pennsylvania, we had a group of men who gathered in the local barbershop each week to listen to the *Town Meeting*, which always ended with a question for listeners to discuss. We stayed late some nights talking about the topic of the week.

A woman in an informal group of listeners wrote to *Town Meeting*, "our discussions often became so heated that it was two or three o'clock before we could calm down enough to think of sleep. This year we decided to ask ten of our friends to meet with us. The group became so interested we decided to make a supper club of it, in order to give more time for discussion." In a 1936 survey by Hadley Cantril, half of *Town Meeting* listeners reported "usually" discussing issues after the program finished.[32]

Town Hall's energized efforts to develop and support listening groups for *America's Town Meeting of the Air* did not continue after 1942. NBC's Blue Network became the independent ABC network, which then attempted to end sustaining support and commercialize the program. Town Hall records indicate no services support staff after that, although the weekly bulletin continued to be published until the show ended in 1956. Given the considerable work put into this effort, funded by Town Hall, the services may have been phased out due to costs. The $30,000 annual budget for services was more than the costs of an expensive radio program, perhaps more than Town Hall could afford, and ABC seemed uninterested.[33]

While most radio programs did not actively organize listening groups, several organizations, independent of programs, recruited listeners to groups and provided agenda and other support for such groups. Most groups were organized by some educational agency, including PTAs, universities, religious organizations, high schools, boards of education, and libraries. Rational discussion was clearly an expectation of agencies promoting groups as well as of members of groups. Discussion was the second most common reason for forming groups, according to leaders. Agencies tended to see radio groups as incorporating into public discussion people that previously were unable to do so. Extending participation in the public sphere was part of the New Deal spirit. According to sociologist Frank Hill, it seemed to have worked. He noted that,

> men's [non-radio] discussion clubs . . . were most plentiful in large cities, and . . . [comprised] almost exclusively business leaders or professional men. The radio groups reached down into strata unable to afford or to have time for the fairly expensive lunches or dinners which in the "regular" discussion clubs were usually the preludes to discussion.

Thus even the participating listeners defined themselves as a public and radio as part of the public sphere.[34]

The flourishing public forum programs in the 1930s arose in part as an antidote to propaganda. As discussed in Chapter 3, some elites feared radio could be used as a tool for propaganda and fill the same role as a demagogue before a crowd, excepting that the audience was the much more numerous mass of the population. George Denny himself expressed this concern in a 1937 speech at Harvard as part of his reasons for wanting to bolster democracy through *America's Town Meeting of the Air*. He was expressing John Dewey's hope that education would save the mass from manipulation. Hadley Cantril expressed a similar hope in his writing in the late 1930s and 1940s. The concerns to provide civic education on the one hand was often linked to the fear of propaganda on the other, not only by Denny and the League of Political Education, but other organizations as well, including the Council for Democracy, B'Nai Brith Anti-Defamation League, *The Nation*, the *New Republic*, *Harper's*, and the *New Yorker*.[35] The discourse promoting publics in this case was an extension of and complement to crowd psychology applied to audiences and to masses.

## Institutional advertising, publics, and consumers

Beside the public forum programs that satisfied the FCC requirement of public service, there were other programs that were less obviously political endeavors, in which radio networks or sponsors framed themselves as civic-minded, uplifting and informing the public, and thus constructed their audiences as self-improving, informed citizens.[36]

In 1932–33, networks broadcast the New York, Boston, Cleveland, and Philadelphia Symphonies and ten other concert music series; in 1937–38, Toscanini directed NBC's own symphony orchestra, the New York Philharmonic played on CBS, Walter Damrosch proselytized for classical music in broadcasts received in 150,000 schools, and four networks broadcast eleven concert music programs on a sustaining basis.[37] Through these programs the networks presented themselves as civic-minded cultural philanthropists to the nation and as responsible caretakers of a public sphere based on cultivating and educating the public.

In a similar vein, radio program sponsorship of cultural and civic programming framed the nation's largest corporations as good citizens. Corporations hoped to use the programs as a means to improve their image, trying to sell themselves more than their products. In the mid to late 1930s, Firestone Tires, Ford Motors, General Motors, Armco Steel, Cities Services, Packard Motors, RCA, Sherwin Williams Paints, Carborundum Abrasives, Chesterfield Tobacco, and American Banks each sponsored concert series. Philco Radio, Scott Paper, Sun Oil, Pall Mall, Bromo Quinine, Jergens Lotion, and Campbell Soups sponsored news and commentary.[38]

Under the guidance of emerging modern advertising agencies, the nation's largest corporations began to fabricate new public images for themselves and to frame radio and its listeners in the process. They crafted a "new vocabulary," more friendly than the former gruff and blunt executive style. The new message was called "Better Living." The term was short for DuPont's slogan, first introduced on its radio program, *Cavalcade of America*, "better things for better living . . . through chemistry," a slogan that lasted for decades. It captured the idea that corporations were the creators and causes of America's high standard of living—ignoring of course the considerable poverty, especially in the depths of the Depression. It placed this idea of domestic comfort at the center of the political agenda by giving it a patriotic quality, as something not only to benefit the individual family but also to make America great. Similarly, *Westinghouse Salutes* and GM's *Parade of the States* adapted civic pageantry to radio.[39] Each weekly episode was a piece of middle-brow eulogy for a city or state. The civic pageantry of these programs used radio to create a representative rather than deliberative public sphere.

Corporate-sponsored high-brow cultural programs concentrated their messages in intermission talks by company spokesmen. Some sponsored programming included opening or closing messages from corporate presidents about public policy, particularly the New Deal. The *General Motors Symphony Concerts* from 1934 to 1937 included brief talks by the "Voice of General Motors." During the sit-down strikes of 1936–37, when auto workers were seeking recognition for a union, GM used these talks more directly for public support. The talk series was relabeled "The American Way of Doing Things," equating GM's views on public issues such as labor legislation with America's and, by implication, the workers' views as un-American. In one message, they drew upon the Declaration of Independence's right to the pursuit of happiness to claim that every worker had the "inalienable right to work," that is, to individually negotiate their own employment and not be bound by a union contract. The talk wove together citizen rights and domestic bliss. It defined the Declaration's "pursuit of happiness" both in domestic terms, "the security, the independence and the welfare of self and family," and as a political right. By speaking to the audience in terms of their domestic circumstances, it framed them as workers and as consumers who through their work would earn enough for their welfare. By addressing the nation on the subject of political rights and labor law they framed radio as a public sphere.[40]

The imagined audience for these shows, despite their high-brow fare, were the masses. In a 1935 internal memo criticizing the musical selections for *Symphony Concerts*, Alfred Sloan of GM remarked that too many compositions "are very low in melody and appeal to the masses." Sloan, speaking for the GM Board, repeatedly called for more popular music, to reach a less sophisticated audience, not one composed, as Denny described, solely of educated opinion leaders.[41] These programs, with their intermission talks, indicate a desire by corporate executives to use radio as a representative public sphere rather than a deliberative one, and envisioned audiences of attentive and obedient listeners rather than informed citizens actively participating in debate and politics.

## Recent talk show publics

American television continued radio's concept of broadcasting as a public sphere by transferring the news and public forum traditions and numerous specific radio programs and personnel to TV. But the participativeness of the early years of *American Town Meeting of the Air* did not transfer to television. They no longer produced pamphlets and other ancillary materials to support listening-group discussion. The voluntary listening groups of the 1930s promoted by a variety of adult education organizations also faded away. By the time of television, the prototype public forum program was a panel of policy experts, journalists, and public officials discussing a current issue with no audience participation or outreach, and the programs were aired at times of lowest ratings, such as Sunday mornings, that reflected their reduced importance for the networks.

From the 1950s through the 1970s, national nightly television news programs became the new standard of the television public sphere.[42] The three commercial television networks produced an imagined national community with their huge audiences. In this era before widespread cable television and VCRs, over 90 percent of prime-time television audiences were watching NBC, ABC, or CBS. The programming of these networks was *the* national culture. People had little choice of what to watch when all networks programmed news at the same hour, creating a shared nightly ritual that reaffirmed the nation, and the audience as its citizens being dutifully informed on public issues. Presidential speeches to the nation were broadcast simultaneously in prime time on all networks and many independent stations. The Republican and Democratic Party conventions and major Congressional hearings were carried live throughout the day and summarized on the national nightly news.

This was a different kind of public sphere, a ritualized representative public sphere in which networks reduced the role of citizen-viewer to that of witness of the national drama. It was a public sphere that elevated national identity above national participation, patriotism above activism. Audiences were invited to watch and learn rather than participate. In public affairs programming, audiences were informed, educated, and included in the nation, but not encouraged to play a part beyond observing. The networks continued this format through the late 1960s, even after many, in the streets if not in the audience, were openly rejecting this passive definition of citizen, and were actively debating the course of the nation.

In this vacuum arose several types of audience participation talk shows. Radio offered the man-in-the-street interview feature and the call-in radio show. On television, in contrast to the public affairs talk show of experts and the late-night celebrity talk shows, another type emerged, featuring ordinary people who were not experts nor celebrities. The *Phil Donahue Show* began in the late 1960s and was unique for two decades, discussing public issues with studio audiences during daytime hours to mostly female viewers. It was closest in intent, although not in form, to *American Town Meeting of the Air*. Donahue did not simply present information about current public issues, but encouraged his television audience to think and talk about them. On *Donahue*, the involvement of studio audiences in the discussion modeled civic participation for viewers at home. *Donahue* brought the studio audience on camera and on stage, giving them a voice as well as a face. The show emphasized a topic or issue rather than guests, and the studio audience was invited to participate. The performance of the studio audience became central to the shows' success, to involve the home audience (through para-social interaction) or to entertain them (as aloof observers).[43]

While *Donahue* was a pioneer, spread of such talk shows awaited changes in regulation and industry structure. Beginning in the 1980s, the regulatory foundation for traditional public affairs programs was dismantled. The FCC replaced the trustee model, to which public service was central, with a new marketplace model, saying that consumers would regulate license-holders through their choices in the marketplace. This new regulatory model eroded "rhetorics of citizenship," as Graham Murdock has phrased them, redefined audiences as consumers rather than as publics, and discarded the conception of mass media as a vital part of the public sphere. The new FCC approach defined radio and television as no more than entertainment businesses, like any other business. The market model was furthered also by the coincident proliferation of stations and networks with cable and the growth of other television uses such as VCR and videogames, beginning in the 1980s, that dismantled the national citizen audience, leaving them to pursue their private interests as individual consumers in niche markets, no longer participating in national political television rituals.[44]

With these changes in regulation as well as industry structure, new programming formats arose. In the late 1980s and 1990s, several new talk shows appeared. The elimination of public service requirements removed any reason to hew these programs to the public sphere model. Broadcasts devoted to discussing public issues dwindled and were replaced by focus on more private, personal matters. The therapeutic model evolved, led by Oprah Winfrey. The *Jerry Springer Show* took the personal in another direction, accentuating confrontation on the show; and the *Robert Downey Show* cast the audience more like a crowd, prompting the studio audience to shout down guests. These shows were constructed not around discussion but intense emotion and conflict.[45] Like the old crowd psychology, the host acted as the instigator, suggesting actions to the audiences.

While there was a range of shows from "classy" to "trashy," even the classy shows no longer emulated a deliberative public sphere, but instead the private personal sphere. There was a good deal of controversy in the 1990s about the "trashy" shows. The people on the shows, in the studio audiences, and, by inference, the viewers, were characterized as trash; bad citizens engaged in emotionally laundering dirty linen in public, instead of cultural uplift, education, and deliberation on public issues. Moreover, criticism of these programs became a vehicle for reinforcing class hierarchy.[46]

Some scholars argue that these shows offered an alternative public sphere, one enacting discursive practices more aligned with non-bourgeois cultures of subordinate groups such as working classes, women, children, and immigrants. However, and perhaps more importantly, the venue compromised the only opportunity for these groups to have a public voice. Some guests attempted to use these trash shows as a public sphere, a place where they could air their views and hope to engage some of the audience in listening to their views. Sociologists Josh Gamson and Laura Grindstaff each interviewed guests who planned to override the program script and tell their stories. Such guests conceived the audience as a public. This is part of what Gamson calls a "brew" of manipulative spectacle and democratic forum. Yet, the primary goal of the programs is entertainment; and even the more "respectable" shows, such as *Oprah Winfrey*, dealt with personal and private matters without linking them to public issues. The form is unstable, at moments public sphere, at other moments therapy, at yet others sentimentalism. The unstable definition of the program made it easier for viewers to interpret the show in terms of their own choosing; viewers differed in their evaluation of the genre, depending on their own predilections.[47]

While talk arose and evolved on television in a more personal direction, a form of talk radio evolved that focused on public issues. All-talk format originated on local radio stations around 1960 and developed in tandem with all-news format. Stations discovered an untapped audience demand to talk on radio. Often that talk veered toward public issues, such as civil rights, race, and Vietnam. According to radio historian Wayne Munson, from the beginning talk radio encouraged "controversy [and] steered conversation toward the 'gut'," in addressing public issues. Two things enabled these local radio talk shows to emerge into nationally syndicated ones: the elimination of the fairness doctrine in the 1980s, allowing shows to become more partisan and outrageous; and the creation of free long-distance 800 phone numbers, making it affordable for people nationwide to phone in. With their combination of focus on public issues and a highly charged emotional and partisan tone, these programs echoed the partisan citizenship of earlier eras, albeit a type of citizenship considered undesirable by many.[48]

This political talk format transferred to television beginning in the mid-1990s with Fox News Network's *O'Reilly Factor*, followed by *Sean Hannity* and similar programs that mixed the expert talk and radio talk formats, with the host attacking their expert guests. These shows seem to have as their goal stirring up their audiences with their mouth-frothing formats, rejecting professional journalistic norms and the concept of the informed, deliberative citizen. This form of radio and television talk show features political questions. But, as with early theater, there is disagreement about its status as a public sphere.[49] Certainly this format is not a deliberative public sphere, but a representative public sphere of performance. The shows are public displays of partisan views, reminiscent of nineteenth-century public party celebrations. The many critics of such programs would go further and characterize these shows as demagogic manipulations of the masses, much as the nineteenth-century middle class and the Progressives criticized urban party political machines. What is clear from all of this history, however, is that even in this media environment, no one questions that programming built upon public discussion of political issues is eminently appropriate to radio and television, despite whatever form it may take and despite the elimination of the FCC public service requirement.

# Part III

# Individuals

Chapter 5

# Mass media, mass man

The 1950s ushered in a new era that came as a blessing to many working Americans after enduring the dire conditions of the Depression and World War II. When the war ended and prosperity followed, people wanted to just live their lives, so long postponed. Millions of young people rushed to marry, find a home, and have a family, producing the baby boom. Many who could not have afforded a new home in the past bought homes in suburban developments subsidized by veteran mortgages and other federal programs. They settled in with a car, a TV, and rear patio. This expanded middle class became the focus of attention of mass media and of retailers. It was they who were talked about in the 1950s, as if all Americans lived in suburban middle-class families. The poor, minorities, and the excluded were invisible in most news, movies, television and music, and in policy.[1]

It was also an era of fear of an external threat from communism and an internal one from a complacent population. Even the optimistic George Denny who created the radio forum program, *America's Town Meeting of the Air*, became pessimistic. Soon, critics began to sound alarms about an emerging mass society. They denigrated suburbs as vacuous and soulless, bemoaned the decline of community, attacked the growing middlebrow culture, and savaged television. They contrasted the mass to a nostalgic remembrance of past community. Instead of a crowd or a public, critics saw isolated individuals and families vulnerable to media manipulation.[2]

The word "mass" became a widely used adjective, modifying production, market, consumption, media, communication, culture, society. The first usage of such terms as mass production and mass media occurred in the 1920s.[3] But these terms became commonplace in the 1950s, entering the conversation and vocabulary of the general reading population. All of these usages implied the same characteristics of mass: large numbers of undifferentiated and interchangeable people; something of disdainful low quality; and the isolated individual within the mass. Rather than referring to class, as "the masses" did, the "mass" referred to an alleged homogeneity among people. According to social and cultural critics of the 1950s, these were the makings of mass culture and mass society.

The term "mass culture" was becoming a catchphrase for a widely shared culture of a large modern society distributed by mass media. The mass was an audience; the mass medium was television. Television neatly fitted the emerging meanings of mass: its large numbers, larger than other media audiences; its dispersed audiences, isolated from each other; its creation of sameness, everyone watching the same programs at the same time; its reputed low quality. Conservatives worried that mass culture degraded civilization and weakened respect for elite leadership. Liberal and left concerns arose from the recent experience of fascism in Europe. They worried that mass culture and mass society threatened democracy by neutralizing the citizenry. Mass society isolated individuals; mass culture pacified and indoctrinated them.

## Television aesthetics

Aesthetic criticism was a central part of the complaints about television through the 1950s and 1960s, cast in terms of cultural hierarchy. The criticism constructed the audiences as persons of little cultivation or motivation, passively consuming whatever TV presented, and depicted the industry as crass commercializers. Arts and humanities advocates judged television with the standards of high culture, literature, and drama. Almost from its beginning, commercial television was lambasted for its low-brow tastes. In 1949, Norman Cousin, editor of *The Saturday Review of Literature*, unleashed a virulent salvo against television. Echoing the same dashed hopes expressed about movies decades earlier, he blamed the TV industry for failing miserably in realizing its potential, which he called "the most magnificent of all forms of communication . . . the supreme triumph of invention, the dream of the ages." He charged that television had produced "such an assault against the human mind, such a mobilized attack on the imagination, such an invasion against good taste as no other communication medium has known, not excepting the motion picture or radio itself," referring to "mass-produced series of plodding stereotypes and low quality programs [reflecting] a grinding lack of imagination and originality." Jack Gould, television critic for the *New York Times*, wrote in 1952, "The medium is hell-bent for the rut of innocuity, mediocrity and sameness that made a drab if blatant jukebox of radio . . . morning, noon and night the channels are cluttered with eye-wearying monstrosities. . . ." Speaking at graduation in 1950, the Boston University president warned that, "if the [television] craze continues with the present level of programs, we are destined to have a nation of morons."[4]

These criticisms prevailed over industry promotional efforts, reaching a peak in the late 1950s. *Time* magazine called it a "reverse status symbol," a measure of negative cultural capital. An article in the *New Republic*, summarizing the decade of criticism of television programming, referred to television as "[t]he country's whipping boy." The article was a response to the famous speech to the National Association of Broadcasters in 1961 by Newton Minow, the newly appointed chairman of the FCC. Speaking to an audience of television executives, he began his speech by accusing network prime-time programming of being "a vast wasteland . . . a procession of game shows, violence, audience-participation shows, formula comedies about totally unbelievable families, blood and thunder, mayhem, violence, sadism, murder, western bad men, western good men, private eyes, gangsters, more violence and cartoons. And, endlessly, commercials—many screaming, cajoling and offending. And most of all, boredom." He then challenged the networks to do better in the public interest.[5]

Some blamed audiences for low-brow taste. Harriet Van Horne, caustic TV critic for the Scripps-Howard newspaper chain, was quoted, "It's utterly appalling that people waste so much time on the trash and trivia the networks throw at them. I'm convinced the audience for westerns, situation comedies and private eyes checks its brains at the door and sits through the dreadful junk in a stupor." The networks consistently blamed "the audience" in their standard retort to criticism that they only gave the people what they wanted. The usual implication of this aesthetic critique was that people did not care to think, that they wanted pre-digested entertainment rather than mind-enhancing, thought-provoking programs.[6] Referring to the audience as "they," these critics set themselves above the audience that they criticized. They reified the audience as a uniform and unvarying mass.

Those who blamed TV often placed the cause in crass commercialism. As Calder Willingham, novelist and screenwriter, phrased it in the *American Mercury*, "Hollywood, Radio and Broadway have dipped heavily into our cultural capital, and put very little back again. A kind of corollary to this belief is the fear that television could exhaust all cultural capital, like a great suction pump or vacuum cleaner, and never put anything whatever back again." John Tebbel, writer for *The New American Mercury*, told a story of "commercialism against culture," as he phrased it, that television was repeating the failure of radio, which began with educators having high hopes of its "spreading of culture and enlightenment," only to have those quality programs eroded away by commercialism with "very little left of radio to which even a [industry] vice president could point with pride." Tebbel noted that television was very expensive, a two billion dollar industry in 1951, and therefore only for rich corporations. He asked, "what are we getting for our two billion dollars?" He answered, "films far below a standard which is none too high . . . shown again and again . . . but the commercials are even worse, and the viewer may get more than a dozen of them in a single hour."[7]

Tebbel was commenting on the struggle at the time between educators who lobbied to reserve part of the spectrum for non-commercial educational and cultural use primarily by universities, and the National Association of Broadcasters who claimed colleges did not have the money and would "waste" their license. In March 1951, the FCC ruled to reserve some channels for education. One of the commissioners, Frieda Barkin Hennock, was instrumental in building public support for this ruling, including involving the Ford Foundation to monitor commercial stations to prove the lack of educational programming. Jack Gould, *New York Times* television critic, in the last of a series of seven articles on "What TV is doing to us," reported that most educators interviewed for the article were critical of the "cultural quality" of commercial programming. He quoted Harold Stassen, perennial Republican primary candidate for Presidential nomination and at the time president of the University of Pennsylvania, that "It is essential that enough channels be reserved throughout the country exclusively for non-commercial educational television stations."[8]

This situation continued through the late 1950s and into the 1960s. In his famous speech, Minow repeatedly said the networks should consider something more than profit. In a less well-known but equally significant speech in 1958, Edward R. Murrow condemned the networks for greed that produced a programming diet of "decadence, escapism and insulation from the realities of the world" and expressed an "abiding fear regarding what [radio and television] are doing to our society, our culture and our heritage." He conceived the news audience as citizens and, in contrast to most critics, claimed that "the American public is more reasonable, restrained and more mature than most of our industry's program planners believe."[9]

Criticisms of television in mass-circulation magazines and news reports were complemented by a broader critique by public intellectuals in literary magazines. Within intellectual circles, television epitomized the problem of mass-produced culture, that is, the culture produced by mass media, specifically commercial media. Such critiques of mass culture were descended from nineteenth-century sacralization and opposition to commercial culture such as theater spectacle and romance novels, the spread of which were blamed on women. Melodrama and dime novels were blamed on the working class.[10] The arrival of television fueled a renewed mass culture criticism. The earliest statement of this new wave was Dwight MacDonald's "Theory of popular culture," published in 1944, before the arrival of commercial television. Norman Cousin's attack on television in its earliest days, quoted above, was another statement of the new wave; Clement

Greenberg joined in 1953, with "The plight of our culture." Articles appeared in *Dissent*, *Commentary*, *Saturday Review*, and almost every other literary magazine. The influential *Partisan Review* published a symposium titled "Our country and our culture" in 1952. Many of the most prominent critiques were collected and published in Bernard Rosenberg and David Manning White's *Mass Culture* in 1957. In 1959, the American Academy of Arts and Sciences sponsored a seminar for the most prominent figures in the debate to discuss the vices and virtues of mass culture. The papers presented were published in the academy's journal, *Daedalus*, and as a book, *Culture for the Millions*. Paul Lazarsfeld summarized the views expressed at the conference as two concerns: that mass media would erode interest in and support for high culture, and that mass culture would erode the mass' ability to understand high culture.[11]

Underlying all the aesthetic criticism was the presumption that people should be doing something more constructive and self-improving during their leisure. The issue was time as well as aesthetics. Minow noted that most programs were not particularly good or bad, but "these time-waster shows are not really neutral fare, at all. By their very absence of positive worth they can be dangerous and destructive."[12] He considered such shows dangerous since democracy requires an informed and involved citizenry, and television was believed by some to be undermining this.

Watching television was easier than just about anything else, the path of least effort, according to the criticism. Not only were people not improving themselves; they were doing nothing. These articles rarely mentioned what people were *doing* with television. Invariably they wrote about what people or children did *not do*. They did not go out as much, did not read as much, did not think as much. Children did not do their homework, did not read, did not get enough exercise or sunshine. Their muscles atrophied, their minds shut down. They vegetated.

The underlying image in this voluminous discourse was a passive audience, adults and children alike. Marya Mannes, cultural critic and columnist for many magazines and the *New York Times*, wrote that "passivity seems to be a prerequisite for the new enlightenment [of television]." In *Education* magazine, a Massachusetts educator declared that children's passivity was a more serious matter than the low-brow programming. The titles of two magazine articles succinctly captured the sense of passivity, "What TV is doing to us" and "What TV is doing to America," instead of asking what we are doing *with* TV. This image persisted for decades, until cable TV and VCRs changed the television landscape.[13]

Critics feared television would sedate people into inertia, to care about nothing except watching the next show, offering bread and circuses. They accused television of drawing audiences away from civic duties. Critics typified audiences as uninterested, passive citizenry, neutralized and removed from the political arena, rather than past descriptions of them as dangerously active crowds or manipulated masses.[14]

Symbolically, the 1950s ended in November 1963 when President Kennedy was assassinated. Different worries supplanted concerns about mass culture. The activism of the 1960s contradicted the image of the passive American and became the new worry of elites. Also, by the mid-1960s the assault in print on television aesthetics had subsided; not because it was defeated, however—there continues to be occasional reiterations of the criticism, even to this day. The decline in numbers of critical articles was likely because it had become a commonplace understanding that television was low brow.

## Institutional advertising and civics

The high-brow criticism of television complemented the strategy of corporations to identify themselves with quality television, building upon the public relations approach that they had used in radio. In the 1950s, America's largest corporations sponsored the showcase programs that defined what would become known as the golden age of television, including most of the anthology series of original dramas. These programs were presented as cultivated educational fair rather than entertainment and offered as a kind of civic philanthropy. They cast corporations as partners with government in making a better America, as well as making better lives for Americans.[15]

*United States Steel Hour*, like the other shows of this genre, set a tone of substantial solemnity, as if it were a civic and cultural ritual for the whole nation's participation and sanctification. Each show opened with celebratory classical music, a Copelandesque patriotic fanfare over dramatic visual footage of molten steel pouring forth from a giant furnace. This was combined with intermission talks by "the Voice of United States Steel," an authoritative baritone describing the company's contributions to America and often relating the company's position on various public issues, especially issues of unions and "right to work" federal legislation intended to weaken unions, which were hot issues for the company through the 1950s.[16]

Like others of its kind, the program was a peculiar hybrid of civic and domestic—United States Steel Corporation branded itself "the industrial family that serves the nation." It was broadcast on Sunday evenings, family night on network prime-time. Industrial product manufacturers like US Steel, DuPont, and General Electric emphasized their "contribution" to American everyday domestic life. They fulfilled a parental role in providing education and culture to their "family" of listeners/viewers through their "award-winning" programs. Even Kraft Foods promoted its consumer products such as Velveeta cheese in this way, framing *Kraft Television Theater* as part of their "gracious living" marketing strategy. At intermission, instead of the usual commercial, they provided domestic instruction, with a recipe featuring one of their food products presented by a disembodied soothing male baritone voice and illustrated by two disembodied female hands.[17] It effectively framed the audience as consumer families; the role of public disappeared into the private suburban home.

At the same time, it framed the corporation as a good citizen. Corporate sponsors in effect claimed credit for American prosperity and standard of living that they said was the source of national strength, simultaneously contributing to both family and nation.[18] Ultimately, these institutional messages appeared to communicate to audiences not that they should become politically active, as did the radio forum programs, but rather that they should be content as consumers and allow these corporations to continue to supply that life of plenty by supporting "free enterprise" as voters.

## Mass society

Televised corporate messages epitomized what social critics of the time were concerned about in the new post-war America, a society in which elites could speak directly to the mass of the population.[19] Mass society critics claimed that mass media, in by-passing local opinion leaders and weakening community, helped to isolate individuals and make them passive and inactive. Variations on this thesis were widespread among academic social science and public intellectuals of the time. It appeared in "high-brow" magazines, as well as academic journals and books, and across the political spectrum. Ernst Van der Haag, conservative social philosopher and writer for the *National Review*, wrote in the 1950s that, "All mass media in the end alienate people from personal experience and though appearing to offset it, intensify their moral isolation from each other, from reality and from themselves." *Dissent* published an even more stark statement about the isolated mass man and how television creates him, by Gunther Anders, social philosopher, leader of the anti-nuclear movement, and husband of Hannah Arendt:

> What [the mass producer] needs is not the compact mass [movie audiences] as such, but a mass broken up or atomized into the largest possible number of customers. . . . The Smiths consumed the mass products *en famille* or even singly; the more isolated they became the more profits they yielded. The

> mass-produced hermit came into being as a new human type, and now millions of them, cut off from each other, yet identical with each other, remain in the seclusion of their homes. Their purpose, however, is not to renounce the world, but to be sure they won't miss the slightest crumb of the world as image on a screen. . . . Le Bon's observations on the psychology of crowds have become obsolete, for each person's individuality can be erased and his rationality leveled down in his own home.[20]

Within academic and intellectual circles this concern about isolation and alienation from civic participation was elaborated not as a unified theory but as a collection of claims about modern society by many authors. These critiques claimed that large modern societies require a set of intermediary institutions between the local and the national, and that a variety of structural changes had undercut these institutions and turned the populations of large societies into a mass composed of isolated, anonymous, and identical individuals. Some of these changes were long-term processes of modernization. But one of the forces was mass media, according to this criticism.[21]

In the 1930s and 1940s, European intellectuals transplanted to the United States tried to explain the rise of fascism in democratic societies such as Germany and Italy. In the 1950s, American academics began to apply these theories to the United States, worrying how it may be drifting toward totalitarian conditions believed to typify both fascism and communism. Critics worried that voluntary associations and community networks would wither away in a mass society, shriveling the public sphere.[22] Post-war mass society theories began with the ideal of the active, informed citizen, and argued that such citizenry required a latticework of institutions and networks to enable being informed and being active in turn, a two-way system of communication from leaders to the mass and responses from the mass to leaders. These theories merged concerns about propaganda as manipulation on the one hand and about mass culture as circus distraction on the other. The main concern was the vulnerability of the mass to manipulation or neutralization. Their vulnerability was presumed to be greater because they were believed to be isolated individuals, without a community to anchor and affirm their views and without means to communicate back to the centers of power. Mass society theories also shared assumptions and foci. They focused on the middle-class mass rather than the working- and lower-class masses. They feared the dissolution of intermediary institutions. They worried about political neutralization, going shopping instead of participating civically.

The theories of the 1950s uniformly saw mass media becoming the only link between center and periphery, even while they differed in other explanations of what caused the dissolution of intermediary institutions. Mass media, as a one-way means of communication, could preoccupy or propagandize the mass audience of isolated individuals. Sociologist Edward Shils summed up the basic premise of mass society theory: that the centralized power of mass society "takes the form of manipulation of the mass through the media of mass communication." According to political scientist William Kornhauser, national leadership could speak directly to each individual and all the mass at once through mass media. As television reduced people's social and civic participation, people would become alienated, unsure of their own values and direction, and highly susceptible to manipulation by the leadership of such mass movements. The same idea was suggested by David Riesman, in his book *The Lonely Crowd*. In a rather intricate psychological argument about the transformation of politics in this new kind of society, he wrote that, "with the mass media behind it, [politics] invades the privacy of the citizen. . . . This invasion destroys the older, easy transition from individual to local, local to national, and national to international interests and plunges the individual directly into the complexities of world politics, without any clear-cut notion of where his interests lie." In other words, politics invades the home via mass media, making a direct connection between the world of national and international politics and the individual family, by-passing the intermediary institutions that mass society theorists argued were so important.[23] These theories implied a gullibility of the mass much like the suggestibility that LeBon, Ross, and others had talked about two generations before, and that underlay both the claims that television would dupe its viewers and the confidence of advertising executives or propaganda analysts that they could manipulate people.

The idea of the isolated individual in the mass evolved from the classical contrast of modern urban-industrial society to traditional society composed of communities. It was an extension of the older concern for the shift from a romanticized pre-industrial Eden with its healthy community relationships to a nightmarish modernity of alienation and anomie. The demise of community had been the central theme of critics of modernity at least since Ferdinand Tönnies 1887 treatise, *Gemeinschaft und Gesellschaft*, contrasting community to association.[24] The idealized community provided a network of interpersonal ties among families, renewed daily through face-to-face interaction. Modern society was believed to be based on interactions among strangers that undermined community and left a population of individuals without stable identities or ties to each other. The mass was contrasted to the community.

Politically, the critique presumed that community provided for a means of communication not only within but also between communities and centers of power, via a chain of relationships from those with lesser to those with greater power. The community was believed to be the fundamental link between the political periphery and the center in large modern societies. The weakening of community implied a weakening of democracy, severing the communication line between the people and political leaders. Within communities, opinion leaders helped to shape local opinion. Such leaders were also the intermediaries for communities to voice opinion to those beyond, influencing centers of power and assuring democratic participation.

## Suburbia, the home of mass man

Criticism of mass society was not confined to academic discourse among scholars. It had its equivalent in 1950's paperbacks that reached a much broader readership, such as John Keats' *The Crack in the Picture Window*, Sloan Wilson's *The Man in the Gray Flannel Suit*, Clare Barnes' *White Collar Zoo*, and Vance Packard's *The Status Seekers*; and in widely read academic books such as William H. Whyte's *Organization Man*, David Riesman's *Lonely Crowd*, and C. Wright Mills' *White Collar*. These books became part of middle-brow discourse of the 1950s and early 1960s.[25]

Common to these books was a criticism of the emptiness of middle-class American life: homogenized suburbanization populated with middle-class families of faceless, homogenous managers and professionals employed by large corporations. Instead of the volatile and dangerous proles that had been thought of as the masses, this new middle class had become recognized as the mass, dangerous not for its potential to revolt but to conform. They were thought by critics to be the prototype of mass man. Post-war suburbia, their quintessential home, became the picture of all the things wrong with American mass society in the 1950s.

John Keats' *Crack in the Picture Window* was typical in its thorough condemnation of middle-class suburban life. Published in 1957, it presented thickly sarcastic portraits of a fictitious family and their neighbors in a development to illustrate statistics about the massive post-war housing rip-offs. It cast developers as the villains, government agencies as their accomplices, and the homeowners as young, inexperienced, unwitting victims, with names like John and Mary Drone, Gladys and Buster Fecund, Maryann and Lawrence Faint, Jane and Henry Amiable. The women stayed at home and contended with the children in their cramped bungalows. The husband, as Keats phrased it, ". . . didn't live in the house. He left in the morning, came home at night for supper and bed . . . [like an] overnight lodger or casual weekend guest." The worst curse was that everyone was the same. All the houses were exactly the same. "Each identical house, with its identical picture window, with its identical dwarf cedar, the identical gullies in the eroding lawns, always the same, same, the same, row on row." All the husbands were twenty-something salaried office workers, with approximately the same income. All the women were young mothers. They dressed alike and furnished their homes in the same way. Every day was monotony. In Keats' words, "Hell was homogeneous." This was the essence of mass society—or so Keats conjured it in his successful book. The same post-war suburban developments were the topic in Vance Packard's *The Status Seekers*, a more serious synopsis of sociological research of the time, in which he noted that new developments were increasing segregation of families by income, "the rather frightening, headlong trend toward social stratification by residential area," making these neighborhoods and their daily living more homogeneous.[26]

Mass society theory and the attitude toward its manifestation as the suburbs, were precisely captured in a popular song written in 1961 by social activist and folk songwriter Malvina Reynolds, *Little Boxes*, that became well known through a popular recording by Dore Previn. Reynold's song belittled the middle class and their homes in post-war suburban developments:

> . . . Little boxes made out of ticky-tacky,
> And they all look just the same . . .
> And the people in the houses,
> All go to the university. . .
> And they all play on the golf-course,
> And drink their Martini dry,
> And they all have pretty children,
> And the children go to school.
> And the children go to summer camp
> And then to the university,
> And they all get put in boxes
> And they all come out the same.

As the song lyrics suggest, the popular expression of mass society theory was manifested in the criticism of suburbia. This criticism at times blamed the suburbanites and consumerism, or "materialism" as it was then termed; at other times it targeted the profiteers of cheap, post-war mass-produced housing. The criticism of suburbs was so widespread that it shaped urban planning theory—but not practice—for decades, despite its simplification and exaggeration of reality. Sociologist and urban planning expert Herbert Gans addressed his second book, *The Levittowners*, to examining the popular claim that suburbs isolated families and destroyed community. He studied one of the largest and most famous post-war developments, Levittown in Willingboro, New Jersey, during its first years of existence from 1958 to 1962. In his introduction, he noted that suburbs were much maligned but little studied. He found a good deal more community participation and a good deal more vitality than critics had claimed.[27]

At the center of this critique of suburbia lay television. It was considered integral to suburbia. Television enabled suburbanites to receive continuous entertainment in their home, so they did not have to go out. TV was described as an important accomplice in the alleged decline in community and civic participation. The demise of places for public conversation such as the corner tavern, gathering place of working-class men, and decline in restaurant and night-club trade, sports event admissions, and civic meeting attendance, were blamed on television.[28]

According to these critics, even more than the tract houses, television produced sameness, with everyone watching the same network programs at the same times every night of the week, week after week. John Keats vividly expressed this view: "Within every shuttered living room gleamed a feeble phosphorescence, a tiny picture flickered . . . it was a common sound, rising above the darkened houses, for everyone watched the same shows." He quoted a sociologist, "Lacking stimulation from their neighbors, oppressed by ennui, people turn to the mass-communications media to find new ideas. Then, because everyone sees the same TV shows, reads the same article in the same magazine, they all come up with the same idea at the same time, and the result is more ennui."[29]

Concern about television's ability to produce this sameness was reinforced by widespread belief in its great power to manipulate minds. This fear of television's power inspired one of the most striking movies of the time, *The Manchurian Candidate*, a 1959 cold war spy novel by Richard Condon and successful 1962 movie by John Frankenheimer. In the movie, an American soldier is captured during the Korean War and, in three days, is "brainwashed" to kill the leading candidate for president of the Unites States so that a puppet president may be elected. The story welded fears of mass culture and of communism into a sinister plot. Explaining his interests in making the book into a movie, Frankenheimer said,

> . . . we believed that we lived in a society that was brainwashed. And I wanted to do something about it. I think that our society is brainwashed by television commercials, by advertising, by politicians, by a censored press (which does exist in this country whether you want to admit it or not) with its biased reporting. More and more I think that our society is becoming manipulated and controlled.[30]

Frankenheimer's statement echoed a best-selling book of the time, by social critic Vance Packard, *The Hidden Persuaders*. Packard warned of the then new "depth" approach in advertising, based on what was called motivational research. Packard opened his book with the remark that we absorb advertising messages "beneath our level of awareness. . . . The result is that many of us are being influenced and manipulated, far more than we realize." Motivational research cobbled together a combination of Pavlovian conditioning and Freudian theory—the same techniques used in *The Manchurian Candidate*. Typically, advertising consultants using this approach would recommend a message loaded with what they believed to be potent Freudian symbolism, and recommend that it be repeated again and again in ads or on packaging to implant—to borrow a term from an earlier time—this message through conditioned reflex.[31]

Frankenheimer and Packard were men of their time and their class. They were voicing beliefs shared by many educated Americans, from liberal to conservative, that most people could be manipulated and controlled by television messages. For a period of time, rumors spread about "subliminal advertising," commercials flashed on movie and television screens too fast to perceive consciously, but believed to be absorbed unconsciously and thus without any resistance.[32] This was an age of fear. Mass culture critics, mass society theorists, anti-communists, and critics of television all shared a common underlying belief that the mass of Americans were dangerously vulnerable to suggestion, whether by television, communist brainwashing, or the deadening effects of suburban sameness.

Cultural and social criticism of the 1950s seemed to insistently return to mass media and especially to television as the explanation of what was wrong. The alleged malaise in a world of affluence, the alleged decline in political interest, the shriveling interest in the arts, the blandness of suburbs, the decline of community, whatever intellectuals criticized, they invariably came around to blaming television as the cause. Television's audiences therefore were of extreme political and social significance, since it was what television did to them that led to their behaving in ways that created all these problems. The audience was political in its inaction and inertia; democracy could not work if its citizens didn't participate.

Critiques of television, mass culture, and mass society faded away during the late 1960s, displaced by issues of social justice and government dishonesty in public discourse, and in intellectual discourse by the demise of public intellectuals and the turn of academics away from broad brush to detailed studies.[33] By the time the ruckus of the various 1960s social movements, of Vietnam, and Watergate had settled, suburbia and television, mass culture, and mass society were so commonplace and pervasive that they were taken for granted by a whole generation of baby boom families who knew nothing else. This was followed in the 1980s by dramatic changes in the structures of mass media, with the unraveling of the three-network hegemony, the spread of cable, VCR and videogames. These changed viewers' relation to TV, so the idea of a passive audience hardly applied anymore, and this changed the issues of concern.

Nor did the criticisms of the suburbs hold up well. Recent re-readings of Gans and rewriting of the history of the post-war suburbs have led historians to discover a community that had existed in these instant "villages," contrary to the core assumptions of the criticisms.[34]

# Chapter 6

# Media effects and passive audiences

While intellectual discourses of the 1950s constructed the image of a mass of isolated individuals vulnerable to media, empirical researchers constructed an effects paradigm, also based on the solitary individual. Both market research and academic research used a paradigm premised on a one-way relationship of a medium's effect on solitary individuals. For market research, the unit of measurement of audiences was the individual consumer, but not as interacting collectivities. Academic research imagined audiences as psychological individuals rather than as social groups. Both constructed these individuals as passive objects rather than as autonomous agents, acted upon rather than acting. As commodities, they were conceived as objects to be bought and sold. As consumers, they were conceived as manipulated by advertising and marketing. As receivers, they were conceived as dependent variables to independent media messages.[1]

This chapter concentrates on the cultural acceptance and the institutionalization of the effects approach that would dominate academic research on media audiences into the 1970s.[2] Two related historical forces shaped academic discourse: public fears about the effects of media, especially on children, and the mobilization of researchers during World War II. To quote communication research historian Jesse Delia, "the particular set of individual and professional interests that gave rise to the field's initial organization served to narrow it in important ways . . . historical research and cultural research were made peripheral, non-statistical approaches to communication science were given marginal treatment, mass communication research was divorced from interpersonal communication studies."[3] This paradigm complemented the mass culture discourse that defined the isolated individuals of the mass as easily manipulated and incapable of fulfilling their role as citizens. Moreover, its preconception of the relation of media to individuals contributed to the reconstruction of citizenship as individuals represented in opinion polls. Thus it had significant political implications.

## Media panics and effects

The effects approach originated in moral panics about new mass media of the twentieth century. British sociologist Stanley Cohen, building on the work of American sociologist Howard Becker, used the term "moral panics" to describe intense public reactions to the spread of a new social behavior, such as movie-going, television viewing, or video-gaming when these media were new. Cohen defines panic as an exaggerated response disproportional to the problem and perhaps counter-productive in seeking solutions. Becker coined the term "moral entrepreneurs" to describe people who take it upon themselves to promote public concern and crusade for government response. Entrepreneurs, government, and media stigmatize the behavior and the people who engage in it. Since the success of moral entrepreneurs depends upon their resources and influence, this tends to result in higher-status entrepreneurs labeling lower-status persons negatively. As public concern grows, authorities and experts begin to investigate and take action to appear to address the problem and mollify the public, after which the panic subsides.[4]

Perhaps the first moral panics about media effects were the reactions to cheap fiction and tabloid journalism during the second half of the nineteenth century.[5] In the early twentieth century, these fears were overshadowed by the shocking popularity of nickelodeons among working-class immigrants and children, feeding a panic over the effects of moving pictures. Media panics are triggered when a new medium or genre becomes popular; deviant uses of the medium are distinguished from good uses; and audiences are divided into those vulnerable to these bad influences and those who can resist them. Media historian Kirsten Drotner argues that all media panics assume that media have a hypodermic effect and affect people individually and directly, ignoring social relationships among users. Some psychological mechanism is offered as the means. The mechanism used to be called suggestion, a concept that emphasized the involuntary intrusion of an idea into the mind. Sometime in the mid-twentieth century, that term went out of academic fashion and was supplanted by a Behaviorist concept of persuasion.[6]

The distinction between good and bad uses of media is also a distinction between good and bad users. Media panics typically focus on people of subordinate status (teens and children, women, subordinate races, and lower classes) as bad, more susceptible users. As audience researcher David Buckingham phrased it, "Debates about the negative effects of the media are almost always debates about *other* people."[7] These distinctions, moreover, were a basis for other distinctions between citizens capable of informed judgment and incapable citizens requiring guidance or guardianship.

Frequently, those considered prone to bad use were children, less bad than innocent and vulnerable. Moral panics about and legal protections for children in the late nineteenth and early twentieth centuries typically were concerned not only for the individual, but the nation. Children were citizens in the making, just as immigrants were. Protecting the morality of children by restricting and supervising their media exposure would assure the quality of their future citizenship. As minors, their rights could be restricted to ensure that they were prepared for full citizenship as adults. At the same time, the vulnerable but protected child symbolized the strength of national morality. In both senses, moral panics about media and audiences had a greater significance.[8]

## Movies, radio, and children

Media research from its inception has been intricately linked to media panics. This began with writers relaying stories of imitation and copycat crimes as a result of watching movies. In the 1920s, the Payne Fund studies (see Chapter 2) adopted psychological research methods that defined the individual as their unit of analysis and as the dependent variable affected by movies. Researchers measured palm sweat as youths watched a movie; measured restlessness during sleep; administered questionnaires and conducted interviews asking what they thought while watching movies. All of this focused on the solitary youth's experience of the movie as if no one else was present and no other presence mattered, neglecting the fact that movie-going was a social activity.[9]

The most striking examples of this assumption are the studies by sociologist Herbert Blumer. One would expect that Blumer's specialty in collective behavior and face-to-face interaction would have led him to consider audiences as groups or crowds. Yet in neither of his two book-length Payne Fund studies did he use research methods that considered the interactions and relationships among members of movie audiences nor any collective acting on their part. Instead, he relied on surveys in which teenagers were individually interviewed or completed questionnaires and "motion picture life histories" about their reactions to movies they had seen. A small but unspecified number of observations of youths in movie theaters were also included. But these were used to corroborate individual mental activity explored by the other methods, rather than to document social interaction.[10]

The Payne Fund studies, perhaps because the moral panic had subsided and the effects of movies ceased to be controversial, did not stimulate further research on movie audiences. Yet the effects approach continued in research on radio and television. In contrast to the immediate rise of concerns about movies, radio was received quite positively in the 1920s. Nevertheless, by the 1930s some began expressing concerns about the effects of radio network drama series and serials on pre-adolescent middle-class children, a different group than the working-class teens who were the primary focus of movie reformers. In 1932, members of a PTA in the wealthy suburb of Scarsdale, New York took exception to thriller radio programs that their own pre-adolescent children were listening to. They cited network programs that "shatter their nerves, stimulate emotions of horror and teach bad grammar," and rated many of them as harmful. Several newspapers and magazines reported their claims, and radio was added to the precautionary lists in parenting guidance literature.[11] Through the 1930s, other groups expressed concern about the dangers of radio programs to pre-adolescent youths and pressured broadcasters for change. These included the National Advisory Council on Radio in Education, the General Federation of Women's Clubs, the American Legion Auxiliary, the National Society of New England Women, the United Parents Association of New York City, the Parents League of New York City, and the executive director of the National Lutheran Council. An article published by the National Committee on Education by Radio claimed about effects on children, ". . . we are confronted with an insidious evil which creeps into our home and, like nitrous oxide gas, does its damage before we are aware of its venom."[12]

In 1933, the Payne Fund began sponsoring research on the effects of radio on children. They established a radio research division at Ohio State University under Werret W. Charters, the director of the Payne movie project, and provided a grant for a Columbia Teachers College dissertation that questioned middle-school children about their individual preferences and reactions to programs—but not about their interactions while listening. In a 1941 survey of research on children and radio, sociologist Herta Herzog catalogued many studies on individual's preferences and reactions, and even raised questions about listening together and effects on family relations, but cited no studies of either of these beyond whether they did or did not listen together, and none that conceived radio audiences as interacting groups. One form of audience interaction frequently reported in magazines was teenagers dancing to radio music. Yet no research studied these interactions and how it shaped use of radio.[13]

Children were the paradigm case of the vulnerable audience. Extensive public discourse on the dangers of media for children cemented an effects approach in the public and research imaginations. It established this as the "natural" way of thinking about media audiences. In the process, it established the relationship of concern as between the medium and the individual. This displaced early accounts by reformers of nickelodeon audiences as interacting groups. Media audience research would not shift from the effects approach for nearly fifty years, and public debate about media continues in this mode today, with the image of the isolated individual and his solitary relation to a medium.

## Adult listeners

That radio audiences were dispersed rather than gathered in theaters made radio listeners invisible. As soon as radio broadcasting became a commercial enterprise and a medium for selling, radio stations became interested in market research as a means to make their invisible audiences visible to advertisers. Both commercial broadcasters and advertisers needed to count individuals or individual households with radios tuned to their advertising, so they knew what they were buying and selling. Neither of them had an interest in audiences as interacting groups such as crowds or publics. To advertisers, audiences were simply the sum of consumers. However, counting presumes that each unit is distinct, indivisible, and independent of each other; counting individuals inevitably disregards their relations with each other and counting households disregards the relationships within households. Further, in asking individuals their choices of radio programs, this effort to measure audiences reduced publics and public opinion to a sum of individual opinions. Whether counting households or individuals, radio audiences were constituted as solitary individuals.

Radio stations' first efforts to tally listeners was through applause cards; postcards printed and distributed by radio manufacturers, radio stations, and advertisers, that listeners could send to stations with their comments about the station or specific programs. The cards provided spaces for the name of the station and program, for name and address of listener, and for a brief comment. The cards did not ask who else and how many were listening. Stations used cards to count radios or households tuned to their station or program, treating radio audiences as isolated households.[14]

When NBC and CBS formed national networks in the late 1920s, they needed national surveys of their programs, bringing into existence the first ratings services. From the beginning, ratings framed the audience as individual households. Marketing researcher Daniel Starch was hired by NBC to conduct a face-to-face survey of listeners in 1927, in which Starch used the household or family as the unit of analysis. The next year, another market researcher and prominent opinion pollster, Archibald Crossley, was the first to use telephones to interview radio listeners nationally, making it feasible to do this regularly. This led to the first national broadcast rating service, the Cooperative Analysis of Broadcasting, established in 1930 jointly by the American Association of Advertising Agencies and the Association of National Advertisers, which became known as the Crossley ratings, after its director. It reported the percent of radio sets tuned to a program in an era when each set effectively represented a household. The Crossley ratings identified households by income, so advertisers could distinguish listeners who could afford their product, but at least in its earlier years did not collect information on the age and sex of each person in the household, nor distinguished who was or was not listening. Pioneering radio market researcher Hugh Beville remembers that the first diaries recording individual radio use were collected as a one-time survey in 1934. But regular surveys including audience composition and individual listening patterns did not begin until the 1940s. By the late 1940s, Hooper ratings included audience composition. Gradually, ratings became more sophisticated and detailed, providing information on each individual in each household by age and sex, so that advertisers could target individual as well as household purchases.[15] Throughout, the conception of audiences by commercial audience measurement and rating services was of disaggregated households and individuals, and ratings methods moved steadily toward counting individuals.

Rating services shared this same conception of populations as sums of individuals with other marketing research, opinion polling, and academic audience research. This conception was at the core of survey research methods. Contributing to the convergence of their methods were the facts that, at that time, most marketing researchers, opinion pollsters, and academics knew each other personally; they often collaborated; and many engaged in commercial as well as academic types of research. For example, Hadley Cantril was friends with George Gallup and used his polling data, and Paul Lazarsfeld funded his academic research by doing market research for consumer products.[16] Surveys are essentially a method of counting individuals' characteristics, which is what each of these research areas were devoted to doing. Marketing research counted potential consumers; opinion polling counted voters rather than parties. In survey research, interactions among individuals were irrelevant. Also, in the psychometric theory that is the basis of survey research, the individual's answer is conceived as a fixed response to a fixed stimulus, the question; individuals are passive reactors, not active agents.[17] Survey method and the underlying psychometric theory constructed audiences and the public as individual passive responders.

An important exception to this research trend was the work of Paul Lazarsfeld, who recognized interactions among audience members with his concept of two-stage communication involving community opinion leaders. Lazarsfeld was director of the Radio Research Project, the first academic center devoted to radio research, initially at Princeton then Columbia University, which focused entirely on adult listeners, in contrast to the focus on children by the Payne Fund. Through the 1940s, Lazarsfeld was an important figure in shaping radio audience research, due to his influential position and his remarkably prolific work. The Project began with the effects approach that predominated in previous radio research. But Lazarsfeld gradually moved toward a different approach. His two classic studies of radio audiences, *People's Choice* and *Personal Influence*, each emphasized the importance of interactions and relationships among audience members—audiences as communities. In *The People's Choice*, a study of the effects of radio on the 1940 presidential election, Lazarsfeld introduced the idea of the "two-step flow of communication" that emphasized the importance of opinion leaders and their interaction with and influence on other listeners in shaping interpretation of radio messages. In *Personal Influence*, he and co-author Elihu Katz emphasized the importance of peers in constructing the meaning of media messages. Lazarsfeld was moving toward a paradigm that focused on audiences as people interacting as groups, rather than as individuals manipulated by media. Some influential social psychologists of the time also shared Lazarsfeld's emphasis on group interaction, such as Kurt Lewin in his group dynamics approach and the social perception research of Hadley Cantril and Solomon Asch.[18]

## Social psychology, communication research, and World War II

Lazarsfeld's influence would be eclipsed by generous government support for a different approach that would dominate post-war audience studies. During World War II, the federal government recruited social and psychological researchers to determine the effectiveness of propaganda, who after the war would develop an experimental approach and institutionalize it in academic discourse as the scientific approach to media audiences.[19] The War Department's Division of Information and Education, responsible for maintaining troop morale, conducted the largest program of research, later published as the four-volume report, *The American Soldier*. Its Research Branch employed dozens of researchers and had unprecedented resources at its disposal, enough to study a half-million soldiers by the end of the war. Its eventual impact on academic discourse was far reaching, as its researchers became the leading figures in post-war social psychology, their names reading like a who's who of the field.[20] The director of the Research Branch, sociologist Samuel Stouffer, preferred quantitative methods and appointed like-minded researchers. One group of researchers, led by Yale psychologist Carl Hovland, were asked to determine the effectiveness of various media, such as film versus lecture, radio commentator versus documentary, and Army newspapers and magazines for soldiers.

Stouffer later reported that the researchers expressed a strong preference for learning theory that reduced phenomena to variables, quantitative measurement of these variables, and experimental testing of effects. Experimental method was considered essential since "social psychology is likely to be limited in its development until the habit of requiring experimental verification is firmly established." This approach would legitimate an image of media audiences, especially for the new medium of television, as passive, isolated individuals with no agency and controlled by the medium and its message. Learning theory reduced human behavior to responses determined by repeated stimuli. Experimental method is similarly based on a deterministic logic in which there is no agency or independent will. Applied to audience research, the viewer's attitude or behavior was defined as the dependent variable controlled by independent variables, the one of focal concern being the medium message.[21] The method produced a body of psychological knowledge about what conditions allegedly produce what thoughts and behavior in media audiences, on the assumption that people could be predictably manipulated and controlled.

Several of the researchers would join Yale University's psychology department after the war to continue experimental research on persuasion that would be central to shaping post-war social psychology and communication research. This program of research resembled Cantril's 1930s experimental research on media effects on audiences, but replaced the crowd psychology terminology of suggestion with the new terms of persuasion and attitude change. Many published research that became required reading for graduate students in social psychology and in communication research.[22] The research at the War Department and at Yale University established persuasion as the dominant topic in social psychology and effects as the paradigm for audience research for over two decades. This was possible because of the availability of considerable funds and resources, first from the Rockefeller Foundation and then the U.S. government, to carry out such a program of research, to travel to spread the word, and to publish it in books. The large amount of money spent on this subject area channeled the fields of social psychology and of communications into the study of media effects.

Communications research emerged from the war as a new academic field. Its formation too was shaped by the War Department's research, but also by another influential wartime program as well. Early in the war, the government created the Office of War Information, devoted to gathering information about propaganda in other nations and to producing and distributing propaganda directed to American and enemy civilians. It recruited writers and literature professors into its ranks. Ironically, one of these literary types became one of the main proponents of quantitative effects research and the single most influential person in establishing communications research as a discipline, Wilbur Schramm.[23]

The war years introduced Schramm to many researchers in the Research Branch and other agencies, and to a new quantitative, social scientific approach to propaganda, opinion, and persuasion research. As part of his work he met two to three times each week with a team of consultants for government research projects, including Lazarsfeld, Stouffer, and Hovland of the Research Branch, as well as survey researcher Rensis Likert, the pollsters George Gallup and Elmo Roper, and propaganda expert Harold Lasswell. Schramm was literally surrounded by the social psychologists and scientists who were formulating the new quantitative and experimental approach to effects research.[24]

This environment shaped his vision of communication research upon which he established three of the first American communication research institutes and degree-granting programs, including the first Ph.D. program in communications research, beginning at the University of Iowa immediately after the war. In 1947, Schramm was recruited to the University of Illinois by its new president, George Stoddard (one of the authors of the Payne Fund studies) to create an Institute of Communication Research. At Illinois, Schramm was very successful at obtaining government funding for research, a quarter million dollars each year (equivalent to two million dollars in 2005). Much of this paid for experimental research on the effects of propaganda. As early as 1947, the Institute submitted a proposal requesting $255,000 to study the comparative effects of different media to persuade Americans what to do in case of intercontinental war. The proposal stated, ". . . they will have to be *prepared by mass communications* and *directed* by whatever communications remain available to them when war comes [emphasis added]." The source of the funding, the topic, and method of the research all suggest a conception of mass media audiences to be manipulated for political purpose, a purpose consistent with elite assertions that the mass is a citizenship that needs to be guided rather than engaged in deliberation. At Stanford, Schramm's doctoral program also concentrated on effects research. It had great influence on the field in the 1950s and 1960s. "Every university wanted to hire one of the new Stanford PhDs in communication," according to communication research historian Everett Rogers. Schramm trained the first generations of PhDs in communication research at a time of great expansion of universities and thus shaped new programs in communications across the country and the academic discourse around the effects model of audiences.[25]

The experimental method of effects research spawned by war-time needs, conceived audiences as solitary individuals controllable through media messages. The paradigm mirrored the premises of mass culture critics and mass society theorists that mass audiences were vulnerable to manipulation and thus, for some, posed a concern about their ability to fulfill their role as informed, independent citizens, and for others, represented a population that needed guidance by elites for the good of the democracy.

## Post-war TV effects, moral panic, and the passive viewer

When television arrived, there soon arose a moral panic about its effects on children. Middle-class parents expressed concern about their children's use of television and about the effects of some programs on children, similar to the parental concerns expressed in the 1930s about radio programs. CBS researcher Joseph Klapper observed that the numbers of popular magazine articles about television and children peaked in 1950 and 1951, when many families were first experiencing television in their homes and the disruptions in family routines that this attractive novelty created. He concluded that popular literature was an expression of what he called "PTA society," a public of parents of school-age children, school teachers and other professionals.[26]

Responding to the widespread debate about television, the U.S. Senate held hearings. The Senate Committee on the Judiciary, Subcommittee on Juvenile Delinquency, chaired by Senator Estes Kefauver, convened the first of these in 1954. This was in response to concerns that violence on television—as well as comics and movies—contributed to juvenile delinquency. In response to these hearings, the TV networks promised to conduct a survey on the impact of television on children, but did not.[27] In 1961, the same committee, now chaired by Senator Thomas Dodd, continued to pursue the issue. Prodded by the committee, the networks cooperated with the U.S. Department of Health, Education and Welfare to create a Joint Committee for Research on Television and Children. However, a presidential commission report later wrote, "Some six and one half years after the formation of the Joint Committee, only one report has been published." In 1964, the Dodd subcommittee held further hearings, at which he concluded that network programming "is 100% worse" than it had been at the time of the previous hearings.[28] In 1968, President Johnson appointed a National Commission on the Causes and Prevention of Violence, after the assassinations of Martin Luther King and Robert Kennedy and the urban riots that ensued after King's death. It issued a report on the effects of television violence. Shortly thereafter, Senator John Pastore, chair of the Senate Commerce Committee, Subcommittee on Communications, requested the Department of Health Education and Welfare to conduct research on the effects of television violence on children's attitudes and behavior. A research budget of one million dollars funded twenty-three separate research projects, demonstrating the federal government concern with effects of television on children. All of this research was directed to answering the same question about effects.[29]

This research, published in five volumes, adopted the effects paradigm implicit in the government charge and the public concern. The first volume reported how much violence appeared on television and what production and programming decisions led to this. The remaining four volumes reported how this television violence affected children's behavior. All of the research was quantitative; all of it focused on the individual viewer; all of it defined television violence as the cause and the individual child's behavior as the effect—although some studies include secondary independent variables, such as family attitude toward violence and social class. Even those critical of the report did not question the paradigm, but simply disputed how significant the effect of television was.

Ironically, this huge project was completed just as public concerns about television effects were beginning to lessen and as new research paradigms emphasizing active audiences were about to rise. The effects paradigm that had grown from public concerns, had been funded by government, and had been incorporated into government policy to control media effects on people, began to become one among several approaches by the late 1970s.[30] Concerns about mass society and mass media ebbed in the face of the civil rights and anti-war movements that filled the streets in the 1960s with active and vocal citizens who were clearly not the passive victims of media that had been feared. Establishment concerns turned instead to how to control these crowds and their riots. Nevertheless, for three decades, the effects paradigm sustained the image of audiences as passive individuals, even while the research itself often contradicted fears about the power of media.

Chapter 7

# Boob tubes, fans, and addicts

## Pathological audiences

Stretching back to the era of silent movie stars but spreading more broadly since World War II are images of audiences that went beyond simply isolated individuals: the characterization of audiences as a public health problem, and even as pathological.[1] These were adults who watched television significantly more than the norm; or children whose health was endangered by too much television or the wrong kinds of programs. Similarly, people who expressed too much interest in movies and movie stars were labeled abnormal. More recently, the image is of the media addict, an individual, usually male, isolating himself from relationships with family, friends, and community, not fulfilling his responsibilities to the family, the community, the polity, and failing to cultivate himself. Moreover, the pathological viewer was a burden on the polity by being a public health problem. Widespread characterizations of audience pathology appeared in newspapers, magazines, and movies, and on television and radio. They circulated in education, science, and medicine as well. They also sedimented, however, in the conversations and concerns of ordinary Americans, who repeatedly encountered such discourse in their roles as audiences, students, and patients.

### The boob and the tube

A mild version of this trend occurred in the common parlance that arose to refer to television users, although perhaps not as pathological. In ordinary conversation, Americans have applied a variety of terms to television and to adults who use it too much: couch potato, boob tube, idiot box, and addict. These names, often used in jest but based on a belief in their essential truth, suggest that some adults lacking intelligence or ambition watch too much television. Their lack of willpower is key to this image. When children watch too much television, the parents are blamed for failing to parent. The diagnosis of heavy viewing was attributed to character rather than to external limitations, and provided the foundation for a pathological characterization of some viewers.[2]

Magazine articles from the late 1940s on fostered images of television over-indulgence. While most discussion focused on the effects of television on children, there were also articles about the behavior of adult viewers. In addition to the assaults on television for low-brow taste (see Chapter 5), other, more slice-of-life and humorous, articles and cartoons depicted early TV viewers watching too much. In 1947, when televisions were an expensive novelty and only a tiny percent of homes had one, a *New Yorker* article satirized a well-to-do family unable to pull themselves away from the television. By the 1960s, when the novelty was long gone and the great majority had a television, an article in the *Saturday Evening Post* sighed, "Oh mass man! Oh lumpen lug! Why do you watch TV?," attributing this weakness for TV to the masses.[3]

Cartoons depicted boob tube and couch potato behavior long before those terms were coined. Magazines published a steady flow of cartoons about TV watching through the 1960s. The *New Yorker*'s picture of television America, as revealed in its many cartoons, is instructive. From the mid-1940s to the early 1950s, the cartoons typically portrayed television families with husbands who wore suits and ties, reflecting the audience skewed to the upper-middle class who then could afford a TV. By the mid-1950s, cartoon characters represented a wider range of classes. But the butt of the humor was frequently heavy viewers, men who were wedded to the television more than to their wives or children, often watching sports. For example, while a husband is watching a ball game, the wife introduces him to her friend by saying "and this is the back of my husband Sam's head." In another cartoon, while a husband watches a baseball game, the wife stands at a window with screens needing to be installed and says, "I wonder if I could interest you in some wonderful 72-inch screens." Yet another depicts a husband with his hands full of a plate of food, a drink, and TV listings, who discovers a sign on his television saying, "Why don't we go out tonight?" *Look* magazine published a cartoon at about the same time, depicting a decidedly down-scale man, unshaved and in t-shirt and socks, in a room with cracked plaster and lit by a bare light bulb, with beer can and newspaper in front of the television, and the wife explaining to a friend, "Have you ever met the quarterback of the L.A. Rams, Marciano's manager. . . ." This pattern continued through the mid-1960s, when a *Saturday Evening Post* cartoon showed a woman telling a delivery man to place a new television in front of her husband, who wears a bow tie and is facing a blank wall.[4]

While cartoons seemed to represent heavy viewing as cutting across classes, researchers more frequently associated heavy viewing with lower classes.[5] The adult viewer was depicted mostly in survey research, often with support from commercial sources and published for general readership in books such as *The Age of Television* (1956), *The Effects of Mass Communication* (1960), *Living with*

*Television* (1962), and *The People Look at Television* (1963). This research established the concept of the heavy viewer, categorizing viewers by how much time they reported watching television.[6] Heavy viewing was then linked to indiscriminate viewing and to lack of parental supervision of children's viewing. These would become known as a syndrome called "passive viewing." It was also identified as a pattern of use common to lower classes. An "active" viewer used television selectively and limited children's television time. These studies contributed to the construction of the image of the inert, slovenly, working-class male television viewer.

In his influential 1956 summary of research to that date, *The Age of Television*, Leo Bogart bluntly stated that, "better educated and wealthier persons, with their greater [mental] resources, are best able to take television in their stride." Two other market researchers, Ira Glick and Sidney Levy, provided a thorough presentation of the working-class boob, making class differences the theme of their book, *Living with Television*. They equated working-class viewers with children, "people with few inner resources that would lead them to cultivate other 'outside' interests," who expect immediate gratification and want programs that are "obvious," "not too complicated or involved," and which don't make them "work at watching." They stated that the stereotype of what we today call the couch potato "fits the working-class viewer more than others, as less motivated to act in an energetic, censoring or selective fashion." Glick and Levy contrasted these working-class viewers to the upper-middle class who were more "active and self-directing, [for whom] selection, discrimination and planning are the keynotes of their viewing." They looked for "worthwhile" programs, and had "little room left for self-indulgence." They exhibited praiseworthy goals by the standards of the dominant culture, high scores on cultural capital. Such descriptions contributed to the larger discourse that used television use as an indicator of status.[7]

These class distinctions were introduced into academic research on children's television use through investigations of parental supervision. Probably the single most important early study was *Television in the Lives of our Children*, by Wilbur Schramm and his graduate students at Stanford, Jack Lyle and Edwin Parker. The book inspired numerous later studies, including the famous Surgeon General's 1972 reports on the effects of television on children. Schramm and his co-authors opened with a statement that effects of television depended upon the family social norms, by which they meant social class differences. Particularly striking is the negative language they used to characterize the working class and to summarize their findings about them. They argued that the middle-class "work ethic" resulted in "less television and a larger proportion of realistic, non-entertaining, self-betterment programs," while what they called the working-class "pleasure ethic" led to "more television and a larger proportion of fantasy and entertainment." Having already identified working-class people as heavy viewers, they labeled these viewers as the "fantasy group," and the middle class who viewed less the "reality group." In another passage, they associated fantasy with surrender, passivity, emotion, and pleasure, and reality with alertness, activity, cognition, and enlightenment. They concluded that the working-class man felt personal problems "are too big for him to solve" and sought relaxation and escape, while the middle-class man faced a challenge and tried to solve his own problems. Finally, they claimed that middle-class children grew into what they labeled a "mature" television use pattern of deferred gratification while working-class children did not. They labeled this the "Principle of Maturation," implying that working-class adults were immature. While acknowledging these were stereotypes, giving a sympathetic explanation of why manual workers watch more television—they are tired and have less money for other choices—and even claiming that they "shall not be using the word [social class] in any pejorative sense," they nevertheless used the stereotypes and thereby gave them the seal of approval of science.[8] All of the traits attributed to the middle-class "reality group" align with good citizenship; the opposite is true for the working-class "fantasy group."

## Pathological audiences

Discourse about fans was more explicit in characterizing some audience members as pathological. Cultural studies scholar Joli Jensen observed that media fans have been characterized either as the obsessed individual, like the celebrity stalker, or the hysterical crowd, like screaming young girls reaching to touch a rock star. She points out how these images draw upon the older mass culture/mass society idea of the alienated individual and mass manipulated masses. Images of fans in mainstream media characterize them as compensating for some inadequacy, developing an imaginary relationship with a media celebrity in lieu of real relationships, the lone and alienated individual dependent upon a media image. In the silent film era, fans were depicted as young women infatuated with a romantic lead such as Rudolph Valentino, building on the image of the matinee girl at the stage door in the late nineteenth century, but with reference to hysterical and obsessive behavior. In 1947, the *New York Times* called movie fan clubs "half-neurotic, half-idiotic intensity of adolescent hero worship." About the same time, the *New Republic* described a crowd of Frank Sinatra's bobby-soxer fans as "a terrifying phenomenon of mass hysteria that is seen only two or three times in a century." In the 1960s, stories about hysterical fans flooded magazines and spawned a new term, Beatlemania. Soap opera fans have long been held in contempt. James Thurber talked about them; and researchers studied their psyches in the 1940s. Half a century later, images of fans as losers or lunatics were still "widely held and rarely questioned."[9]

While several scholars have studied fandom, a more recent pathological depiction of audience obsession, the media addict, has received less attention. Whereas the fan's obsession is with the content of a medium, a movie, or an actor, the addict is obsessed with the medium itself. Cartoons that depict a person watching a blank TV screen illustrate an addict, not a fan.[10] Addiction is a very pejorative label that feeds moral panic. Definitions of addiction invariably focus on its destructive nature; the addict abandons healthy relationships and activities to single-mindedly pursue the addiction. Relationships crumble, jobs are lost, and families are abandoned. However, the term does little to shed light on solutions to problem behaviors. It has come to be defined as a psychological rather than a physical illness. Even when identified as a physical illness, treatment has typically centered on psychological solutions and the will to resist.

The concept of addiction describes a person who is the antithesis of a good citizen. The addict is represented as self-possessed and incapable of considering the group or community interest. He is irrational, his pursuit of the addiction leading to his own self-destruction. He lacks independence, being controlled by his addiction. His affliction and his cure often have been attributed to a matter of willpower, necessary for independence as well as strong moral character or civic virtue. Last, he is a threat to the community, destroying the ties of family and friends that make up a community and constituting a public safety as well as public health problem.

Addiction is a vague concept and one that has repeatedly changed through history. Addiction discourse has been a mélange of popular, political/legal, and medical usage of the term. Post-war American dictionaries narrowed earlier definitions to one focused on habitual use that persists despite harmful consequences. *Webster's New Twentieth Century Dictionary*, in 1968, noted that the term was, "as now used, generally in a bad sense." It has been used interchangeably with and not clearly distinguished from other terms such as "habit," "compulsion," or "dependence." Etiology or explanations of the cause of addictions have vacillated from a focus on the addictive substance to a focus on the individual's religious, moral, psychological, or biological weakness. Explanations of excessive alcohol consumption alternately blamed the drinker and the drink. With the rise of a disease model in the mid-twentieth century, promoted by Alcoholics Anonymous and some medical researchers, the focus shifted to a minority of drinkers afflicted with a disease. According to AA, the alcoholic is different than other people: "He seemed quite rational and well-balanced with respect to other problems. Yet he had no control whatever over alcohol."[11] Willpower, in the form of recognizing the problem and a commitment to fight it, was necessary but not sufficient for the alcoholic. The addict needed assistance. For AA, the answer was religion; only with God's help could the addict resist.

Medical and scientific definitions of addiction also have varied. In the first edition of the standard reference, the American Psychiatric Association's *Diagnostic and Statistical Manual of Mental Disorders*, in 1952, drug addiction was defined as "symptomatic of a personality disorder," that is, some pre-existing psychological flaw in the person that caused them to become addicted. This was distinguished from alcohol addiction that appeared "without recognizable underlying disorder," that is, without a personal flaw, confirming the AA's position. In 1968, the *DSM II* reserved the term for physical addiction to alcohol and, by contrast, declared drug "dependence" to be "habitual use or a clear sense of need for the drug," that is, a psychological issue. The third edition (*DSM III*, 1980) shifted to descriptions based strictly upon behavioral symptoms rather than explaining underlying causes. It banished the term "addiction" entirely and for alcohol, tobacco, and drugs distinguished two levels of misuse: "substance abuse," an inability to cut down or stop use, or the more severe "substance dependence," indicated by increasing physiological tolerance or withdrawal symptoms. The fourth and current edition (*DSM IV*, 1994) continues to use the term "dependence" and avoid the term "addiction."[12]

Criminologist Ronald Akers observes that there was a significant break in the 1960s from a medical focus on physiological addiction to the psychological. In what he terms the "traditional concept of addiction," certain drugs were classified as addictive if they produced physiological dependence and increased tolerance with sustained use, indicating that body chemistry had adjusted to and become dependent on the drug to function. This definition gave primacy to the drug as the source of addiction. Without these physical symptoms, drug use was simply not defined as addiction. Psychologist Stanton Peele notes the uniqueness of such a concept, writing that, "no other scientific formulation attributes a complex human phenomenon to the nature of a particular stimulus." Psychological dependence and abuse were introduced as new categories in the mid-1960s and at least partly encoded in the *DSM* in 1968, to refer to a craving for a drug, with or without the effects of physical addiction. The criterion of craving confused "addiction" and "compulsion." Peele refers to the "conventional idea [in the 1980s] of addiction [as] a substance or activity that can produce a compulsion to act that is beyond self-control." This definition combined the "pull" of the drug to the "push" of the compulsion.[13] Using the term "compulsion" or its older, commonplace alternate, "habit," to define addiction, gave greater attention to the user's actions, and opened the door to defining many behaviors as addictions. The newer term "abuse" targets the person for blame even more. "Addict" and "dependence" are more ambivalent in their suggestive etiology.

Legal status of addiction and drugs also changed with the times and targeted particular subordinate groups as problem users. In the nineteenth-century United States, opiates were legal, prescribed by doctors and widely used. By the turn of the century, federal, state, and local governments began to curtail their use. The Harrison Narcotics Act of 1914 blocked sale of opiates or cocaine, and the Marijuana Tax Act in 1937 suppressed its use and sale. During the 1930s, the federal government launched an educational campaign emphasizing the dangers of drugs to discourage use, contributing to the negative discourse about addiction. It associated opiates, cocaine, and marijuana with Chinese, African, and Latino Americans, respectively; in the 1950s, heroin was associated with African Americans and marijuana with Mexican Americans. Such claims emphasized these groups' unsuitability for citizenship.[14]

## Media addiction

Eve Sedgewick argues that since the 1970s there has been a growing list of consumption behaviors that have been defined as uncontrolled and conceived as paralyses of the will. Behavior addictions such as exercise, gambling, and sex are claimed to arise in the addicted person rather than from the substance or behavior, which by itself is normal and even healthy.[15] Excessive media use is such a behavior. However, the discourse on media addiction has mixed blaming the individual and the medium, similar to the vacillating discourse on alcohol and drugs. The addict is weak-willed and/or dependent on the "drug."

As discussed in previous chapters, through the twentieth century movies, popular music, and especially television were the subjects of moral panics. The concept of media addiction is an extension of the thesis of heavy media users displacing healthier activities, and has been used mostly by non-professionals to talk about the strong attractions of new media. Debates recurred each time a new medium became widespread, from movies to radio to television and the internet, from tango to jazz to rock'n'roll to rap. In earlier decades of the twentieth century, subordinate peoples of all sorts were identified as more susceptible than others to media. Immigrants, the working class, poor, and unemployed, the uneducated, African Americans and Latinos, women, and children were variously described as spellbound, mesmerized, or narcotized by early movies.

However, for most of the twentieth century, references and anecdotes that told of strong attractions to media rarely used the term addiction. During the silent movie era, reformers such as Jane Addams worried about the strong hold movies had on working-class adolescents. She cited some girls who forfeited a day in the country for fear they would not be able to go to the movies that night. Most comment was about the grip movies had, once the person was watching, rather than upon a compulsion to go to the movies. These concerns, in other words, were part of the effects debate, not part of the thesis that overuse displaced healthier activities. Similarly with popular music, the fear was about the effect music had on youth when they listened and danced, not about a compulsion to listen. Sociologists Paul Lazarsfeld and Robert Merton introduced the term "narcotizing dysfunction" of the media in 1948, but again, this was not meant to indicate addiction. Rather, they referred metaphorically to the effect of the flood of media information that immobilized people from acting, because they come "to mistake knowing about problems of the day for *doing* something about them . . . inadvertently transforming the energies of men from active participation into passive knowledge." Moreover, these allusions to "narcotic" effects were infrequent. Various synonyms of addiction were used occasionally in reference to early radio users, but typically this usage also was metaphorical. Magazine articles in the early days of radio humorously depicted men addicted to their hobby of building their own radios or trying to tune in distant broadcast stations on their radio sets, sometimes referring to them as "fiends." Sociologist Herta Herzog reported a nine-year-old girl commenting in an interview that her mother removed the tubes from the radio because she decided the children were becoming "radio fiends."[16] But, as radios rapidly became commonplace household appliances, comments suggesting addiction to radio disappeared.

It was when television came on the scene after World War II that articles appeared in the mainstream press discussing uncontrolled over-use of television and addiction. The household magazine *Coronet* in 1955 titled an article: "I was cured of TV: the story of a confirmed addict and his long hard fight back to life." In a more serious article that same year, *US News and World Report* quoted several people saying they could not control their television use, suggesting an addiction. A Princeton, New Jersey wife said, ". . . this creature seemed to have come into our lives and taken over . . . [we] seem to be mesmerized by it." A single San Francisco secretary was quoted, "If I didn't watch myself carefully, I'd watch TV all the time and get nothing done." Again in 1955, in *Reader's Digest* a medical doctor advised melodramatically,[17]

> That's the insidious thing about television. You pause a moment on your way upstairs to adjust the knobs and make the image sharper. Before you know it, you are kneeling in front of the screen, turning the dials to see what's on channel 7. Three hours later your children have gone off to bed sobbing,

> your wife has missed the Philharmonic, and the cathode curse has darkened another happy home.

A few references to TV addiction even dribbled into scientific papers. Two influential researchers, Eleanor Maccoby and Wilbur Schramm, each suggested that children may become addicted. Both made these comments not as interpretations of their research data, but as personal observations. Medical professionals expressed concern about dangers of television to children, but published very little research about TV addiction.[18]

Paralleling the occasional mention of addiction was a more general tendency to cast the problem primarily in terms of the new medium, television, as a dangerous "substance" and the principal cause of the problem. Television was described in very much the same language as prescription medicine: powerful and dangerous if not used strictly as prescribed—and medical associations published prescriptions for media use. Like alcohol and tobacco, they were legal but use needed to be regulated. The main focus of public discourse was protecting "innocent" children from television. *Parents Magazine*, for example, warned parents to limit the hours of their children's viewing, supervise what they see, plan their viewing week, discourage programs that upset, and to not use television as a babysitter, but to watch with their children and explain.[19] Linking over-use to less education, medical professionals blamed lower-class parents for irresponsible behavior in their own and their children's use of television, and for the delinquency that was claimed to result.

Articles and passing remarks about addiction continued to be scattered through the popular press, referring to "TV addiction," being "hooked," and how to "break the habit." Most authors used the language of addiction melodramatically to accent the degree to which people watch, and let their children watch, too much television. These articles consistently addressed the reader or someone they knew as a potential TV addict, and either faulted him for lack of willpower or television for its magnetic addictiveness. In 1962, *Reader's Digest* reprinted from *TV Guide*—two magazines with amongst the largest circulation in the nation—an article titled, "Don't just sit there—reach for the switch!," in which humorist Leo Rosten wrote in a serious vein that: "[Those who blame television] act as if television mysteriously forces them to abdicate their time-honored role as guides, teachers, and yes, censors for the young."[20]

After a flurry of such articles in the early 1960s,[21] addiction references seemed to subside for about a decade, as Americans became accustomed to television and concerned about more pressing issues such as urban riots, the Vietnam War, and youth rebellion, and as researchers focused more on effects of television violence than on over-use and displacement. Then, in the late 1970s, a steady stream of new assertions developed, part of the growth of self-help literature that Sedgewick noticed.[22] The self-help literature labeled a set of symptoms as media addiction and relied on anecdotes for evidence. It typically offered no explanation of causes. Most significant, this second wave promoted the idea of media addiction as a real illness, not just a metaphor.

Most successful was Marie Winn's *The Plug-in Drug*, the pioneering book on the subject, first published in 1977, reprinted and reincarnated several times over twenty-five years, and inspiring graphic spin-offs of the title. Even respected psychologists Jerome and Dorothy Singer cited Winn approvingly in their influential 1981 book on television violence. Swimming against the tide of the 1970s when others worried about the violence children saw on television, Winn argued that the question was not what we watch, but how much. Based on what she read and on "lengthy talks" she had with people about television, she claimed that television is truly addictive just like drugs. She specified criteria for determining addiction and said that people identified these characteristics in themselves or others. Two similar books on television addiction followed in the wake of Winn's success.[23]

Video games appeared in the 1980s, followed by computer games and the internet in the 1990s, and charges of addictiveness began to be raised about them. Adolescent enthusiasm for these games stimulated a continuing stream of magazine articles into the new millennium.[24] Another self-help book, *Caught in the Net*, by clinical psychologist Kimberly Young, claimed that internet addiction was real and briefly received wide attention. Magazine articles of the 1990s also used the term literally, especially in relation to video and computer games and the internet. They cited examples of both boys and adults as addicted to games, and both men and women as addicted to the internet, for stock trading, sex, chat rooms, and email. The idea of internet addiction became so widespread that it was the basis for a *New Yorker* cartoon in which a person in a self-help group confesses that he checks his email two hundred times a day.

Ironically, this stream began just as some psychologists were beginning to question the general concept of addiction.[25] The first research on media addiction also began in the 1980s.[26] A few communication research studies claimed media addiction as a real illness. A parallel body of research was produced by medical professionals rooted in addiction research. This spawned articles by other academics in the 1990s highly critical of claims that media addiction is anything more than a metaphor.[27] The self-help literature as well as the academic proponents of media addiction diagnoses began with the premise that everyone is susceptible, and therefore the problem lies less in weak individuals than in the irresistible power of the medium. They offered remedies on how to combat and control their seductiveness. The idea of media addiction, then, grows out of a long-term discourse that defines media as dangerous. Within this discourse the medium continues to bear a large part of the blame, even in the case of "addiction." The media are problematic; they are seductive. "Addiction" is a term used to emphasize the strong hold that media have on some people, to highlight the time consumed by media use and the consequent displacement of healthier activities, including relationships and the damage resulting from their neglect. It emphasizes the difficulty of resisting, regardless of how unsatisfying the entertainment.

Each of these elements has also been a traditional symptom for identifying addiction. The term "addiction" was already highly charged, familiar, and well suited to the purpose of emphasizing the dangers of television and the internet. The addiction discourse is a classic melodrama of good against evil that applies well to media. Media are "dangerous" and "destructive." People who use them are "weak"; people who promote them are "bad"; people who oppose them are "good." Since the discourse is so familiar, it is easy to adopt it in talking about media and audiences. Labeling media use as addictive signifies its dangers by simply transferring the negativity packaged in the label from drugs to television, video games, or the internet. The media addiction discourse however has emphasized the dangers of media over the weakness of people, due to the persistent demonizing of television for decades before the term "addiction" began to be widely applied to media. Similarly, while computer and internet technologies in a variety of ways have erased the idea of a passive audience, the image of addiction has reinstated it.

These claims have been part of the "moral panic" and public debate that recurred with the rapid proliferation of each new entertainment medium. These moral panics characterized audience pathologies as a public health problem, particularly for children, endangering not only their individual health but also, by extension, the health and future of the nation. They complemented other criticism, such as Robert Putnam's *Bowling Alone*, that heavy use of media causes citizens to neglect their civic responsibilities generally.[28] While not expressed explicitly, descriptions of pathological audiences depicted them as devoid of the very traits at the core of good citizenship. They were dependent upon and controlled by the medium instead of being free and independent in their judgment; their excessive use of media left little time for civic participation; their excessive use also was irrational, bringing into question their ability to act as reasoning citizens; their inability to resist the temptation indicated a weak will, in contrast to the moral character expected for the civic virtue that would lead a citizen to put public interest above personal interest.

# Epilogue

How we have imagined audiences and what we have expected of them reveal much about our sense of citizenship and equality. The representations of audiences discussed in these chapters complement discourses about what constitutes citizenship and why some, more than others, deserve its rights and privileges. They build on and reinforce broader discursive frameworks of social and cultural hierarchies that distinguish and separate classes, races, sexes, and others.

Images of crowds, publics, and isolated individuals have and continue to mobilize these effects. Through American audience history, the idea of publics has been the standard for evaluating audiences as citizens. Measured against this ideal, audiences at different times have been denounced as dangerous crowds or isolated individuals, inadequate for citizenship. These images are not exclusive to any particular era. Historical discourses don't die, but they do shift in dominance and older discourses reconfigure their past forms to suit new eras. While current academic discourses challenge the old characterizations of audiences as isolated individuals and irrational crowds, nevertheless popular, journalistic, and even legal discourses continue to rely on traditional categories. Echoes of dangerous crowds and crowd psychology still ring in discourses on live audiences. Representations of active autonomous audiences have revived in popular discourses on new digital media and in critical academic discourses—and yet images of isolated individuals submerged in virtual reality are equally important characterizations of new media audiences.

Popular music has given rise not only to the image of the hysterical fan, but also has re-produced images of riotous crowds. These are images of an active audience, a shift away from the image of a mass-mediated, passive audience, but a bad audience, a crowd rather than a public. Young males were the targets of this representation, and particularly working-class youth depicted as trouble-makers. Fifties images associated rock 'n' roll and its working-class base of popularity with dangerous crowds of juvenile delinquents.[1] A decade later, the language of crowd psychology was again recruited, this time focused on a "generation gap" without reference to class, to explain riots and other destructive incidents at rock concerts, defining youths as problems of public order, whether due to drugs, sex, or violence.[2] The exception was the overwhelmingly favorable news coverage of the original Woodstock concert in 1969 precisely because of its claimed peacefulness. News and editorials elevated this image to an ideal, contrasting that audience as community to other audiences as crowds creating disorder and committing violence. This very contrast, however, emphasized that the bad audiences were immature and ill suited to citizenship if they could not behave civilly and live for a few hours in harmony.[3]

In sharp contrast to the original concert, news reports on the thirtieth anniversary Woodstock concert in 1999 depicted a crowd that raped and rioted. At the end of a three-day concert attended by 200,000, some audience members started bonfires, first with trash cans, then a car, and then supply and equipment trucks, after which some began to loot concessions. A cover story in *Rolling Stone* was titled "Moshing and looting." The *New York Times* reports called it a "violent and frightening rampage by thousands of young people," and claimed that the hard rock/hip-hop music and performers had incited the mostly male crowd. Accompanying these stories were reports of rapes in mosh pits. A couple months later, *US News and World Report* claimed that the rioting at Woodstock '99 and outside another concert that August was a result of a male youth music culture and that minor violence was becoming the norm at concerts. It quoted a researcher saying, "when you have a mass amount of people of the same generation, usually young, congregated in one area, [they] get the feeling that rules don't apply anymore." Several articles labeled concert audiences as chaotic and called for more security to control them. By mid-2000, *Billboard* reported that safety was a growing concern for the concert business.[4] Reports were beginning to represent not just specific incidents but young male concert audiences generally as a problem for public order and requiring more policing. Crowd psychology crept back into the descriptions: the focus was on live audiences, crowded together and insufficiently policed, becoming excited and then violent. The reports' language (violent, frightening, rampage, riot) and claims that the behavior was incited by the music could have been taken from accounts of the Astor Place riot of 1849.

Sports spectators also have been represented as crowds out of control. A 2002 opinion column in the *New York Times* about spectators rushing the field at the end of a few college football games labeled the scenes "mayhem," and condemned crowds as "intrinsically dangerous." In 2001, fans at a Cleveland Browns professional football game, irate at a referee's call, threw plastic bottles and other debris on the field. The newspaper report took for granted this was unacceptable behavior and focused on whether the home team officials were sufficiently stern in reprimanding the fans and protecting the players—echoing rock concert critics' calls for more policing. The article cited a similar example of fans throwing snowballs at players in a 1995 game, referred to this incident as "chaos," and quoted players and other personnel who claimed it was dangerous—for brawny, helmeted, and armored players to be hit with plastic bottles.[5] Other complaints about sport spectators linked their misbehavior to too much beer, the drink of youth. Compared to the reports about privileged young Ivy League football spectators of the last turn of the century, recent depictions were far less tolerant. The concern underlying the intolerance was that audiences at professional sport events were of mixed age, race, gender, and class, so that violence by some threatened the safety, not of the players, but of the other spectators who were lucrative customers that expected the audience to behave as respectable and responsible citizens in a public place. The underlying message was that a good audience should behave as a good public, a message made explicit in the recent call for more civility generally in public places.[6]

Discourses on new media have included images of an ideal autonomous audience, claiming the new technologies liberated their users and opened vistas of a vital new public sphere—the usual high hopes raised for each new medium, as we have seen—but they also have been accused of manipulating, controlling, and enslaving their users—the usual fears.[7] The growth of internet use in the 1990s and 2000s has been accompanied by a wave of claims that internet technology liberates people from the one-way, top-down mass media that dominated the twentieth century—neglecting the internet's increasing similarity to a mass medium. One widespread claim focused on the explicit use of the internet as a public forum, epitomized by political blogs and listservs, providing easy access and equality through anonymity. Another described the combination of search engines and downloading as providing access to a much broader array not only of music but also many other forms of information and entertainment, such as ebooks and on-line newspapers and databases, for a much wider range of users, loosening control over these forms by corporations and other organizations, promising a creative commons, and enabling people to sample a far wider range of ideas than they could find in a store, on television, or even in a library.[8] The internet has been represented as providing the means to turn the mass into a public through universal availability of the knowledge and participation that marks the informed citizen. These claims reflect a faith in the technology producing a competitive market/forum in which users are not only autonomous, but also influence the shape of ideas and events, both commercial and political. Much like Habermas' original formulation of public sphere, however, they have ignored the exclusion of those without sufficient education and income from sharing this form of citizen participation.

Academic discourse moved similarly toward a conception of active audiences. In the 1970s, a new ethnographic approach in the United States and cultural studies in Britain gained institutional footholds for approaches that presumed active audiences. By the 1990s, the active audience had become a widely-accepted academic construct. But this was formulated as individual, consumer autonomy more than collective crowds or citizen publics. Some within cultural studies began to criticize exaggerated claims of agency. Others called for an approach that recognized both the power of media as well as that of audiences, proposing an approach of autonomy with limits.[9]

Other popular discourses, however, have sustained images of pathological users. Fears of commercialization and corporate control have contributed predictions that the internet is quickly becoming just another mass medium with a passive audience.[10] Claims of internet addictiveness reveal a fear of the technology's mesmerizing power that allegedly devours time and lives. The image of the asocial computer nerd similarly depicts an isolated individual, incapable of healthy social relationships and finding refuge in these new technologies. This image sometimes includes a fear that an avenging monster may suddenly burst forth from the meek nerd. Early news reports about the student who slaughtered 32 students and teachers at Virginia Polytechnic Institute in 2007 emphasized his quiet nerd-like characteristics that belied murderous rage underneath. This followed the same pattern as reports for several other school shootings in the 1990s and 2000s, which at first suggested that the killer was an asocial youth who overindulged in consuming violent media.[11]

In sum, dangerous crowds, ideal publics, and isolated individuals continue to be features of discourses on audiences. Two centuries of representing audiences in terms relevant to citizenship and evaluating the worthiness of audiences in terms of their social inequality indicate that discourses on audiences, whether academic, elite, intellectual, journalistic, or popular, are neither innocent description nor private opinion, but are filled with political implications that sustain mainstream conceptions of citizenship and worthiness. Whatever our assertions about audiences, we need to be cognizant that we speak in the context of these long-term discourses and that our claims may be incorporated into and our meaning transformed by them.

# Notes

## Introduction: the politics of audiences in America

1 *Statistical Abstracts of the United States 2007* (Washington DC: US Government Printing Office), Table 1110, 709.

2 On moral panics and media audiences, see Kirsten Drotner, "Modernity and Media Panics," in Michael Skovmand and Kim Christian Schroder, eds, *Media Cultures: Reappraising Transnational Media* (London: Routledge, 1992), 42–62; Chas Critcher, *Moral Panics and the Media* (Buckingham: Open University Press, 2003), 155; Stanley Cohen, *Folk Devils and Moral Panics*, third edition (London: Routledge, 2002), xxviii–xxxv; Howard Becker, *The Outsiders* (New York: Free Press, 1963), Ch. 8.

3 Class structure differs by era. But to simplify and provide continuity in discussion, I sometimes will use the terms lower class or working class loosely to mean artisans, servants, small leaseholders, and those without land leases or employment in earlier eras, and to mean their proletarianized descendants in the later periods.

4 A verb, "auditing" or "audiencing," would make this more evident, but such unconventional usage would disrupt the flow of reading.

5 While I focus on dominant discourse, I do not discount the importance of alternative and oppositional discourses. But in order to cover the scope of two centuries over which these major changes occur, I cannot examine the dialog of discourses in depth and have deliberately left many threads hanging. I leave these stories for others to tell.

6 These discourses on audiences parallel those on other subjects, such as intelligence, illness or criminality, that also represent subordinate groups as emotional, impulsive, or suggestible in contrast to good citizenship, and are used interchangeably for subordinate status whether race, sex, class, or other category. See Evelyn Nakano Glenn, *Unequal Freedom: How Race and Gender Shaped American Citizenship and Labor* (Harvard University Press, 2002), 3; Genevieve Lloyd, *The Man of Reason: "Male" and "Female" in Western Philosophy* (University of Minnesota Press, 1984); Nicole Hahn Rafter, ed., *White Trash: The Eugenic Family Studies, 1877–1919* (Boston: Northeastern University Press, 1988); Michael Sokal, *Psychological Testing and American Society, 1890–1930* (New Brunswick: Rutgers University Press, 1987).

7 Scholars have devised many different typologies to dissect the history of citizenship. See Derek Heater, *Citizenship: The Civic Ideal in World History, Politics and Education*, third edition (Manchester University Press, 2004); Michael Schudson, *The Good Citizen: A History of American Civic Life* (Harvard University Press, 1998); T. H. Marshall and Tom Bottomore, *Citizenship and Social Class* (London: Pluto Press, 1992); Rogers Brubaker, *Citizenship and Nationhood in France and Germany* (Harvard University Press, 1992); Rogers Smith, *Civic Ideals: Conflicting Visions of Citizenship in US History* (Yale University Press, 1997); Ginafranco Poggi, "Citizens and the state: retrospect and prospect," in Quentin Skinner and Bo Straith, eds, *States and Citizens: History, Theory, Prospects* (Cambridge University Press, 2003); Dawn Oliver and Derek Heater, *The Foundations of Citizenship* (London: Harvester Wheatsheaf, 1994), Chs 1, 6; Margaret Somers, "The privatization of citizenship: how to un-think a knowledge culture," in Victoria Bonnel and Lynn Hunt, eds, *Beyond the Cultural Turn: New Directions in the Study of Society and Culture* (University of California Press, 1999), 121–64; David Ricci, *Good Citizenship in America* (Cambridge University Press, 2004), Ch. 1; James Kettner, *The Development of American Citizenship, 1608–1870* (University of North Carolina Press, 1978).

8 Undemocratic governments require citizens merely to be obedient subjects. Scholars distinguish between citizenship as simple residence within a nation, and active citizenship mentioned here. See, e.g., Bernard Crick, "Foreword," in Derek Heater, *Citizenship*, third edition, xi; James Kettner, "Prologue," *The Development of American Citizenship*, 3–10.

9 On ancient citizenship, see Derek Heater, *Citizenship*, 3–21. It presumed a common interest shared between privileged male citizens and subordinate women, slaves, etc.

10 David J. Manning, *Liberalism* (New York: St. Martin's Press, 1976), 121–2; John Locke, *Second Treatise*; John Stuart Mill, *On Liberty*, and *Representative Government*.

11 Derek Heater, *Citizenship*, 33, 74; Catherine Hall, Keith McClelland, and Jane Rendall, *Defining the Victorian Nation: Class, Race, Gender and the British Reform Act of 1867* (Cambridge University Press, 2000), 62–70, 165, Mill quote on 63; George Marcus, *The Sentimental Citizen: Emotion in Democratic Politics* (Penn State University Press, 2002), Ch. 3.

12 Charles Tilly "A Primer on Citizenship," *Theory and Society* 26 (1997): 601; Kathleen Canning and Sonya Rose, *Gender, Citizenship, and Subjectivities* (Oxford: Blackwell, 2002); T. H. Marshall, *Citizenship and Social Class*; Frank Van Nuys, *Americanization and the West: Race, Immigration and Citizenship, 1890–1930* (University Press of Kansas, 2002); Hall et al., *Defining the Victorian Nation*; Joan Gunderson, "Independence, Citizenship and the American Revolution," *Signs* 13 (1987): 59–77; Ali Behdad, *A Forgetful Nation: On Immigration and Cultural Identity in the United States* (Duke University Press, 2005).

13 On the application of civic virtue in American citizenship, see Philip Gould, "Virtue, Ideology and the American Revolution: The Legacy of the Republican Synthesis," *American Literary History* 5 (1993): 564–77; Kettner [but see Smith, 27, on Kettner's optimism]. On the gendered construction of virtue, see Ruth Bloch, "The Gendered Meaning of Virtue in Revolutionary America," *Signs* 11 (1987): 37–58.

14 Schudson, *The Good Citizen*, 5–9; Ricci, 72; Joyce Appleby, *Liberalism and Republicanism in the Historical Imagination* (Harvard University Press, 1992), 1.

15 On deference, see Gordon Wood, *Radicalism of the American Revolution* (Knopf, 1992), 104–5; Appleby, *Capitalism and a New Social Order*, 9; Appleby, *Liberalism and Republicanism in the Historical Imagination*, 14; Jack Pole, "Historians and the Problem of Early American Democracy," *American Historical* 67 (1961).

16 For a historiography of republicanism, see Daniel Rogers, "Republicanism: The Career of a Concept," *Journal of American History* 79 (1992): 11–38.

17 Ricci, 81–93; Wilentz, *Chants Democratic*.

18 Stuart Blumin, *The Emergence of the Middle Class: Social Experience in the American City, 1760–1900* (Cambridge University Press, 1989); Glenn Altschuler and Stuart Blumin, *Rude Republicans: Americans and Their Politics in the Nineteenth Century* (Princeton University Press, 2001); Mary Ann Clawson, *Brotherhood: Class, Gender, Fraternalism* (Princeton University Press, 1989).

19 John Dewey, *The Public and Its Problems* (New York: Henry Holt, 1927), 111–13; Hall and McClelland, 62, 63; Heater, 4–21.

20 Rogers Smith, *Civic Ideals*, 1, 16–17; John T. Wheelwright, "Public Opinion as a Force," *Harvard Monthly* 8 (1889): 47–8; Schudson, 1–3. Also see Evelyn Nakano Glenn, *Unequal Freedom*.

21 Rogers Smith, *Civic Ideals*, 6, 7.

22 Michael Schudson, *The Good Citizen*, 5–9; Rogers Smith, *Civic Ideals*, 410.

23 Smith, 27

24 David Snow and Ronnelle Paulsen, "Crowds and Riots," in Edgar and Marie L. Borgatta, eds, *Encyclopedia of Sociology*, Vol. 1 (New York: Macmillan, 1992), 395–402; Ralph Turner and Lewis Killian, *Collective Behavior*, second edition (Prentice Hall, 1972), 12, 79–80, 112, 179; Clark McPhail, *The Myth of the Madding Crowd* (New York: Aldine, 1991); Ian Munro, *The Figure of the Crowd in Early Modern London* (London: Palgrave-Macmillan, 2005).

25 John S. McClelland, *The Crowd and The Mob: From Plato to Canetti* (London: Unwin Hyman, 1989), 1–7; *The Compact Edition of the Oxford English Dictionary* (Oxford University Press, 1971), 1825; Salvadore Giner, *Mass Society* (New York: Academic Press), 138; Raymond Williams, *Keywords* (New York: Oxford University Press, 1976), 159. English and American novels of the nineteenth century regularly depicted the working class as a mob. See Alan Swingewood, *The Myth of Mass Culture* (Atlantic Highlands, NJ: Humanities Press), 47; Mary Esteve, "Representations of Crowds and Anonymity in Late Nineteenth and Early Twentieth-Century Urban America," dissertation (University of Washington, 1995).

26 On distinctions between subject and citizen, see Jeffrey Merrick, "Subjects and Citizens in the Remonstrances of the Parlement of Paris in the Eighteenth Century," *Journal of the History of Ideas* 51 (1990): 453–60. On crowds, see George Rude, *The Crowd in History* (New York: Wiley, 1964); Edward P. Thompson, "The Moral Economy of the English Crowd in the Eighteenth Century," *Past and Present* 50 (1971): 76–136; Charles Tilly, *Popular Contention in Great Britain, 1758–1834* (Harvard University Press, 1995).

27 Natalie Davis, "The Reason of Misrule: Youth Groups and Charivaris in Sixteenth Century France," *Past and Present* 1 (1971): 41–75; Tim Harris, ed., *The Politics of the Excluded, 1500–1850* (London: Palgrave, 2001); Michael Bristol, *Carnival and Theater: Plebian Culture and the Structure of Authority in Renaissance England* (London: Methuen, 1985); Peter Borsay, "'All the Town's a Stage': Urban Ritual and

Ceremony, 1600–1800," in Peter Clark, ed., *The Transformation of the English Provincial towns, 1600–1800* (London: Hutchinson, 1984), 228–58. On audience crowds, see Robert J. Holton, "The Crowd in History: Some Problems of Theory and Method," *Social History* 3 (1978): 223.

28 On importance of familiarity for the self-regulation of the crowd and for the restraint of authorities, see John Bohstedt, *Riots and Community Politics in England and Wales, 1790–1810*, (Harvard University Press, 1983); Andrew Charlesworth, "From the Moral Economy to the Political Economy of Manchester, 1790–1812," *Social History* 18 (1993): 205–17.

29 Charles MacKay, *Memoirs of Extraordinary Popular Delusions* (London: Richard Bentley, 1841); Robert Nye, *Gustave Le Bon and the Crisis of Mass Democracy in the Third Republic* (Beverly Hills and London: Sage 1975), 63, 3.

30 Gustave Le Bon, *The Crowd* (New York: Viking Press, 1960; orig. 1895); Robert Park, *The Crowd and the Public and Other Essays* (University of Chicago Press, 1972, orig.1904, Charlotte Elsner, trans.), 47. Le Bon's concern about crowds apparently arose from his experience as a member of the bourgeoisie living through the Revolution of 1848 and the Paris Commune.

31 Nye, 62–3, 67; Le Bon, 28, 38, 81–2.

32 Craig Calhoun and Joseph Karaganis, "Public Sphere," *Encyclopedia of American Studies*, 446–7; *Encyclopedia of Sociology*, 1395; Turner and Killian, 179–80, 196–7. On the equation of public and rationality, see Elisabeth Noelle-Neumann, "Public Opinion and Rationality," in Theodore Glasser and Charles Salmon, eds, *Public Opinion and the Communication of Dissent* (New York: Guilford Press, 1995), 33–54; Mike Hill and Warren Montag, eds, *Masses, Classes and the Public Sphere* (New York: Verso, 2000) 6; Turner and Killian, 196–7.

33 Jeff Weintraub, "The Theory and Politics of the Public/Private Distinction," in J. Weintraub and Krishan Kumar, *Public and Private in Thought and Practice*; on another typology of public, see John Durham Peters, "Historical Tensions in the Concept of Public Opinion," in Glasser and Salmon.

34 Turner and Killian, *Collective Behavior*, second edition (Englewood Cliffs: Prentice Hall, 1972); Gabriel Tarde, "The Public and the Crowd" and "Opinion and Conversation," in *On Communication and Social Influence*, Terry Clark, ed. (University of Chicago Press, 1969), 277–94, 297–318; Jurgen Habermas, *The Structural Transformation of the Public Sphere*, Thomas Burger, trans. (MIT Press, 1989, orig. 1962). Historically, Habermas places the beginnings of the public sphere in merchant trade communication, secondarily in literary conversations, and only then in political communication. The means at first were conversation and letters, followed later by print.

35 Gabriel Tarde, "The Public and the Crowd," *On Communication and Social Influence*, 281.

36 Tarde, "Opinion and Conversation," in *On Communication and Social Influence*, 307–8; Jaap van Ginneken, *Crowds, Psychology and Politics, 1871–1899* (Cambridge University Press, 1992). Tarde quoted Diderot, who described public opinion formed by a small number of notable men "who speak after having thought and who continuously form centers of instruction. . . from which errors and well formed truths flow by degrees until they reach the outer confines of the city." Conversation also fed back into the newspapers as well, according to French historian Robert

Darnton, in *American Historical Review* online discussion of his "An Early Information Society," March 13–27, 2000

37 Tarde, 300. Tarde distinguished opinion formation from his narrower concept of reason, which he identified with intellectual elites. Tarde, 298–9.

38 Robert Park, "News as a Form of Knowledge" and "News and the Power of the Press," in *Collected Papers of Robert Ezra Park, Volume 3: Society* (Glencoe, IL: Free Press, 1955); Robert Park, *The Crowd and the Public* (University of Chicago Press, 1972), trans. by Charlotte Elsner from *Masse und Publikum* 1904, 55–60, 80–1; Barnhurst and Nerone, *The Form of News: A History* (New York: Guilford Press, 2001), 32–43.

39 Robert Park, *Collected Papers of Robert Ezra Park, Volume 3: Society*, 79, 116. Robert Park linked his concept of publics to the tradition of liberal political philosophers in a brief discussion of public opinion and social control, where he said they "looked upon freedom of discussion and free speech as the breath of life of a free society." See *Introduction to the Science of Sociology* (University of Chicago Press, 1921), 850–1.

40 Walter Lippmann, *Liberty and the News* (New York: Harcourt, Brace and Howe, 1920), 10–11.

41 John Dewey, *The Public and its Problems*; also see Herbert Blumer, "The Field of Collective Behavior," in Robert Park, ed., *An Outline of the Principles of Sociology* (New York: Barnes and Noble, 1939), 245–7. Turner and Killian, *Collective Behavior*, 199ff, ground publics in communities and their relationships. Lazarsfeld's idea of opinion leaders presumes the existence of networks of relationship within a community. See Katz and Lazarsfeld, *Personal Influence* (New York: Free Press, 1955; Peter Simonson, special editor, "Politics, Social Networks and the History of Mass Communication Research: Rereading *Personal Influence*," *Annals of the American Academy of Political and Social Science* 608 (2006). Alan Wolfe's (in Wientraub) critique of Habermas' public sphere is that it does not consider the social relations upon which it depends.

42 On differences of interpretation, see Myra Marx Ferree, "The Political Context of Rational Choice: Rational Choice Theory and Resource Mobilization," in Aldon Morri and Carol Mueller, eds, *Frontiers in Social Movement Theory* (Yale University Press, 1992), 47; Marc W. Steinberg, *Fighting Words: Working-class Formation, Collective Action, and Discourse in Early Nineteenth Century England* (Cornell University Press, 1999), 11–12.

43 Steinberg, 231; Christine Kelly, *Tangled Up in Red, White, and Blue: New Social Movements in America* (Lanham, MD: Rowman and Littlefield, 2001).

44 George Lefebre, "Revolutionary Crowds," in J. Kaplow, ed., *New Perspectives on the French Revolution* (New York: Wiley, 1965, 173–90; George Rude, *Crowd in History*, 1964; Robert Holton, "The Crowd in History: Some Problems of Theory and method" *Social History* 3 (1978): 219–33; John Bohstedt, *Riots and Community Politics in England and Wales, 1790–1810* (Harvard University Press, 1983); A. Randall and A. Charlesworth, eds, *Moral Economy and Social Protest: Crowds, Conflict and Authority* (London: Macmillan, 2000).

45 For examples of labeling collective actions as publics, see Geoff Eley, "Nations, Publics and Political Cultures," in Calhoun and Karaganis, 289–339; Jeffrey Ravel, *The Contested Parterre: Public Theater and French Political Culture, 1680–1791* (Cornell University Press, 1999).

46 Williams, *Keywords*, 158–63; *The Compact Edition of the Oxford English Dictionary* (Oxford University Press, 1971), 1736–7; Asa Briggs, "The Language of 'Mass' and 'Masses' in Nineteenth Century England," in *The Collected Essays of Asa Briggs*, Vol. 1 (Urbana: University of Illinois Press, 1985), 34–54.

47 Howard Zinn, *A People's History of the United States* (New York: Harper Perennial, 2005), 96.

48 William H. Whyte, *The Organization Man* (New York: Simon and Schuster, 1956); C. Wright Mills, *White Collar: The American Middle Class* (New York: Oxford University Press, 1951).

49 Quote from Turner and Killian, 112; Williams, *Keywords*, 158–63.

50 On the concept of community, see Gunnar Almgren, "Community," in Edgar and Marie Borgatta, eds, *Encyclopedia of Sociology*, Vol. 1 (New York: Macmillan, 1992), 244–9; For classic theories of transition from traditional to modern, see Emile Durkheim, *The Division of Labor in Society*, trans. George Simpson (Glencoe, IL: Free Press, 1949) and Ferdinand Tonnies, *Community and Society*, trans. Charles Loomis (New York: Harper & Row, 1963, orig. 1887); on public sociability, see Ray Oldenburg, *The Great Good Place: Cafes, Coffee Shops, Community Centers, Beauty Parlors, General Stores, Bars, Hangouts and How They Get You Through the Day* (New York: Paragon, 1989).

51 John T. Wheelwright, "Public Opinion as a Force," *Harvard Monthly* 8 (1889): 43–52; E. L. Godkin, "The Growth and Expression of Public Opinion," *Atlantic Monthly* 81 (1898): 1–15. Godkin noted that public opinion did not exist in the colonies before the Revolution, as only the opinion of "leading men" was important and the majority deferred to them; but it began to appear as a result of the Revolution. See also Susan Herbst, "On the Disappearance of Groups: 19th and Early 20th Century Conceptions of Public Opinion," in Theodore Glasser and Charles Salmon, *Public Opinion and the Communication of Consent* (New York: Guilford Press, 1995), 100, on the expression of public opinion via parties versus polls.

52 Herbert Blumer, "Public Opinion and Public Opinion Polling," *American Sociological Review* 13 (1948): 542–9; John Durham Peters, "Historical Tensions in the Concept of Public Opinion," 3–32; Susan Herbst, 89–104, quote from Peters, 20.

## 1 Theater audiences, crowds, and publics

1 This representation of auditors of lower sorts had a long and continuous history, going back to Elizabethan theater and to street performers before that. See, e.g., Steven Mullaney, *The Place of the Stage: License, Play and Power in Renaissance England* (University of Chicago Press, 1988); Jeffrey Ravel, *The Contested Parterre: Public Theater ad French Political Culture, 1680–1791* (Cornell University Press, 1999).

2 Richard Butsch, *The Making of American Audiences, from Stage to Television, 1750–1990* (Cambridge University Press, 2000), Ch. 1. Theaters were divided into pit, box, and gallery. The pit was the section of the theater that we now call the orchestra between the stage and surrounding boxes, but then was an inexpensive open area without fixed seats or raked floor. It could be quite crowded; auditors often stood and might mill about. The gallery held the disreputable: prostitutes, servants, apprentices, and so on. Boxes were for the respectable classes.

3 Tice Miller, *Bohemians and Critics: American Theatre Criticism in the Nineteenth Century* (Metuchen, NJ: Scarecrow Press, 1981), 2; "Introduction to the Dramatic Censor," *Mirror of Taste and Dramatic Censor* 1 (1810): 51.

4 *Mirror of Taste and Dramatic Censor* 3 (1811): 367, 369.

5 For other examples of audiences defining themselves as publics and authorities defining them as crowds, see Marc Baer, *Theatre and Disorder in Late Georgian London* (Oxford University Press, 1992); Jeffrey Ravel, *The Contested Parterre: Public Theater and French Political Culture, 1680–1791* (Cornell University Press, 1999).

6 Butsch, *The Making of American Audiences*, 39–40.

7 Edward Countryman, "Moral economy, political economy and the American bourgeois revolution," Adrian Randall and Andrew Charlesworth, eds, *Moral Economy and Popular Protest: Crowds, Conflict and Authority* (London: St. Martin's Press, 2000), 153–4, 156. On the discourse on liberty, see Pauline Maier, *From Resistance to Revolution* (New York: Knopf, 1972), Ch. 1 and *American Scripture: Making the Declaration of Independence* (New York: Knopf, 1997). On *Mose*, see Peter Buckley, "To the Opera House: Culture and Society in New York City, 1820–1860," Ph.D. thesis (SUNY Stony Brook, 1984); on Whitman, see "The Bowery," in Justin Kaplan, *Walt Whitman: Prose and Poetry* (New York: Library of America, 1982), 1186–9, and David Reynolds, *Walt Whitman's America: A Cultural Biography* (New York: Knopf, 1995), Ch. 4. On work and civic virtue, see Ricci, *Good Citizenship in America* (Cambridge University Press, 2004), 81–7, 90–1.

8 Jean Harvey Baker, "Politics, Paradigms, and Public Culture," *Journal of American History* 84 (1997): 894–9; Paul Starr, *The Creation of the Media* (New York: Basic Books, 2004; Susan Davis, *Parades and Power: Street Theatre in Nineteenth-century Philadelphia* (Philadelphia: Temple University Press, 1986); William Pencak, Matthew Dennis, and Simon Newman, eds, *Riot and Revelry in Early America* (Pennsylvania State University Press, 2002). On colonial development of a public sphere, see Michael Warner, *The Letters of the Republic: Publication and the Public Sphere in Eighteenth-century America* (Harvard University Press, 1990).

9 Also in France, see Jeffrey Ravel, *The Contested Parterre*, and James Johnson, *Listening in Paris* (University of California Press, 1995).

10 See Geoff Eley's conception of a contentious public, in Craig Calhoun, *Habermas and the Public Sphere* (MIT Press, 1992), 306.

11 Ruth Harsha McKensie, "Organization, Production and Management at the Chestnut Street Theatre, Phildelphia, 1791–1820," Ph.D. thesis (Stanford University, 1952), 271–8.

12 Arthur Hobson Quinn, *A History of the American Drama from the Beginning to the Civil War* (New York: Appleton Century Crofts, 1923), 81–131; Richard Moody, *Dramas from the American Theatre, 1762–1909* (World Publishing Company, 1966), 61–114.

13 Joyce Appleby, *Capitalism and a New Social Order* (New York University Press, 1984), 75–8.

14 Bruce Laurie, *Artisans into Workers: Labor in Nineteenth Century America* (Illinois University Press, 1997); Stuart Blumin, *The Emergence of the Middle Class* (Cambridge University Press, 1989).

15 Richard Stott, *Workers in the Metropolis: Class, Ethnicity, and Youth in Antebellum New York City* (Cornell University Press, 1990); Sean Wilentz, *Chants Democratic: New*

*York City and the Rise of the American Working Class, 1789–1850* (New York: Oxford University Press, 1984); Butsch, *American Audiences*, Ch. 3.

16 Buckley, Ch. 4.

17 Yankee Doodle, "The Italian Opera House and the Bowery, New York," *Spirit of the Times*, February 6, 1847, 590.

18 On images of riverboatmen and frontiersmen, see Richard Slotkin, *The Fatal Environment: The Myth of the Frontier in the Age of Industrialization, 1800–1890* (New York: Atheneum, 1985).

19 Paul Boyer, *Urban Reform and Moral Order* (Harvard University Press, 1978), 69, 70; John Kasson, *Rudeness and Civility: Manners in Nineteenth Century America* (New York: Hill and Wang, 1990), 74–80.

20 Allan Nevins and Milton Halsey Thomas, eds, *The Diary of George Templeton Strong*, Vol. 1 (New York: Macmillan, 1952), 293; Hone, quoted in Lawrence Levine, *High Brow/Low Brow: The Emergence of Cultural Hierarchy in America* (Harvard University Press, 1988), 173; on imagery of impurity, see Mary Douglas, *Purity and Danger: An Analysis of Concepts of Pollution and Taboo* (New York: Praeger, 1966).

21 On police departments, see James Richardson, *The New York Police: Colonial Times to 1901* (Oxford University Press, 1971); Roger Lane, *Policing the City: Boston, 1822–1885* (Harvard University Press, 1967); n.a. *The Iron Fist and the Velvet Glove*, revised edition (Berkeley: Center for Research on Criminal Justice, 1977), 23–6.

22 Historian Peter Buckley, p. 10, describes the diverging discourses; Paul Gilje, *Rioting in America* (Indiana University Press, 1996) 20–4, 32–3, 37–8, 51–2.

23 Officers and witnesses at the coroner's inquest reported that the first volley was directed over the heads of the rioters, but two or three additional volleys were directed into the crowds. See Richard Moody, *The Astor Place Riot* (Indiana University Press, 1958), 152–6; Peter G. Buckley, "To the Opera House: Culture and Society in New York City, 1820–1860," Ph.D. thesis (SUNY Stony Brook, 1984), 75.

24 *New York Evening Post*, May 8, 9, 11, 14 and 15, 1849, all page 2. This same dispute over conflicting rights and classes underlay the 1809 Old Price riots at London's Covent Garden that marked the end of audience sovereignty in England. See Marc Baer, *Theatre and Disorder in Late Georgian London* (Oxford University Press, 1992).

25 New York *Evening Post*, May 16, 1849, 2.

26 *Courier and Enquirer*, May 9 and 15, 1849, both page 2.

27 "Theatrical and Musical," *Herald*, May 8, 1849, 4; "The great theatrical war," *Herald*, May 10, 1849, 4

28 On parceling blame, see *Tribune*, "The outrage on Macready," May 7, 2, "The Astor Place tragedy," May 12, 1, "The late riot," May 12, 2, "The moral of the riot," May 15, 2; *Herald*, "The tragedy at Astor Place," May 12, 2, and "The recent tragedy," May 15, 4; *Brooklyn Daily Eagle*, "The tragedy of last night," May 11, 2 and "The dead," May 14, 2. Among artisan papers, the *Pennsylvanian* declared that the authorities and "fifteen of the 'upper crust' aristocracy" had prodded the masses. The *Albany Atlas* called the firing on the crowd a "massacre . . . most sanguinary and cruel," but did not condone the behavior of the crowd. The *Boston Atlas* acknowledged the legitimate resentment of the working classes against the "upper ten thousand," but praised the city authorities. All quotes reprinted in the New York *Herald*, May 16, 1849, 1.

29 Buckley, 19–20, 27, 31
30 Sean Wilenz, *Chants Democratic: New York City and the Rise of the American Working Class, 1788–1850* (Oxford University Press, 1984), 372–81.
31 Joel Tyler Headley, *The Great Riots of New York* (New York: E. B. Treat, 1873), Ch. 8; Edward Winslow Martin [James Dabney McCabe], *The History of the Great Riots and of the Molly Maguires* (Philadelphia: National Publishing Company, 1877); for a short vivid description of conditions in the 1870s, see Robert Bruce, *1877: Year of Violence* (Indianapolis: Bobbs-Merrill, 1959), Ch. 1.
32 Philip Foner, *History of the Labor Movement in the United States*, Vol. 2 (New York: International Publishers, 1955).
33 Robert Merton, "Introduction" to Gustave Le Bon, *The Crowd* (New York: Viking Press, 1960), xix–xxvii; Allport quote from Gardner Lindzey, *Handbook of Social Psychology* (Boston: Addison-Wesley, 1954). See also Robert Nye, *The Origins of Crowd Psychology: Gustave Le Bon and the Crisis of Mass Democracy in the Third Republic* (London: Sage, 1975); Jaap Van Ginneken, *Crowds, Psychology, Politics 1871–1899* (Cambridge University Press, 1992); Erika King, *Crowd Theory as a Psychology of the Leader and the Led* (New York: Mellen, 1990); Susanna Barrows, *Distorting Mirrors: Visions of the Crowd in Late Nineteenth Century France* (Yale University Press, 1981).
34 Le Bon, *The Crowd*, 18
35 Ibid., 15, 18.
36 Ibid., 124.
37 Ibid., 31–2.
38 Ginneken, 116–21.
39 Le Bon, 32, 36, 158; Barrow, 46.
40 Le Bon, 118, 120, 121.
41 Boris Sidis, *The Psychology of Suggestion* (New York: D. Appleton, 1899), vii, Ch. 27; Sidis, "A Study of the Mob," *Atlantic Monthly*, February, 1895, 362; Eugene Leach, "'Mental Epidemics': Crowd Psychology and American Culture, 1890–1940," *American Studies*, 33 (1992): 5–29; Edward A. Ross, "The Mob Mind," *Popular Science Monthly* July (1897): 390–98.
42 Clark McPhail, *The Myth of the Madding Crowd* (New York: Aldine, 1991), 5–20.
43 Sidis, *Psychology of Suggestion,* 301, 302, 305, 362; *Current Literature*, 47 (1909): 550, 551. Producer, writer, and director David Belasco, however, countered that, "The theory is as absurd as the fact is non-existent."
44 Gideon Diall, *The Psychology of the Aggregate Mind of an Audience* (Terre Haute: Inland Publishing Co., 1897), 11, 24–5, 27, 41ff, 49ff.
45 Diall, 15, 26, 60, 73.
46 From the New York *Herald*, "A riot of rahs," November 25, 1887, 6, "All the town wore yellow," November 29, 1889, 4, and "Dungeon cells for college boys," December 1, 1893, 7. A similar though somewhat less florid prose characterized the briefer reports in the New York *Tribune* and the *New York Times*.
47 "Wesleyan defeats the University of Pennsylvania," *New York Times*, November 25, 1887, 2. At the time, newspapers characterized striking workers' actions in negative terms, even when sympathetic to the workers' plight. Yet newspapers presented college boys as heroes having another jolly time assaulting workers to break up strikes. See Stephen Norwood, *Strike-breaking and Intimidation: Mercenaries*

*and Masculinity in Twentieth-century America* (University of North Carolina Press, 2002), Ch. 1.

48 "Theatrical gossip," *New York Times*, November 24, 1887, 2.

49 Michael Oriard, *Reading Football: How the Popular Press Created an American Spectacle* (University of North Carolina Press, 1993), 288; from the New York *Herald*, "Dungeon cells for college boys," December 1, 1893, 7, "They didn't celebrate," December 2, 1894, 4, and "Jubilators in blue," November 24 1895, 7.

50 "O'Connor's Hamlet," New York *Herald*, April 10, 1888, 6; "Star Theatre," New York *Tribune*, April 10, 1888, 4; "A howling mob in a theatre," New York *Tribune*, July 16, 1893, 1; George C. D. O'Dell, *Annals of the New York Stage*, Vol. 15 (Columbia University Press, 1927), 401.

## 2 From crowds to masses: movies, radio, and advertising

1 Mary Gabrielle Esteve, "Of Being Numerous: Representations of Crowds and Anonymity in Late Nineteenth and Early Twentieth Century Urban America," Ph.D. thesis (University of Washington, 1995); Edmund Leach, "'Mental Epidemics': Crowd Psychology and American Culture, 1890–1940," *American Studies* 33 (1992): 5.

2 Stuart Ewen, *PR! A Social History of Spin* (New York: Basic Books), 42–3.

3 Brett Gary, *The Nervous Liberals: Propaganda Anxieties from World War I to the Cold War* (Columbia University Press, 1999), 254 n14.

4 To recount the long debate about nickelodeon audiences, see Ben Singer, "Manhattan Nickelodeons: New Data on Audiences and Exhibitors" and Robert C. Allen, "Manhattan Myopia; or Oh! Iowa!," *Cinema Journal* 35 (1995): 5–128, and the articles cited therein.

5 Gustave Le Bon, *The Crowd* (New York: Viking Press, 1960, orig. 1895), 67–8. By contrast, print media were language-based and thus not considered effective stimuli for suggestion, according to Le Bon. Similarly, Tarde thought print better suited to the birth of publics.

6 On representations of women and voting, see Paula Baker, in Linda Gordon, ed., *Women, the State and Welfare* (University of Wisconsin Press, 1990), 69–70; Samuel Hays, "Political Parties and the Community–Society Continuum," in William Nisbet Chandler and Walter Dean Burnam, *The American Party Systems: Stages of Political Development*, second edition (Oxford University Press, 1975). On women's gaze at movies, see Miriam Hansen, *Babel in Babylon* (Harvard University Press, 1991); Nan Enstad, *Ladies of Labor, Girls of Adventure: Working Women, Popular Culture and Labor Politics at the Turn of the Twentieth Century* (Columbia University Press, 1999).

7 On social control in reform movements, see Reverend H. A. Jump, "The Social Influence of the Moving Picture" (New York: Playground and Recreation Association of America, 1911); Jane Addams, *The Spirit of Youth and the City Streets* (New York: Macmillan, 1912), 91–3; Paul Boyer, *Urban Masses and Moral Reform in America, 1820–1920* (Harvard University Press, 1978).

8 Hugo Munsterberg, *The Film: A Psychological Study* (New York: Dover Publications, 1970).

9 Matthew Hale, Jr., *Human Science and Social Order* (Philadelphia: Temple University

Press, 1980), 145. Boris Sidis thanked Munsterberg in his book, *The Psychology of Suggestion*, 28.

10 Frank Landy, "Hugo Munsterberg: Victim or Visionary," *Journal of Applied Psychology* 77 (1992): 792–3; Allan Langdale, "Introduction", *Hugo Munsterberg on Film* (Routledge 2002) 6, n36; on links between mysticism, spiritualism, hypnotism, and suggestibility, see Jeffrey Sconce, *Haunted Media: Electronic Presence from Telegraphy to Television* (Duke University Press, 2001); Hale, 186; *Photoplay*, 96–9.

11 Langdale, *Hugo Munsterberg on Film*, 19; Hugo Munsterberg, *The Film: A Psychological Study* (New York: Dover, 1970), 46–7, 95, 96.

12 Edward A. Ross, *In Worlds Drift* (New York: Macmillan, 1928), 179; Edward A. Ross, *Social Control: A Survey of the Foundations of Order* (New York: Macmillan, 1929); Carl Richard Greer, *Advertising and Its Mechanical Reproduction* (New York: Tudor Publishing, 1931), 68. For other academics on movies and on crowd psychology, see Norman Denzin, *Symbolic Interactionism and Cultural Studies* (New York: Basil Blackwell, 1992), 104ff; Ellsworth Faris, "The Concept of Imitation," *American Journal of Sociology* 32 (1926): 367–78; Jesse Steiner, "Community Organization and The Crowd Spirit," *Journal of Social Forces* 1 (1923): 221.

13 On movie reform, see Garth Jowett, Ian Jarvie, and Kathryn Fuller, *Children and the Movies* (Cambridge University Press, 1996); Lee Grieveson, *Policing Cinema: Movies and Censorship in Early Twentieth Century America* (University of California Press, 2004). Munsterberg's article reprinted in Langdale was an exception. On the contrast of tone from Le Bon to Park, see Leon Bramson, *The Political Context of Sociology* (Princeton University Press, 1961), 64.

14 Jowett et al., *Children and the Movies*, 30–6. Most of the reports were researched and authored by academics who were or had been affiliated with the University of Chicago.

15 Jowett et al., 64.

16 Henry Forman, *Our Movie Made Children* (New York: Macmillan, 1933), 1–3, 125, 134, 139–40, 159, 274.

17 Jowett et al., 65, 71. On Blumer, see Stanford Lyman and Arthur Vidich, "Introduction," *Selected Works of Herbert Blumer* (University of Illinois Press, 2000).

18 Blumer, "Moulding of Mass Behavior through the Motion Picture," *Publications of the American Sociological Society* 29 (1935): 115–27; Blumer, "The Field of Collective Behavior," in Robert Park, *Outline of Principles of Sociology* (New York: Barnes & Noble, 1939), 221–54; Clark McPhail, *Myth of the Madding Crowd* (Chicago: Aldine), 9–20.

19 Herbert Blumer, *Movies and Conduct* (New York: Macmillan, 1933), 74; Blumer and Philip M. Hauser, *Movies, Delinquency and Crime*. Hauser also became a prominent sociologist. On *Movies and Conduct*, also see Norman Denzin, *Symbolic Interaction and Cultural Studies: The Politics of Interpretation* (Oxford: Blackwell, 1992), 106–12; Patricia Clough, "The Movies and Social Observation; Reading Blumer's *Movies and Conduct*," *Symbolic Interaction* 11 (1988): 85–97.

20 "Moulding of Mass Behavior," 1935, 116, 118; see also Martin Hammersley, *The Dilemma of Qualitative Method: Herbert Blumer and the Chicago Tradition* (New York: Routledge, 1989), 88.

21 *Movies, Delinquency and Crime*, 201–2; Stanford Lyman and Arthur Vidich, *Social Order and the Public Philosophy: An Analysis and Interpretation of the Work of Herbert*

*Blumer* (University of Arkansas Press, 1988), 38; Blumer, "Moulding of Mass Behavior," 115–27. Forman, *Our Movie Made Children*, 280, also described Thrasher and Cressey's Payne study of congested areas as focusing on "immigrant stock."

22 Roy Rosenzweig, *Eight Hours for What We Will: Workers and Leisure in an Industrial City, 1870–1920* (Cambridge University Press, 1983), Ch. 8; Elizabeth Ewen, "City Lights: Immigrant Women and the Rise of the Movies," in Catherine Stimpson, Elsa Dixler, Martha Nelson, and Kathryn Yatrakis, eds, *Women and the American City* (University of Chicago Press, 1981), 42–63; Kathy Peiss, *Cheap Amusements: Working Women and Leisure in Turn-of-the-Century New York* (Philadelphia: Temple University Press, 1986), Ch. 6.

23 Miriam Hansen, *Babel and Babylon: Spectatorship in Early Silent Film* (Harvard University Press, 1991); John Dewey, *The Public and Its Problems* (New York: Henry Holt, 1927).

24 Hansen, *Babel and Babylon*, Ch. 3; David Bordwell, Kristin Thompson, and Janet Staiger, *The Classical Hollywood Cinema: Film Style and Mode of Production to 1960* (Columbia University Press, 1985).

25 Richard Butsch, "American Movie Audiences in the 1930s," *International Labor and Working Class History* 59 (2001): 106–20; Thomas Doherty, "This is Where We Came In: The Audible Screen and the Voluble Audience of Early Sound Cinema," in Melvin Stokes and Richard Maltby, eds, *American Movie Audiences* (London: British Film Institute, 1999), 143–63.

26 Everett Dean Martin, *The Behavior of Crowds: A Psychological Study* (New York: W. W. Norton, 1920), 44–50; Hadley Cantril, *The Invasion from Mars: A Study in the Psychology of Panic* (Princeton University Press, 1940). Le Bon considered that a crowd need not be gathered together to be susceptible. See *The Crowd*, 24.

27 Hadley Cantril and Gordon Allport, *The Psychology of Radio* (New York: Harper and Bros., 1935); Hadley Cantril, *The Invasion from Mars*. Rockefeller foundations were central to creating a field of communication research. See Everett Rogers, *A History of Communication Study* (San Francisco: Jossey-Bass), 142–5, 267–71, 219–20; David Morrison, *The Search for a Method* (University of Luton Press, 1998), 68–77; Paul Lazarsfeld, "An Episode in the History of Social Research: A Memoir," in Donald Fleming and Bernard Bailyn, eds, *The Intellectual Migration: Europe and America, 1930–1960* (Harvard University Press, 1969), 304ff; Hadley Cantril, *The Invasion from Mars*, xiv–xv; Gary, 87.

28 Cantril, *Social Movement*, xi, Ch. 1. While raised in Utah, Cantril worked among the influential Eastern elite. He was an undergraduate at Dartmouth, a graduate student at Harvard, and a professor at Princeton. The Rockefeller Foundation supported his research; and he conducted opinion polls for Roosevelt and advised several U.S. administrations on propaganda and psychological warfare. See Albert Cantril, *Psychology, Humanism and Scientific Inquiry: The Selected Essays of Hadley Cantril* (New Brunswick: Transaction Books, 1988), 234; George Gallup, "In Memoriam: Hadley Cantril, 1906–1969," *Public Opinion Quarterly* 33 (1969): 506; R. M. Eisinger and J. Brown, "Polling as a Means to Presidential Autonomy," *International Journal of Public Opinion Research* 10 (1998): 237–56.

29 Hadley Cantril and Gordon Allport, *The Psychology of Radio*, 21, 60, 172, 178, 242.

30 Hadley Cantril, *The Psychology of Social Movements* (New York: Wiley, 1941), xi, 256–61; Cantril, *Invasion from Mars*, 75–6,

31 Other crowd behavior terms were fads, crazes, and mass hysteria. See Turner and Killian, *Collective Behavior*, second edition (Englewood Cliffs, NJ: Prentice Hall, 1972), 119. Such behaviors were commented upon even before crowd psychology, e.g. in Charles MacKay, *Extraordinary Popular Delusions and the Madness of Crowds* (London: Richard Bentley, 1841).

32 Cantril, *Invasion from Mars*, 3, 47–55; "Boo!," *Time*, November 7, 1938, 13; "Panic from Mars" *The Nation*, November 12, 1938, 498. David Culbert, *News for Everyman* (Greenwood Press, 1976) said 3 percent believed it was real.

33 Cantril, *Invasion from Mars,* xii; editorial "Terror by Radio," *New York Times*, November 1, 1938.

34 Cantril, *Invasion from Mars*, 68, 111–14, 148, 157.

35 Ibid., 70–1, 119–24.

36 Michael Denning, *The Cultural Front* (New York: Verso, 1996), 382–3, n39. "Boo!," *Time*, November 7, 1938, 13 and "Panic from Mars," *The Nation*, November 12, 1938, 498, both mentioned fears of war in Europe to explain the ease with which people were panicked.

37 Cantril, *Social Movements*, xiii, 5; Hadley Cantril, "The Role of the Radio Commentator," *Public Opinion Quarterly* October (1939): 662. Albert Hastorf and Hadley Cantril, "They saw a Game," *Journal of Abnormal and Social Psychology* 49 (1954): 129–34, also focused on how emotion affected belief and perception, and became a classic in social psychology.

38 George Creel, *How We Advertised America: The First Telling of the Amazing Story of the Committee on Public Information that Carried the Gospel of Americanism to Every Corner of the Globe* (New York: Harper and Brothers, 1920), 5–8.

39 Everett Rogers, *A History of Communication Study: A Biographical Approach* (New York: Free Press, 1994), 211; Gary, *The Nervous Liberals: Propaganda Anxiety from World War I to the Cold War*, 1, 18–19; J. Michael Sproule, "Propaganda Studies in American Social Science: The Rise and Fall of the Critical Paradigm," *Quarterly Journal of Speech* 73 (1987): 74–5; Gary, *The Nervous Liberals*, 9–10.

40 Gary, *Nervous Liberals*, 3; Walter Lippmann, *The Phantom Public* (New York: Harcourt, Brace, 1925), 64–5; Lippmann, *Public Opinion*, quoted by Gary, 30, 31. Lippmann grew up in a wealthy German Jewish family and community who dissociated themselves from Judaism and from working-class Eastern European Jews of the Lower East Side. As an undergraduate at Harvard, he studied with Hugo Munsterberg. Ronald Steel, *Walter Lippmann and the American Century* (New York: Little Brown, 1980), Ch. 1.

41 Everett Dean Martin, *The Behavior of Crowds* (New York: Harper and Bros, 1920), 6–7; Gary 65ff; Everett Rogers, *A History of Communication Study*, 205, 210–14. Lasswell's analysis of propaganda during World War I became the basis for academic study of propaganda and of media through the 1920s and 1930s.

42 Cantril and Allport, *The Psychology of Radio*, 48, 3. Cantril and Lasswell both participated in the Rockefeller seminars and co-founded *Public Opinion Quarterly*.

43 Dewey, *The Public and Its Problems*, 178–81,114, 139.

44 Cantril and Allport, *Psychology of Radio*, 60; Marc Crispin Miller, 'Introduction," in Edward Bernays, *Propaganda* (Brooklyn: IG Publishing, 2005), 9–15, 48; Leach, "Mental Epidemics," 24–5.

45 Paul Lazarsfeld and Robert Merton, "Mass Communication, Popular Taste and

Organized Social Action," in Lyman Bryson, ed., *The Communication of Ideas* (New York: Harper Bros., 1948), 96.

46 James Norris, *Advertising and the Transformation of American Society, 1865–1920* (New York: Greenwood Press, 1990); Frank Luther Mott, *A History of American Magazines*, Volume 4, 1885–1905 (Harvard University Press, 1957), 20–5.

47 Roland Marchand, *Advertising the American Dream: Making Way for Modernity, 1920–1940* (University of California Press, 1985), 69; Ewen, *PR!: A Social History of Spin* (New York: Basic Books, 1996 ), 132.

48 Marchand, *Advertising the American Dream*, 63, 65, 69, 77. Indicating their elite status, Bernays never learned to drive because his family always had a chauffer; Ivy Lee, Rockefeller's publicist, graduated from Princeton in 1898. See Ewen, *PR!*, 12, 74.

49 Edward Bernays, *Propaganda*; Ewen, *PR!*, 9–10.

50 Marchand, 70; W. Trotter, *Instincts of the Herd* (London: Unwin, 1916); Bernays, 71, 73. IQ pioneer and eugenicist Henry Goddard similarly stated at Princeton University: "That man has a mental age of 13 while you have one of 30." See Leon Kamin, *The Science and Politics of IQ* (Potomac, MD: Erlbaum, 1974).

51 Marchand, 65, 66, 67, 68, 85.

52 Marchand, 61–2, 67, 70, 80, 84; on the construction of movie fans as female, hysterical, and consumers, see Kathryn Fuller, *At the Picture Show: Small-town Audiences and the Creation of Movie Fan Culture* (Washington, DC: Smithsonian Press, 1996), Chs 6–8.

53 Marchand, 88–92; Jennifer Wang, "Clubwomen v Drudges," Transnational Radio Conference Madison, Wisconsin, 2003, 1.

## 3 From cultivated individual to public citizen

1 Stuart Blumin, *The Emergence of the Middle Class: Social Experience in the American City, 1760–1900* (Cambridge University Press, 1989); Michael Katz, "The Urban 'Underclass' as a Metaphor of Social Transformation," in M. Katz, ed., *The "Underclass" Debate: Views from History* (Princeton University Press, 1993), 6–9.

2 Glenn Altschuler and Stuart Blumin, *Rude Republic: Americans and their Politics in the Nineteenth Century* (Princeton University Press, 2000); Mark Lawrence Kornbluh, "From Participatory to Administrative Politics: A Social History of American Political Behavior, 1880–1918," Ph.D. thesis (Johns Hopkins University, 1987); Samuel P. Hays, "Political Parties and the Community–Society Continuum," in William Nisbet and Walter Dean Burnham, eds, *The American Party Systems: Stages of Political Development*, second edition (Oxford University Press, 1975), 152–81.

3 Karen Halttunen, *Confidence Men and Painted Ladies: A Study of Middle Class Culture in America, 1830–1870* (Yale University Press, 1982), 14–15.

4 *Gleason's Drawing Room Companion*, 136, emphasis added; Altschuler and Blumin, 137. Paula Baker describes this as a masculine political culture in "The Domestication of Politics: Women and American Political Society, 1780–1920," in Linda Gordon, ed., *Women, the State and Welfare* (University of Wisconsin Press, 1990), 70, 88 fn55. The distinction between republicanism and liberalism in the early republic is nicely summarized by John Nerone, *Violence Against the Press* (Oxford University Press, 1994), 18–20.

5 Tocqueville quoted in Elizabeth Wilson, *The Sphinx in the City: Urban Life, the Control of Disorder and Women* (University of California Press, 1991), 7; Thomas Sugrue, "The Structures of Urban Poverty: The Reorganization of Space and Work in Three Periods of American History," in Michael Katz, ed., *The "Underclass" Debate: Views from History* (Princeton, 1993), 93–4; Nancy Cott, *Bonds of Womanhood*; Barbara Welter, "The Cult of True Womanhood, 1820–1860," in Michael Gordon, *The American Family in Social Historical Perspective*, third edition (New York: St. Martin's Press, 1983); on women representing class as well as gender, see Haltunnen, 56–9, and David Scobey, "Anatomy of the Promenade: The Politics of Bourgeois Sociability in Nineteenth Century New York," *Social History* 17 (1992): 214–15.

6 Christopher Lasch, *Haven in a Heartless World: The Family Besieged* (New York: Basic Books, 1977). Women's public role as citizen was also dependent upon her husband's status. See Nancy Cott, "Marriage and Women's Citizenship in the United States, 1830–1934," *American Historical Review* 103 (1998), 1440–74.

7 Mona Donash, "The 'Gorgeous Incongruities': Polite Politics and Public Space in the Streets of Nineteenth Century New York City," *Annals of the Association of American Geographers* 88 (1998): 218; Mary Ryan, *Women in Public: Between Banners and Ballots, 1825–1880* (Johns Hopkins University Press, 1990), 68–76; John Kasson, *Rudeness and Civility: Manners in Nineteenth Century Urban America* (New York: Hill and Wang, 1990), Ch. 3; Karen Halttunen, *Confidence Men and Painted Women: A Study of Middle Class Culture in America, 1830–1870* (Yale University Press, 1982), Chs 2–3. The organic street patterns of old European cities abetted crowds and crowding, with constricted lanes that slowed movement and squares that invited stopping and forming standing crowds. See Richard Sennett, *Flesh and Stone: The Body and the City in Western Civilization* (New York: W. W. Norton, 1994), 328–9.

8 Kasson, *Rudeness and Civility*; Arthur Schlesinger, *Learning How to Behave: A Historical Study of American Etiquette Books* (New York: Macmillan, 1946).

9 Richard Butsch, *Making of American Audiences*, 70, on constraints on going to theater. On the opening of public spaces for women, see William Leach, *Land of Desire: Merchants, Power and the Rise of a New American Culture* (New York: Pantheon, 1993); and David Scobey, "Anatomy of the Promenade: The Politics of Bourgeois Sociability in Nineteenth Century New York," *Social History* 17 (1992): 203–28.

10 "Editor's Easy Chair," *Harper's Monthly* March (1870): 605–6; quote in Lawrence Levine, *High Brow/Low Brow* (Harvard University Press, 1998), 185; on earlier commingling, see Peter Buckley, "To the Opera House: Culture and Society in New York City, 1820–1860," Ph.D. thesis (SUNY Stony Brook, 1984), 102–25, especially 120–1.

11 "Editor's Easy Chair," *Harper's Monthly*, February (1880): 463; *The Illustrated Manners Book* (New York: Leland Clay and Co., 1855), 247–8; Alice Ives, *The Social Mirror: A Complete Treatise on the Laws, Rules, and Usages that Govern our most Refined Homes and Social Circles* (Detroit: F. B. Dickerson, 1886) 35–7; Julia Dewey, *Lessons on Manners: Arranged for Grammar Schools, High Schools and Academies* (New York: Hinds and Noble, 1899), 87–91.

12 Also implied was a change from conceiving the theater as a public forum to a private enterprise. A similar conflict of rights occurred in the London Old Price riots of 1809. See Marc Baer, *Theatre and Disorder in Late Georgian London* (Oxford University Press, 1992).

13 S. H. Emery, Jr., "Culture and Discipline" *The Western: A Journal of Literature, Education and Art* 3 (1877): 319–20. On origins of self-cultivation, see Steven Lukes, *Individualism* (Oxford: Basil Blackwell, 1973) Ch. 10. On cultivation and citizenship, see John Tehranian, "Performing Whiteness: Naturalization Litigation and the Construction of Racial Identity in America," *Yale Law Journal* 109 (2000): 817–48; Brian Walker, "Thoreau on Democratic Cultivation," *Political Theory* 29 (2001): 155–89. Even appreciation of nature was to be intellectual rather than sensual. See Levine, 183, 186, 192. Middle-class Progressives condemned the self-indulgent individualism of the noveau riche industrial class. See Michael McGerr, *A Fierce Discontent: The Rise and Fall of the Progressive Movement in America, 1870–1920* (New York: Free Press, 2003), 54–9.

14 On constructing the subject position of theater-goers, see Dorothy Chansky, *Composing Ourselves: The Little Theatre Movement and the American Audience* (Southern Illinois University Press, 2004), 7–8; William B. Worthen, *Modern Drama and the Rhetoric of Theater* (University of California Press, 1991), 20, 24, 148–9; on Laura Keene, see Faye Dudden, *Women in the American Theatre* (Yale University Press, 1994), 124–5; on Lester Wallack, see Arthur Hornblow, *A History of the Theatre in America* (New York: Benjamin Blom, 1965), Ch. 23; on taming audiences and dramatic realism, see Bruce McConachie, *Melodramatic Formations* (University of Iowa Press, 1992); also see Patricia Denison, "The Legacy of James A. Herne," in William DeMastes, *Realism and the American Dramatic Tradition* (University of Alabama Press, 1996); "The Easy Chair," *Harper's New Monthly Magazine* March (1870): 606.

15 Quotes reprinted in Bernard Hewitt, *Theatre U.S.A., 1665–1957* (New York: McGraw-Hill, 1959), 226–7. Realism gradually introduced the fourth wall, an imaginary window through which audiences watched events on stage; by the turn of the century, actors seldom addressed the audience.

16 Darkness was not initially preferred by audiences. See Marilyn Casto, *Actors, Audiences and Historic Theaters of Kentucky* (University Press of Kentucky, 2000), 108–11; Henneke, 56–63.

17 Benjamin McArthur, *Actors and American Culture, 1880–1920* (PhiladelphiaTemple University Press, 1984), 146; Tice Miller, *Bohemians and Critics: American Theatre Criticism in the Nineteenth Century* (Metuchen, NJ: Scarecrow Press, 1981), 83, 86. Winter nevertheless rejected dramatic realism for displaying the "ulcers" of society.

18 Miller, 80, 87; Levine, 1998.

19 On institutionalization, see Paul DiMaggio, "Cultural Entrepreneurship in Nineteenth Century Boston," Parts 1 and 2, *Media Culture and Society* 4 (1982): 33–50, 303–22, and "Cultural Boundaries and Structural Change: The Extension of the High Culture Model to Theater, Opera and the Dance, 1900–1940," in Michele Lamont and Marcel Fournier, eds, *Cultivating Differences* (University of Chicago Press, 1992), 21–57. On the Syndicate, see Jack Poggi, *Theater in America: The Impact of Economic Forces, 1870–1967* (Cornell University Press, 1968), 11–14; Harrison Fiske, "The Usher," *New York Dramatic Mirror* October 23, 1897, 15; Norman Hapgood, "The Theatrical Syndicate," *International Monthly* 1 (1900): 117, 121; Howell quote from Hapgood 106; John Ranken Towse, *Sixty Years of the Theater: An Old Critic's Memoir* (New York: Funk and Wagnall, 1916), 462–4. Famous actors and playwrights Joseph Jefferson, Richard Mansfield, James

O'Neill, Minnie Maddern Fiske (wife of Harrison Fiske), and James Herne opposed the Syndicate.

20 William Winter, *Other Days, Being Chronicles and Memories of the Stage* (New York: Moffat, Yard, 1908), 303, 307, 328, 311–12, 313–14.

21 Charlton Andrews, "Elevating the Audience" *Theatre* 25 (1917): 102, 120.

22 The middle-class efforts of self-cultivation can be understood as individual cultural capital accumulation, as Bourdieu defines it. At the end of the century, Progressives conceived their efforts at cultural uplift as enhancing the community and nation's social capital, as Putnam formulates it. See Pierre Bourdieu, *Distinction: A Social Critique of the Judgement of Taste*, Richard Nice, trans. (Harvard University Press, 1984); Robert Putnam, *Bowling Alone: The Collapse and Revival of American Community* (New York: Simon and Schuster, 2000).

23 Carlyle quote from Mina Carson, *Settlement Folk: Social Thought and the American Settlement Movement, 1885–1930* (University of Chicago Press, 1990), 1–2; on lower classes as filth, disease, and disorder in the Progressive era, see Daniel Bender, *Sweated Work, Weak Bodies: Anti-Sweatshop Campaigns and Languages of Labor* (Rutgers University Press, 2004), 48–52; Alan Kraut, *Germs, Genes and the "Immigrant Menace"* (New York: Basic Books, 1994); Mark Pittinger, "A World of Difference: Constructing the Underclass in Progressive America," *American Quarterly* 49 (1997), 26–65; Elizabeth Wilson, *The Sphinx of the City*, Ch. 3.

24 Robin Muncy, *Creating a Female Dominion in American Reform, 1890–1935* (Oxford University Press, 1991); Helen L. Horowitz, "Varieties of Cultural Experience in Jane Addams' Chicago," *History of Education Quarterly* 14 (1974): 71.

25 By 1911 there were over 400 settlement houses in the United States. See Allen F. Davis, *Spearheads for Reform: The Social Settlements and the Progressive Movement 1890-1914* (New York: Oxford University Press, 1967), 8; Mina Carson, *Settlement Folk*, 136; Horowitz, 72; Jane Addams, *Twenty Years at Hull House* (New York: Macmillan, 1922), 372

26 Helen L. Horowitz, *Culture and the City: Cultural Philanthropy in Chicago from the 1880s to 1917* (University Press of Kentucky, 1976), 126–44; Jane Addams, *The Spirit of Youth and the City Streets* (New York: Macmillan, 1912), 75–6; also see Addams, *Twenty Years*, 384–5

27 Carson, *Settlement Folk*, 116; Jane Addams, "A Function of the Social Settlement," *Annals of the American Academy of Political and Social Science* 13 (1899): 336, quoted in Helen Horowitz, "Varieties of Cultural Experience," 75.

28 Carson, *Settlement Folk*, 116; Irving Howe, *World of Our Fathers* (New York: Harcourt, 1976), 229–35; Lillian D. Wald, *The House on Henry Street* (New York: Henry Holt, 1915), 184–8; Lillian D. Wald, *Windows on Henry Street* (Boston: Little, Brown, 1934), 165–74; also see Cathy James "'Not merely for the sake of an evening's entertainment': the educational use of theater in Toronto's settlement houses, 1910–1930," *History of Education Quarterly* 38 (1998): 299, 306.

29 Ruth Crocker, *Social Work and Social Order: The Settlement Movement in Two Industrial Cities, 1889–1930* (University of Illinois Press, 1992), 61, 145; Irving Howe, *World of Our Fathers*, 230ff.

30 Lydia Kingsmill Commander, "The Significance of Yellow Journalism," *Arena* 34 (1905), 154–5. On Americanization, see Edward George Hartmann, *The Movement to Americanize the Immigrant* (Columbia University Press, 1948), 19–21; Roberta

Carlson, *The Quest for Conformity: Americanization through Education* (New York: Wiley, 1975), Chs 5–7. On nationalism, see Benedict Anderson, *Imagined Communities: Reflections on the Origin and Spread of Nationalism*, revised edition (London: Verso, 2006); Geoff Eley and Ronald Grigor Suny, "Introduction," in Eley and Suny, eds, *Becoming National* (Oxford University Press, 1996), 4–8.

31 Hartmann, 22–37, 143.

32 Daniel Chauncey Brewer, "A Patriotic Movement for the Assimilation of Immigrants," *The Editorial Review* August (1910): 788; North American Civic League for Immigrants, *Annual Report 1909–10* (Boston: NACLI, 1910), 21; Thomas Winter, *Making Men, Making Class: The YMCA and Workingmen, 1877–1920* (University of Chicago Press, 2002), 48.

33 John Dewey, *The Public and Its Problems* (New York: Henry Holt, 1927) 139; Richard Abel, *The Red Rooster Scare: Making Cinema American, 1900–1910* (University of California Press, 1999); Lee Grieveson, *Policing the Cinema: Movies and Censorship in Early Twentieth-century America* (University of California Press, 2004), 156, on Addams; Lee Grieveson, "Visualizing Citizenship," presented at the Society for Cinema and Media Studies, Chicago, 2007; Alice Guy, director, *Making an American Citizen* (New York: Solax Co., 1912); Guy Hedlund, director, *The Making of an American* (State of Connecticut Department of Americanization, 1920). In *The Immigrant Press and Its Control*, Robert Park proposed using foreign language newspapers. Radio would be recruited to the task of creating a nation in the 1930s. See Michele Hilmes, *Radio Voices, American Broadcasting, 1922–1952* (University of Minnesota Press, 1997); Inge Marszolek, "Radio Days: Did Radio Change Social Life in Germany and the United States?," in Norbert Finzsch and Ursula Lehmkuhl, eds, *Atlantic Communications: The Media in American and German History* (New York: Berg, 2004), 254–6.

34 Horowitz, *Culture and the City*, on Dewey and Addams; John Dewey, *The Public and Its Problems* (New York: Henry Holt, 1927) 35, 112–13, 149.

35 Barbara Sicherman, "Sense and Sensibility: A Case Study of Women's Reading in Late Victorian America," in Dorothy Helly and Susan Reverby, eds, *Gendered Domains* (Cornell University Press, 1992), 71–89, for an example of a reading family; Elizabeth Long, *Book Clubs: Women and the Uses of Reading in Everyday Life* (University of Chicago Press, 2003), 37, 43–5, 52–3; also Megan Seaholm, "Earnest Women: The White Women's Movement in Progressive era Texas, 1880–1920, Ph.D. thesis (Rice University, 1988).

36 Karen Blair, *The Clubwoman as Feminist: True Womanhood Refined, 1868–1914* (New York: Holmes and Meier, 1980); and *The Torchbearers: Women and their Amateur Arts Associations in America, 1890–1930* (Indiana University Press, 1994); Daniel Scott Smith, "Family Limitation, Sexual Control and Domestic Feminism in Victorian America," Mary Hartman and Lois Banner, eds, *Clio's Consciousness Raised* (New York: Harper and Row, 1974).

37 Dorothy Chansky, *Composing Ourselves: The Little Theatre Movement and the American Audience* (Southern Illinois University Press, 2004), 2, 4, 8, 29, 37.

38 Chansky, Chs 1–2, especially 8–9, 41; also W. B. Worthen, *Modern Drama and the Rhetoric of Theater* (University of California Press, 1992), "Introduction"; E. C. Mabie, "Opportunities for Service in Departments of Speech," *Quarterly Journal of Speech Education* 6 (1920): 3.

39 David Glassberg, *Sense of History: The Place of the Past in American Life* (University of Massachusetts Press, 2001), 65–71; Naima Prevots, *American Pageantry: A Movement for Art & Democracy* (Ann Arbor, MI: UMI Research Press, 1990), 4.
40 David Glassberg, *American Historical Pageantry: The Uses of Tradition in the Early Twentieth Century* (University of North Carolina Press, 1990), 4, 24–5, Ch. 2.
41 Naima Prevots, 1, 3. On events sponsored earlier by political parties, see Mark Lawrence Kornbluh, 94–104.
42 Percy MacKaye, *The Civic Theatre in Relation to the Redemption of Leisure* (New York: Mitchell Kennerley, 1912) 14, 29–31; Glassberg, 67–8.
43 Gerald Rabkin, *Drama and Commitment: Politics in the American Theatre of the Thirties* (Indiana University Press, 1964), 96–7, 101.
44 Hallie Flanagan, *Arena: The History of the Federal Theatre* (New York: Benjamin Blom, 1940); Rabkin, 120.
45 Jack Poggi, *Theater in America: The Impact of Economic Forces, 1870–1967* (Cornell University Press, 1968); *Arena*, 170, 65, 70–1, 124–5, 115.
46 *Arena*, 174, 193, 150, 255; Barry Witham, *The Federal Theater Project: A Case Study* (Cambridge University Press, 2003), 6, 85, 89; John O'Connor, "The Federal Theater Project's Search for an Audience," in McConachie, 182. The Project's audience reports noted that many in their audiences had never before seen a live play.

## 4 Broadcast publics

1 John Nerone, *Violence Against the Press: Policing the Public Sphere in US History* (Oxford University Press, 1994), 55); Michael Schudson, *The Good Citizen: A History of American Civic Life* (Harvard University Press, 1998), 69–77. The newspaper as watchdog over the government on behalf of the public was not established until after 1801, when the Alien and Sedition Act that had been used to silence presses expired. See Nerone, Ch. 3 and Leonard Levy, *Emergence of a Free Press* (Chicago: Ivan R. Dee, 1985).
2 Kevin Barnhurst and John Nerone, *The Form of News: A History* (New York: Guilford Press, 2001); on phases of citizenship, see Schudson, *The Good Citizen.*
3 Barnhurst and Nerone, 31–50; on republican citizenship, see Dawn Oliver and Derek Heater, *The Foundations of Citizenship* (London: Harvester Wheatsheaf, 1994), 11–16; on deference, see Gordon Wood, *The Radicalism of the American Revolution* (Knopf, 1992), 63.
4 Schudson, Ch. 3; Barnhurst and Nerone, 50, 58–9, 67, 101; Oliver and Heater, 16–19; Joyce Appleby, *Capitalism and a New Social Order: The Republican Vision of the 1790s* (New York University Press, 1984) on the shift. On technological change, see Alfred McClung Lee, *The Daily Newspaper in America: The Evolution of a Social Instrument* (New York: Macmillan, 1937), 113–19; Michael Schudson, *Discovering the News: A Social History of American Newspaper* (New York: Basic Books, 1978), 31–5.
5 Barnhurst and Nerone, 84–5, 186–7. Habermas considered this the demise of the bourgeois public sphere, the re-feudalization of the public sphere, as newspapers became integral to capital.
6 Barnhurst and Nerone, 88–9.

7 Michael Schudson, *Discovering the News*, 106–20; Schudson, *The Good Citizen*, 177–9; "Business Announcement," *New York Times*, August 19, 1896, 4. Ironically, a *Times* editor attributed Ochs' success not to creating a public but to manipulating a crowd at the same time he wished to publish a paper for "intelligent" people. See R. C. Cornuelle, "Remembrance of the *Times*," *American Scholar* 36 (1967): 433–4, 444.

8 Jeremiah W. Jenks, "The Guidance of Public Opinion," *American Journal of Sociology* 1 (1895): 160; E. L. Godkin, "The Growth and Expression of Public Opinion," *The Atlantic Monthly*, January (1898): 1–15.

9 W. Joseph Campbell, *Yellow Journalism: Puncturing the Myths, Defining the Legacies* (New York: Praeger, 2001), Ch. 1, quote from p. 32. See also "Newspapers' Sensations and Suggestions," *Independent* 67 (1910): 449–51; "Lessons in Crime Fifty Cents Per Month," *Outlook* February 1908, 276; "Newspaper Responsibility for Lawlessness," *Nation* 77, 131.

10 Campbell, 34–8, 52–3.

11 Eugene Leach, "Tuning Out Education," *Current*, January–March, 1983.

12 Louise Benjamin, *Freedom of the Air and the Public Interest: First Amendment Rights in Broadcasting to 1935* (Southern Illinois University Press, 2001); F. Leslie Smith, Milan D. Meeske, and John W. Wright, *Electronic Media and Government: The Regulation of Wireless and Wired Mass Communication in the United States* (New York: Longman, 1994), 256.

13 *Congressional Record*, 67, Part 11, 5558, cited in Benjamin, 70.

14 On the struggle between public and commercial, see Robert McChesney, *Telecommunication, Mass Media and Democracy: The Battle for Control of US Broadcasting, 1928–1935* (Oxford University Press, 1993); Susan Smulyan, *Selling Radio: The Commercialization of American Broadcasting, 1920–1934* (Smithsonian Institution Press, 1994).

15 Erik Barnouw, *A Tower in Babel: A History of Broadcasting in the United States*, Vol. 1 (Oxford University Press, 1966), 31; Susan Douglas, *Inventing American Broadcasting, 1899–1922* (Johns Hopkins University Press, 1987), Ch. 6, 279–85.

16 *Wireless Age*, October 1924, 24.

17 Barnouw, 178ff; Smith et al., 238; Sections 9 and 11 of the Radio Act of 1927, in Barnouw, *A Tower in Babel*, 305–6; also see Section 307 of the Communications Act of 1934; Barnouw, *The Golden Web: A History of Broadcasting in the United States*, Vol. 2 (Oxford University Press, 1968), 321.

18 Smulyan, 148–53; Barnouw, *The Golden Web*, 26–7; McChesney, Ch. 8.

19 NBC v US, 319-US, 190, 213 (1943), quoted in *Network Broadcasting, Report of the Committee on Interstate and Foreign Commerce* (Washington, DC: Eighty-Fifth Congress, Second Session, 1954), 54.

20 Barnouw, *A Tower in Babel*, 219; McChesney, 18–28; Elizabeth Fones-Wolf, *Waves of Opposition, Labor and the Struggle for Democratic Radio* (University of Illinois Press, 2006); Benjamin, Ch. 11; Barnouw, *The Golden Web*, 34.

21 *Wireless Age* November (1923): 30; Richard Butsch, *The Making of American Audiences* (Cambridge University Press, 2000), Ch. 14; Derek Vaillant, "'Your voice came in last night . . .': rural radio listening and 'talking back' during the Progressive era in Wisconsin, 1920–1932," in Michele Hilmes and Jason Loviglio, eds, *Radio Reader: Essays in the Cultural History of Radio* (New York: Routledge, 2002), 63–112.

22 "A Non-partisan Political Medium," *Wireless Age*, December (1922), 27–9.

23 William Hurd, "The Dawn of Radio in Politics," 17; Assistant Secretary Davis, "The Foundation Laid by Radio for Our Social Edifice," 21; Senator Wadsworth, "How Broadcasting . . ., 24, all in *Wireless Age*, October, 1924.

24 Smith et al., *Electronic Media and Government*, 252, on the 1946 Blue Book, an FCC guide to stations that specified programming that discussed public issues, such as these forums, as serving the public interest; Douglas Craig, *Fireside Politics: Radio and Political Culture in the United States, 1920–1940* (Johns Hopkins University Press, 2000), 216ff.

25 Harrison Summers, *A Thirty Year History of Radio Programs, 1926–1956* (New York: Arno, 1971), 17ff; FCC, *Public Service Responsibility of Broadcast Licensees*, March 7, 1946. Summers did not report ratings for sustaining programs; apparently rating services did not rate such programs, since their customers were commercial sponsors of programs.

26 Tim Brooks and Earle Marsh, *The Complete Directory to Prime Time Network and Cable TV Shows, 1946–Present*, seventh edition (New York: Ballantine Books, 1999), 38, 1275; *American Forum* 4 (1942): 14; *University of Chicago Round Table* pamphlets, 1938–55. Number 1 was published for broadcast on March 20, 1938.

27 *Good Evening Neighbors*, 1950, 14. It broadcast as a live hour-long show until it was reduced to a half-hour after being televised in 1950. Schudson, *The Good Citizen*, 222–3, briefly discusses the show and its listener participation.

28 *Readers Digest* sponsored it in 1944–45; for local sponsors of radio broadcasts from 1948–55, see Summers.

29 *Good Evening Neighbors*, Town Hall, 1950, 14; David Goodman, "Programming in the Public Interest: America's Town Meeting of the Air," in Michele Hilmes, ed., *NBC: America's Network* (University of California Press, 2007), 49 ; Denny, "Bring Back the Town Meeting," speech at Harvard University July 26, 1937, New York Public Library Manuscripts Division, Town Hall collection, box 156; *Good Evening Neighbors*, Town Hall, 1950, 23.

30 New York Public Library Manuscripts Division, Town Hall collection, box 29, Advisory Service file, Rockefeller Foundation file; Frank Hill and W. E. Williams, *Radio's Listening Groups: The United States and Great Britain* (Columbia University Press, 1941), 53.

31 Hill and Williams, 12, 45, 60, 64, 69.

32 Ray Barfield, *Listening to Radio: 1920–1950* (Westport, CT: Praeger, 1996), 93; *New York Sun*, December 5, 1936, cited by Goodman, 76; Hill and Williams, 27.

33 "Estimated Weekly Network Program Costs," *Variety*, November 15, 1950, 32; NYPL Town Hall collection, box 61.

34 Hill and Williams, 53, 54; Amanda Bruce "Strangers in the Living Room: Radio, Television, and American Childhood, 1930–1960," Ph.D. thesis (SUNY Stony Brook, 2006), Ch. 2; Jennifer Wang, "Clubwomen versus Drudges: The Battle to Define the Daytime Radio Audience," presented at the Radio Conference: A Transnational Forum, University of Wisconsin, 2003.

35 George Denny, "Bring Back the Town Meeting," presented at Harvard University, July 26, 1937; Brett Gary, *The Nervous Liberals: Propaganda Anxieties from World War I to the Cold War* (Columbia University Press, 1999), 79; David Goodman, "Programming in the Public Interest," 58-60.

36 On the public service framing of entertainment programs for television, see Anna McCarthy, "Governing by Television? Public Service Films and the Early TV archive," *Montage/AV* (Marburg: Schuren Verlag, 2005).
37 Fred MacDonald *Don't Touch that Dial!: Radio Programming in American Life from 1920 to 1960* (Chicago: Nelson-Hall, 1979), 54; Barnouw, *Tower of Babel*, 205, 250, 279; Summers, 31, 67–8.
38 Summers, 51–2, 54, 59–60, 67–8, 70. On institutional advertising, see William Bird, *Better Living: Advertising, Media and the New Vocabulary of Business Leadership, 1935–1955* (Northwestern University Press, 1999); Roland Marchand, *Creating the Corporate Soul: The Rise of Public Relations and Corporate Imagery in American Big Business* (University of California Press, 1998).
39 Bird, 23, 29–30.
40 Ibid., 41–5.
41 Bird, 43–4. *American Family Robinson* used a third approach, weaving pro-business, anti-New Deal messages into the stories of a middle-brow drama series. See Bird, 54–9.
42 Renowned newsman Edward R. Murrow concluded that they failed even at providing the information. In a 1958 speech shortly after his news program, *See It Now*, had been cancelled by CBS, he condemned the executives of all the networks for their failure to live up to their duty to provide public service in the form of top quality news. See his "Speech at Radio and Television News Directors Association," October 15, 1958, Chicago.
43 Loviglio, "*Vox Pop*: Network Radio and the Voice of the People," in Michele Hilmes and Jason Loviglio, eds, *Radio Reader: Essays in the Cultural History of Radio* (New York: Routledge, 2002), 89–111; Paolo Carpignano, Robin Andersen, Stanley Aronowitz, and William DeFazio, "Chatter in the Age of Electronic Reproduction: Talk Television and the 'Public Mind'," in Bruce Robbins, *The Phantom Public Sphere* (University of Minnesota Press, 1993), 93–120; Bernard Timberg, *Television Talk: A History of the TV Talk Show* (University of Texas Press, 2002).
44 Smith et al., 256, 260; Graham Murdock, "Back to Work: Cultural Labor in Altered Times," in Andrew Beck, ed., *Cultural Work: Understanding the Cultural Industries* (New York: Routledge, 2003), 22.
45 Laura Grindstaff, *The Money Shot: Trash, Class, and the Making of TV Talk Shows* (University of Chicago Press 2002).
46 Grindstaff, 18–28, reports a ten to one ratio of critics to defenders in the press.
47 Josh Gamson, *Freaks Talk Back: Talk Shows and Sexual Nonconformity* (University of Chicago Press, 1998), 18–19, 174; Grindstaff, *The Money Shot*; Sonia Livingstone and Peter Lunt, *Talk on Television: Audience Participation and Public Debate* (London: Routledge, 1994), 62, 76, 87; Peter Lunt and P. Stenner, "The Jerry Springer Show as an Emotional Public Sphere," *Media, Culture and Society* 27 (2005): 59–81. On the venue undercutting the voice, see "Disruptive access," in Harvey Molotch and Marilyn Lester, "News as Purposive Behavior: On the Strategic Use of Routine Events, Accidents, and Scandals," *American Sociological Review* 39 (1974): 101–12.
48 Wayne Munson, *All Talk* (Temple University Press, 1993), 36–8, 41, 47. According to Munson, the level of audience participation has been overestimated. Less than half of one percent of talk show listeners *ever* call. Munson traces participative talk radio back to game shows, amateur hours, and "man in the street"

interviews. See Jason Loviglio, "*Vox Pop*: Network Radio and the Voice of the People," in Hilmes and Lovigolio, eds, *Radio Reader*.

49 On alternative forms of public sphere discourse, see Myra Marx Ferree, "The Political Context of Rational Choice: Rational Choice Theory and Resource Mobilization," in Aldon Morri and Carol Mueller, eds, *Frontiers in Social Movement Theory* (Yale University Press, 1992), 47; Marc W. Steinberg, *Fighting Words: Working-class Formation, Collective Action, and Discourse in Early Nineteenth Century England* (Cornell University Press, 1999), 11–12.

## 5 Mass media, mass man

1 Elaine Tyler May, *Homeward Bound: American Families in the Cold War Era* (New York: Basic Books, 1988); Kenneth Jackson, *Crabgrass Frontier: The Suburbanization of the United States* (Oxford University Press, 1985); Stephanie Coontz, *The Way We Never Were: American Families and the Nostalgia Trap* (New York: Basic Books, 1992).

2 David Goodman, "Programming in the Public Interest: *America's Town Meeting of the Air*," in Michele Hilmes, ed., *NBC: America's Network* (New York: Routledge, 2007).

3 Raymond Williams, *Keywords* (Oxford University Press, 1976), 16–2; Online Etymological Dictionary, http://www.etymonline.com/index.php?term=mass. *The Compact Edition of the Oxford English Dictionary* (Oxford University Press, 1971), 1737, using nineteenth-century sources, lists none of these uses of the term, referring only to "mass meeting" and "mass vote." Everett Rogers, *A History of Communication Study* (New York: Free Press, 1994), 222, claims the term "mass communication" was coined in 1939 by John Marshall of the Rockefeller Foundation.

4 Norman Cousin, "The Time Trap," *Saturday Review of Literature*, December 24, 1949, 20; Jack Gould, "The Low State of TV," *New York Times*, October 19, 1952, X13; n.a. "Television," *Time*, June 19, 1950, 68. On the attractions of television, see Clifton Utley, "How Illiterate Can Television Make Us?," *The Commonweal*, November 19, 1948, 137–9.

5 "The Audience," *Time*, November 8, 1968, 98; John Cogley, "The Country's Whipping Boy," *New Republic*, May 23, 1961, 28–9; Newton Minow, "The Vast Wasteland," speech to the National Association of Broadcasters, May 9, 1961.

6 Van Horne, quoted in S. Frank, "TV Makes Her Tired," *Saturday Evening Post*, June 3, 1961, 27.

7 Calder Willingham, "Television: Giant in the Living Room," *American Mercury*, February 1952, 115; John Tebbel, "What Hath Two Billion Wrought?," *New American Mercury* 72 (1951): 235–8. Other critics contrasted the suspect motives of commercial culture to the authenticity of folk culture (e.g. Ernst Van der Haag, "Of Happiness and of Despair We Have No Measure," in Bernard Rosenberg and David Manning White, eds., *Mass Culture: The Popular Arts in America* (New York: Free Press, 1957), 522.

8 Lucy Liggett, "Biography of Frieda Barkin Hennock," Museum of Broadcast Communications, www.museum.tv/archives; on educational TV, see Joe Alex Morris, "TV Without Terror," *Saturday Evening Post*, March 12, 1955, 32–3, 134–8; Jack Gould, "What TV is doing to us," pamphlet reprint from *New York Times*, June 24–31, 1951.

9 Edward R. Murrow, speech at the annual meeting of the Radio and Television News Directors Association, October 15, 1958.

10 On mass culture critiques, see Alan Swingewood, *The Myth of Mass Culture* (Atlantic Highlands, NJ: Humanities Press, 1977); Patrick Brantlinger, *Bread and Circuses: Theories of Mass Culture as Social Decay* (Cornell University Press, 1983); Paul Gorman, *Left Intellectuals and Popular Culture in Twentieth Century America* (University of North Carolina Press, 1996); Martin Jay, *The Dialectical Imagination: A History of the Frankfurt School* (New York: Little, Brown, 1973), Ch. 6; James Gilbert, *A Cycle of Outrage* (Oxford University Press, 1986), Ch. 7; Michael Denning, "The End of Mass Culture," and discussion, *ILWCH* 37–39 (1990–1991). On blame, see Andreas Huyssen, *After the Great Divide: Modernism, Mass Culture, Postmodernism* (Indiana University Press, 1986); Ann Douglas, *The Feminization of American Culture* (New York: Knopf, 1977); Michael Denning, *Mechanic Accents: Dime Novels and Working-Class Culture in America* (New York: Verso, 1987), Ch. 4.

11 Dwight MacDonald, "A Theory of Popular Culture", *Politics* 1 (1944); Norman Cousins, "The Time Trap," *Saturday Review*, December 24, 1949, 20; Clement Greenberg, "The Plight of Our Culture," *Commentary* 15 (1953): 558–66 and 16 (1953): 54–62; Bernard Rosenberg and David Manning White, *Mass Culture* (New York: Free Press, 1957); Norman Jacobs, *Culture for the Millions* (Boston: Beacon Press, 1959). Many contributors to "Our Country and Our Culture" in *Partisan Review*, May 1952, 281–326, and July 1952, 420–51, saw relatively little danger from mass culture to intellectual life.

12 Newton Minow, "Is TV Cheating Our Children?," *Parents Magazine*, February 1962, 116.

13 Marya Mannes, "Channels: Enlightening the Jerks," *The Reporter*, March 24, 1955, 39; John Harmon, Jr., "Television and the Leisure Time Activities of Children," *Education*, October 1950, 126–8; Jack Gould, "What TV is Doing To Us,"*New York Times*, 1951; n.a., "What TV is Doing to America," *US News and World Report*, September 2, 1955, 36–50; Joel Swerdlow, "What is Television Doing to Real People," *Today's Education*, September 1981, 58–66.

14 William Kornhauser, *The Politics of Mass Society* (New York: Free Press, 1959); Robert Putnam, *Bowling Alone* (New York: Simon and Schuster, 2000).

15 William L. Bird, Jr., *"Better Living": Advertising, Media and the New Vocabulary of Business Leadership, 1935–1955* (Northwestern University Press, 1999); on the public service framing of entertainment programs for television, see Anna McCarthy, "Governing by Television? Public Service Films and the Early TV Archive," *Montage/AV* (Marburg: Schuren Verlag, 2005); also see Lizabeth Cohen, *A Consumer's Republic: The Politics of Mass Consumption in Postwar America* (New York: Knopf, 2003).

16 www.classicthemes.com/50sTVThemes/seriesListA-B.html; Bird, 1999, 195; on steel union issues in the 1950s, see Paul Tiffany, *The Decline of American Steel: How Management, Labor, and Government Went Wrong* (Oxford University Press, 1988); Jack Metzgar, *Striking Steel: Solidarity Remembered* (Temple University Press, 2000).

17 Bird, "Introduction" and p. 17 on the "better living" campaign; http://museum.tv/archives/etv/K/htmlK/krafttelevis/krafttelevis.html.

18 Bird, 44–5, 47, 209.

19 By contrast in the 1920s, Edward Bernays specialized in a two-step process targeting opinion leaders. See Bird, 37.

20 Rosenberg and White, 529, 358–9.
21 Salvador Giner, *Mass Society* (New York: Academic Press, 1976), 117, Ch. 4; Alan Swingewood, *The Myth of Mass Culture* (Atlantic Highlands, NJ: Humanities Press, 1977); Eugene Leach, "Just Atoms Massed Together: The Evolution of Mass Society Theory from Ortega y Gasset to Riesman and Mills," *Mid-America* 71 (1989): 31–49.
22 Eugene Leach, "Just Atoms . . .," *Mid-America* 71 (1989): 31–49. Ironically, in contrast to the critics of the time, Putnam's *Bowling Alone* claims that the 1950s was a "golden era" of civic participation.
23 Edward Shils, "The Theory of Mass Society," in *Center and Periphery: Essays in Macro-sociology* (University of Chicago, 1975), 91; William Kornhauser, *The Politics of Mass Society*, 94, 108–9; David Riesman, *The Lonely Crowd* (Yale University Press, 1950), 176.
24 Gunnar Almgren, "Community," in Edgar Borgatta, *Encyclopedia of Sociology*, Vol. 1 (New York: Macmillan, 1992), 244; Giner, 91; Robert Nisbet, *The Quest for Community: A Study in the Ethics of Order and Freedom* (Oxford University Press, 1953). American literature similarly criticized modernity. See Richard Slotkin, *Gunfighter Nation: The Myth of the Frontier in Twentieth-century America* (New York: Atheneun, 1992).
25 John Keats, *The Crack in the Picture Window* (New York: Houghton Mifflin, 1956); Vance Packard, *The Status Seekers* (New York: David McKay Co., 1959); Sloan Wilson, *The Man in the Gray Flannel Suit*, (New York: Simon and Schuster, 1955), Clare Barnes, *White Collar Zoo* (London; Methuen, 1949) and *White Collar Zoo Revisited* (Garden City, LI: Doubleday, 1961); C. Wright Mills, *White Collar: The American Middle Classes* (Oxford University Press, 1951); William H. Whyte, *The Organization Man*, (New York: Simon and Schuster, 1956); David Reisman, *The Lonely Crowd: A Study of the Changing American Character* (Yale University Press, 1953).
26 Keats, 47, 60, 63, 64; Packard, 269.
27 Herbert Gans, *The Levittowners: Ways of Life and Politics in a New Suburban Community* (New York: Pantheon, 1967). Gans emphasized that his study might not apply to an established older suburb in which residents are not new. The dynamic Gans captured was that of a community entirely of young newcomers, eager to meet and make friends with their neighbors and find playmates for their children.
28 Jack Gould, "What TV is Doing To Us," series of seven articles from June 24–31, 1951, reprinted in booklet by *New York Times*, np. For a recent look at the demise of public places, see Ray Oldenburg, *The Great Good Place: Cafes, Coffee Shops, Community Centers, Beauty Parlors, General Stores, Bars, Hangouts and How They Get You through the Day* (New York: Paragon, 1989).
29 Keats, 79, 81. Interestingly, critics today worry that sameness crucial to national identity is threatened by the replacement of the mass market with niche markets.
30 Gerald Pratley, *The Cinema of John Frankenheimer* (New York: A. S. Barnes,1969).
31 Vance Packard, *The Hidden Persuaders* (New York: Pocket Books Inc., 1958), 1. A list of motivational researchers published by the Advertising Research Foundation in 1954 included prominent psychologists, including Kurt Back, Donald T. Campbell, Raymond Cattell, and Richard Centers. *Directory of Social Scientists Interested in Motivational Research* (New York: Advertising Research Foundation, 1954).

32 Packard, 35–6.

33 Russell Jacoby, *The Last Intellectuals* (New York: Basic Books, 2000). By contrast, in 1952 Philip Rahv saw the integration of the public intellectual into academia with the expansion of higher education in the post-war era as a good thing.

34 Rosalyn Baxandall and Elizabeth Ewen, *Picture Windows: How the Suburbs Happened* (New York: Basic Books, 2001).

## 6 Media effects and passive audiences

1 The categories of audiences conceived as commodities, consumers, receivers (victims), and citizens are borrowed from Oscar Gandy, "The Real Digital Divide: Citizens Versus Consumers," in Leah Lieverouw and Sonia Livingstone, eds, *Handbook of New Media* (London: Sage, 2002), 448, commenting on James Webster and Patricia Phelan, *The Mass Audience: Rediscovering the Dominant Model* (Mahwah, NJ: Erlbaum, 1997).

2 I will not review the numerous critiques of the effects model that have accumulated since the 1970s. See, e.g., Herbert Blumer, "Sociological Analysis and the 'Variable'," *American Sociological Review* 21 (1956): 683–90; Elihu Katz, Jay G. Blumler, and Michael Gurevitch, "Uses and Gratifications Research," *Public Opinion Quarterly* 37 (1973), 509–23; Stuart Hall, "Encoding, Decoding," in Simon During, ed., *The Cultural Studies Reader* (London: Routledge, 1993) 90–103.

3 Jesse Delia, "Communication Research: A History," in Charles Berger and Steven Chaffee, eds, *Handbook of Communication Science* (Thousand Oaks, CA: Sage, 1987), 69.

4 Stanley Cohen, *Folk Devils and Moral Panics*, third edition (New York: Routledge, 2002), xxvi–xxxi; Howard Becker, *Outsiders: Studies in the Sociology of Deviance* (Glencoe, IL: Free Press, 1963), Ch. 8, "Moral Entrepreneurs," 147–63. On the relation of media to moral panics, see Chas Critcher, *Moral Panics and the Media* (Buckingham: Open University Press, 2003). Cohen argues that in recent years moral panics, which are discrete events, have been to a degree displaced by a diffuse "risk society" or "culture of fear" that is pervasive and on-going. See Barbara Adam, Ulrich Beck, and Joost van Loon, eds, *Risk Society and Beyond* (London: Sage, 2000); Barry Glassner, *The Culture of Fear: Why Americans are Afraid of the Wrong Things* (New York: Basic Books, 1999); John Jost, Arie Kruglanski, Jack Glaser, and Frank Sulloway "Political Conservatism as Motivated Social Cognition," *Psychological Bulletin* 129 (2003): 339–75.

5 Michael Denning, *Mechanic Accents: Dime Novels and Working-Class Culture in America* (New York: Verso, 1987), Ch. 4; W. I. Thomas, "The Psychology of the Yellow Journal," *American Magazine*, March 1908, 491.

6 Kirsten Drotner, "Modernity and media panics," in Michael Skovmand and Kim Christian Schroder, eds, *Media Cultures: Reappraising Transnational Media* (London: Routledge, 1992); Martin Barker and Julian Petley, eds, *Ill Effects: The Media/Violence Debate* (London: Routledge, 1997), 156; James Gilbert, *A Cycle of Outrage: America's Reaction to the Juvenile Delinquent in the 1950s* (Oxford University Press, 1986). On definitions of suggestion, see Frances Fenton, "The Influence of Newspaper Presentations upon the Growth of Crime and Other Anti-social Activity," *American Journal of Sociology* 16 (1910): 360–4; Sheron Lowery and

Melvin DeFleur, *Milestones in Mass Communication Research* (New York: Longman, 1983), Chps 5–7. A term that bridged these two periods, but changed conceptually, is the idea of imitation. Compare Gabriel Tarde, *Laws of Imitation*, Elsie Clews Parson, trans. (New York: Henry Holt, 1903) to Albert Bandura and Richard Walters, *Social Learning and Personality Development* (New York: Holt Rinehart and Winston, 1963).

7 David Buckingham, in Barker and Petley,64, 69. Also see Drotner, 56–57; Julian Petley, "Us and Them," in Barker and Petley, 170–85; Herbert Gans, *Popular Culture and High Culture: An Analysis and Evaluation of Taste* (New York: Basic Books, 1974), 61; Geoffrey Pearson, *Hooligan* (New York: Macmillan, 1983).

8 On some aspects of this, see Lauren Berlant, "Live Sex Acts (Parental Advisory: Explicit Material)," in Joan Landes, ed., *Feminism, the Public and the Private* (Oxford University Press, 1998), 285–7.

9 See the eight-volume set of reports published under the series title, *Motion Pictures and Youth*, by Macmillan in 1933, and also Garth Jowett, Ian Jarvie, and Kathryn Fuller, *Children and the Movies: Media Influence and the Payne Fund Controversy* (Cambridge University Press, 1996).

10 Herbert Blumer, *Movies and Conduct* (New York: Macmillan, 1933), 3–11; Herbert Blumer and Philip Hauser, *Movies, Delinquency and Crime* (New York: Macmillan, 1933). Blumer also later gained fame for his opposition to behaviorism's "effects" approach. See his "Sociological Analysis and the 'Variable'."

11 "The Children's Hour," *The Nation*, April 5, 1933, 362; "Mothers Protest 'Bogeyman' on Radio," *New York Times*, February 27, 1933, 17, and "A 'New Deal' for Youth," *New York Times*, September 10, 1933, X, 7; Amanda Bruce, "Strangers in the Living Room: Radio, Television, and American Childhood, 1930–1960," Ph.D. thesis (SUNY, Stony Brook, 2006). By the 1940s, a new movement grew alongside the reform of children's radio, a movement against daytime serials and their effects on less-educated working-class housewives. See Jennifer Hyland Wang, "Clubwomen vs. Drudges: The Battle to Define the Daytime Radio Audience," Transnational Radio Conference, Madison Wisconsin, 2003; Herta Herzog, "What We Really Know About the Day-time Serial Listeners," and Helen Kaufman, "The Appeal of Specific Daytime Serials," both in Paul Lazarsfeld and Frank Stanton, eds, *Radio Research, 1942–43* (New York: Duell, Sloane, 1944), 3–33, 86–107.

12 Neita Oviatt Friend, "A Mother's Viewpoint," *Education By Radio*, May 10, 1934, 17; on the National Advisory Council, see Azriel Eisenberg, *Children and Radio Programs* (New York: Columbia University Press, 1936), 18–21, and its annual proceedings in Levering Tyson, *Radio and Education*, Vols. 1–4 (University of Chicago Press, 1931–1934); "W.C.T.U. Speaker Assails the Radio," *New York Times*, September 12, 1935, 27; on the General Federation, and so on, see "Radio Reforms for Youth, Aim of Joint Drive," *New York Times*, April 30, 1939, II 4; also see "Radio Denounced as Peril to Young," *New York Times*, March 31, 1938, 35; "Radio's Effect on Youth," *New York Times*, November 13, 1938 IX, 12; "Radio Thrillers Scored," *New York Times*, January 25, 1940, 42.

13 Payne Fund Records register, p. 36, Western Reserve Historical Society; Eisenberg, viii, 24–5, 32, 138–9; Frederick Lumley, *Measurement in Radio* (Ohio State University Press, 1934), v; John James De Boer, *The Emotional Responses of*

*Children to Radio Drama* (University of Chicago Libraries, 1940); Herta Herzog, *Children and Their Leisure Time Listening to Radio: A Survey of the Literature in the Field* (Radio Council on Children's Programs, 1941).

14 On applause cards, see Lumley, *Measurement in Radio*; Mark James Banks, "A History of Broadcast Audience Research in the United States, 1920–1980," Ph.D. thesis (University of Tennessee, 1981). Fan mail often emphasized the intimacy of listening, as if they alone were the audience. On intimacy, see Richard Butsch, *The Making of American Audiences from Stage to Television, 1750–1990* (Cambridge University Press, 2000), 213–16. Many radio archives hold collections of applause cards.

15 Daniel Starch, "Revised Study of Radio Broadcasting Covering the Entire United States," National Broadcasting Company, 1930; Hugh Beville, *Audience Ratings: Radio, Television, Cable*, first edition (Mahwah, NJ: Erlbaum, 1985), 29–31, 64–8; W. Phillips Davison, "In Memoriam: Archibald Maddock Crossley, 1896–1985," *Public Opinion Quarterly* 49 (1985): 396–7; Mark James Banks, 28–36, 55–9; Erik Barnouw, *A Tower in Babel: A History of Broadcasting in the United States, Volume 1 – to 1933* (New York: Oxford University, Press, 1966), 270; Karen Buzzard, *Chains of Gold: Marketing the Ratings and Rating the Markets* (Metuchen: Scarecrow Press, 1990), 26. Broadcast audiences are artificially constructed by ratings services. On the other hand, they can constitute imagined and interpretive communities.

16 Hadley Cantril, *The Human Dimension: Experiences in Policy Reearch* (New Brunswick, NJ: Rutgers University Press, 1967), 23; Paul Lazarsfeld, "An Episode in the History of Social Research: A Memoir," in Donald Fleming and Bernard Bailyn eds, *The Intellectual Migration: Europe and America, 1930–1960* (Harvard University Press, 1969), 279, 295, 297, 310, 327, 332, and acknowledgments in Lazarsfeld's publications.

17 Michael Sproule, *Propaganda and Democracy* (Cambridge University Press, 1997), 65; Jum C. Nunnally, *Psychometric Theory* (New York: McGraw-Hill, 1967).

18 Lazarsfeld, in Fleming and Bailyn, 310; Paul Lazarsfeld, Bernard Berelson, and Hazel Gaudet, *The People's Choice* (Columbia University Press, 1948); Elihu Katz and Paul Lazarsfeld, *Personal Influence* (New York: Free Press 1955); Peter Simonson, special editor, "Politics, Social Networks, and the History of Mass Communications Research: Rereading *Personal Influence*," *Annals of the American Academy of Political and Social Science* 108 (2006); Elihu Katz, "Diffusion Research at Columbia," in Everette Dennis and Ellen Wartella, eds, *American Communication Research: The Remembered History* (Mahwah, NJ: Erlbaum, 1996), 63. Lazarsfeld's student and co-author, Elihu Katz, would keep this focus on interaction alive in his uses and gratifications paradigm. See Katz, "Uses and Gratifications," *Public Opinion Quarterly* 37 (1973): 509–23. Lazarsfeld also recognized the importance of measuring long-term and broad effects on audiences that would become the central concern of "cultivation analysis" developed by George Gerbner in the 1970s.

19 See Everett Rogers, *A History of Communication Study* (New York: Free Press, 1994), Ch. 6, on the shift from qualitative to quantitative study in propaganda analysis. Groundwork for this mobilization was laid before the war. In 1939, the Rockefeller Foundation funded a seminar of prominent researchers to conceive a new field of communications research. With Germany's invasion of Poland, the seminar turned to proposing how the U.S. government could use communications in the coming

war effort and focused the discussions around effects research. In January 1941, the Foundation organized an exclusive conference between communication scholars and government officials to discuss government use of communication. Rogers, 224–7.

20 National Archive, Records of the War Department General and Special Staffs, records group 165.14, History; Samuel Stouffer, Edward Suchman, Leland DeVinney, Shirley Star, and Robin Williams, Jr., *The American Soldier: Adjustment During Army Life*, Vol. 1 (Princeton University Press, 1949), xi–xii, 9–10, 22–7.

21 Stouffer et al., *The American Soldier*, Vol. 3, v–vi ; Vol. 1, 31, 51. Subject variables internal to the individual being studied may appear to consider the person as actively shaping his own behavior, but are conceived as other pre-determined conditions within the individual and not as agency.

22 Compare names in the preface to Carl I. Hovland, Irving L. Janis, and Harold H. Kelley, *Communication and Persuasion; Psychological Studies of Opinion Change* (Yale University Press, 1953) and cited in William McGuire, "Attitude Change," in Elliott Aronson and Gardner Lindzey, *Handbook of Social Psychology*, third edition (Reading, MA: Addison-Wesley, 1968), 136–314, to those listed in *The American Soldier*, Vol. 1, xi–xii, 22–7.

23 On OWI, see Everett Rogers, 13–15; Charles Siepmann, "American Radio in Wartime," in Lazarsfeld and Stanton, 111–50; Allan Winkler, *The Politics of Propaganda: The Office of War Information, 1942–1945* (Yale University Press, 1978).

24 Rogers, 11–15; Jacqueline Marie Cartier, "Wilbur Schramm and the Beginnings of American Communication Theory," Ph.D. thesis (University of Iowa, 1988), 170–5.

25 Timothy Glander, *The Origins of Mass Communication Research* (Mahwah, NJ: Erlbaum, 2000), 76; Rogers, 446–7; Cartier, 170–81; on research at Schramm's Illinois Institute, see Glander, 154–72; Schramm quote from Glander, 176, fn 83; also Rogers, 453; quote from Rogers, 459–60.

26 Joseph T. Klapper, "Children and Television—A Review of Socially Prevalent Concerns," Bureau of Applied Social Research report, Columbia University, 1953, 3–4, 7. Magazine articles mostly reassured parents that TV was not as bad as they feared, and recommended moderate and selective use.

27 Hearings before the Subcommittee to Investigate Juvenile Delinquency of the Committee on the Judiciary U.S. Senate 84th Congress first session, *Television Programs* (US Government Printing Office, 1955); for a summary on Congressional investigation into effects of television, see Sandra Ball and Robert K. Baker, *Violence and the Media, Mass Media Hearings* v 9A, report to the National Commission on the Causes and Prevention of Violence, 1969, 393–7. The only survey conducted by CBS was Gary Steiner, *The People Look at Television* (New York: Knopf, 1963), which did not examine effects of television on children but, in the words of the author, parents' self-report on their own "beliefs, attitudes and behavior with respect to the television set vis-à-vis the child," p. 82. On the Kefauver hearings, see James Gilbert, *A Cycle of Outrage* (Oxford University Press 1986), Ch. 9.

28 Dodd quotes from Ball and Baker, 395. The Joint Committee ultimately funded research in 1971, which concluded that violence on television does not cause violent behavior. See Seymour Feshbach and Robert Singer, *Television and Aggression: An Experimental Field Study* (San Francisco: Jossey-Bass, 1971), xv, 145.

29 The Surgeon General's Scientific Advisory Committee on Television and Social Behavior, *Television and Growing Up: The Impact of Television Violence*, Report to the Surgeon General USGPO, 1972, 21–2.

30 A second Surgeon General report was published in 1982 and received far less attention. See David Pearl, Lorraine Bouthilet, and Joyce Lazar, eds, *Television and Behavior: Ten Years of Scientific Progress and Implications for the Eighties*, Vol. II, Technical Reviews (Washington, DC: U.S. Department of Health and Human Services, NIMH).

## 7 Boob tubes, fans, and addicts: pathological audiences

1 Affluent young girls swooning over matinee idols appear in the late nineteenth century, but the references characterize this as adolescent romanticism rather than pathology.

2 On the origin of the term couch potato in the 1970s, see David K. Barnhart and Allan A. Metcalf, *America in So Many Words* (New York: Houghton Mifflin, 1997). According to Answer.com, the term boob tube originated in the 1960s. Researchers labeled such people "heavy viewers" rather than "frequent" or "extensive" or "intensive," suggesting something negative as in heavy drug use.

3 Robert Rice, "Onward and Upward with the Arts: Diary of a Viewer," *New Yorker*, August 30, 1947, 44–55; Wallace Markfield, "Oh Mass Man! Oh Lumpen Lug! Why Do You Watch TV?" *Saturday Evening Post*, November 30, 1968, 28–9, 72.

4 See cartoons in "The New Cyclops," *Business Week* March 10, 1956, 76–94; Charles Preston, *The $64,000,000 Answer* (New York: Berkley Publishing, 1955); Steven Pettinga, *The Best Cartoons of the* Saturday Evening Post (Grand Rapids, MI: Zondervan Publishing, 1993); Paul Ritts, *The TV Jeebies* (Philadelphia: John C Winston Co., 1951); and the television cartoons file of the New York Public Library Picture Collection. Robert Mankoff, ed., *The Complete Cartoons of the New Yorker* (New York: Black Dog and Leventhal, 2004), which includes searchable CDs of all cartoons published in the magazine from 1925 to 2004.

5 Science writer Joel Swerdlow, in "What is Television Doing to Real People?," *Today's Education*, September 1981, 58, suggested that the negative traits attributed to heavy viewing pre-existed in "people at the lower end of the income/education ladder." That image is now being publicly contested and rejected by white trash studies and Appalachian studies, by the Republican Party political machine, and by the very successful Blue Collar Comedy Tour, which, like past ethnic comedians, make fun of their own kind, while at the same time expressing pride in their subculture. Academic research also differed in neglecting adult viewers and focusing on children's television viewing, about which there was more public concern and eventually generous government funding.

6 Leo Bogart, *The Age of Television: A Study Viewing Habits and the Impact of Television on American Life*, third edition (New York: Frederick Ungar, 1972); Joseph Klapper, *The Effects of Mass Communication* (New York: Free Press, 1960); Ira Glick and Sidney Levy, *Living with Television* (New York: Aldine, 1962); Gary Steiner, *The People Look at Television: A Study of Audience Attitudes* (New York: Knopf, 1963). Bogart (xl, xliv) was a researcher at McCann-Erickson advertising agency; he declared television a "wholly neutral instrument in human hands." Klapper's (xi–xii) survey of existing

research was supported by a grant from CBS. Glick and Levy (15–16, 229–30) used their marketing studies for McCann Erickson, Campbell-Ewald, and other advertising agencies. *The People Look at Television* (x–xiii) was funded by CBS. One of the earliest studies to distinguish heavy from light viewers was Thomas Coffin, 1952, under contract to NBC. See Bogart, 1972, 68.

7 Bogart, 108; Glick and Levy, *Living with Television*, Part Two. Bogart's book was originally published in 1956 and reissued in 1958 and 1972. Bogart's equation of wealth with mental resources went beyond Hadley Cantril's and Herbert Blumer's beliefs in formal education as a prerequisite to proper media use.

8 Wilbur Schramm, Jack Lyle, and Edwin Parker, *Television in the Lives of Our Children* (Stanford University Press, 1961), 35, 47, 63–4, 98–9, 109, 112, 117. See Everett Rogers, *A History of Communication Study* (New York: Free Press, 1994), 471, on its influence. Two other television research pioneers, Eleanor Maccoby and Hilda Himmelweit, also expressed similar views. See Schramm et al., 109–11.

9 Joli Jensen, "Fandom as Pathology: The Consequences of Characterization," in Lisa Lewis, ed., *The Adoring Audience: Fan Culture and Popular Media* (New York: Routledge, 1992), 9–29; Kathryn Fuller, *At the Picture Show: Small Town Audiences and the Creation of Movie Fan Culture* (Smithsonian Institution Press, 1996), Ch. 6; Thomas Brady, "Hollywood Resume: Fans Out," *New York Times*, April 6, 1947, X5; Samantha Barbas, *Movie Crazy: Fans, Stars and the Cult of Celebrity* (New York: Palgrave, 2001), 172, illustration 15; David Dempsey, "Why the Girls Scream, Weep, Flip," *New York Times Magazine*, February 23, 1964, 15, 69–71; James Thurber, "The Listening Women," *The New Yorker*, July 24, 1948, 63–8; Herta Herzog, "What Do We Really Know about Daytime Serial Listeners," in Paul Lazarsfeld and Frank Stanton, eds, *Radio Research 1942–43* (New York: Duell Sloan Pierce, 1944), 3–33; C. Lee Harrington and Denise Bielby, *Soap Fans: Pursuing Pleasure and Making Meaning* (Philadelphia: Temple University Press, 1995), 1–2; also see Pertti Alasuutari, "I'm Ashamed to Admit It, But I Have Watched *Dallas*," *Media, Culture and Society* 14 (1992): 561–82.

10 George Humphrey, "Do the Movies Help or Harm Us?," *Collier's*, May 24, 1924, 5. See cartoon depictions of media addiction in *The New Yorker*, October 29, 1949, 69; May 17, 1969, 46; May 16, 1977, 45; *Saturday Evening Post*, April 10, 1965, 80; Preston, Ch. 6, 7.

11 Ronald Akers, "Addiction, the Troublesome Concept," *Journal of Drug Issues* 21 (1991): 777; G. D. Walters, *The Addiction Concept* (New York: Allyn & Bacon, 1999; *Webster's New Twentieth Century Dictionary*, second edition (World Publishing 1968), 22; *Webster's New World Dictionary, College Edition*, 1966, 16; *Compact Edition of the Oxford English Dictionary* (Oxford University Press, 1971), 103–4; *Alcoholics Anonymous* (New York: Works Publishing, 1939), 37; on cycles of acceptance to condemnation, see Joseph Gusfield, *Contested Meanings: The Construction of Alcohol Problems* (University of Wisconsin Press, 1996), 192–3; David Musto, ed., *Drugs in America: A Documentary History* (New York University Press, 2002), 3.

12 *Diagnostic and Statistical Manual: Mental Disorders* (Washington, DC: American Psychiatric Association, 1952), 39; *DSM II*, 1968, 45; *DSM III*, 1980; *DSM IV*, 1994. For a lay history of the change to behavioral descriptions in the 1980 edition, see Alix Spiegel, "The Dictionary of Disorder," *The New Yorker*, January 3, 2005, 56–63; Virginia Berridge and Griffith Edwards, *Opium and the People: Opiate Use in*

*Nineteenth Century England* (Yale University Press, 1987), discuss the historical substitution of dependence for addiction in England.

13 Akers, "Addiction, the Troublesome Concept;" Stanton Peele, *The Meaning of Addiction: Compulsive Experience and Its Interpretation* (Lexington, MA: D. C. Heath, 1985), xi, 1; *DSM II*, 45. Compulsion is an urge to repeat certain behaviors to stave off an unpleasant condition, such as anxiety, not to obtain the pleasurable stimulus of an addictive substance.

14 David Musto, *The American Disease: Origins of Narcotics Control* (Yale University Press, 1987); David Musto, ed., *Drugs in America: A Documentary History* (New York University Press, 2002); Timothy Hickman, "Drugs and Race in American Culture," *American Studies* 41 (2000): 71–91; Jill Jonnes, *Hep Cats, Narcs and Pipe Dreams* (Johns Hopkins University Press, 1996).

15 Eve Kosofsky Sedgewick, "Epidemics of the Will," in *Tendencies* (New York: Routledge 1994); also see Mariana Valverde, *Diseases of the Will: Alcohol and the Dilemmas of Freedom* (Cambridge University Press, 1998); Jacque Derrida, "The Rhetoric of Drugs," *Differences: A Journal of Feminist Cultural Studies* 5 (1993): 1–25

16 Paul Lazarsfeld and Robert Merton, "Mass Communication, Popular Taste and Organized Social Action," in Lyman Bryson, ed., *The Communication of Ideas: A Series of Addresses* (New York: Harper Bros, 1948), 105–6; Herta Herzog, "Children and their Leisure Time Listening," in *Radio Research* (New York: Radio Council on Children's Programs, 1941), 73. On the few occasions it was used, it was done metaphorically or humorously, such as when the editor of the reform magazine *Outlook* confessed to being "reasonably addicted" to movies. See "The Spectator [editorial]," *Outlook*, January 25, 1913, 230.

17 *Coronet*, February 1955, 38–40; Corey Ford, "How to Give Up TV," *Reader's Digest*, March 1955, 62–4.

18 Eleanor Maccoby, "Why Children Watch Television," *Public Opinion Quarterly* 15 (1951): 443; Schramm et al., 167–8. English television audience research pioneer Hilda Himmelweit made a similar observation, labeling 30 percent of the heaviest viewers as addicts. See Himmelweit, A. N. Oppenheim, and Pamela Vince, *Television and the Child* (Oxford University Press, 1958), 28–9. Two papers by medical professionals mentioned TV addiction: J. A. M. Meerlo, "Television Addiction and Reactive Apathy," *Journal of Nervous and Mental Disease* 120 (1954): 29–91; and E. D. Glynn, "Television and the American Character: A Psychiatrist Looks at Television," in W. Y. Elliot, ed., *Television's Impact on American Culture* (Michigan State University Press, 1956). The AMA made a public statement in 1952 about the dangers of television programs to children, but included no mention of addiction: "Influence of TV Crime Program on Children's Mental Health," *Journal of the American Medical Association* 150 (1952): 37.

19 Robert Goldenson, "Television and Our Children: The Experts Speak Up," *Parents Magazine* December (1954): 36–7, 76, 78–81.

20 Leo Rosten, "Don't Just Sit There—Reach for the Switch," *Reader's Digest*, January 1962, 197–8.

21 Robert Alan Aurthur, "Farewell, farewell TV. . .," *The Nation*, March 4, 1961, 184; Markfield, 28–9, 72; Thomas Meehan, "Add Hot Water; Serves Fourteen Million," *The New Yorker*, March 28, 1964, 35–7; Robert Lewis Shayon, "Father Television Knows Best," *Saturday Review*, December 5, 1964, 42; "The Habit,"

*Time*, March 26, 1965, 52, 57. "Videophobes," *Time*, November 8, 1968, 98, examined those who refused to watch.

22 Marie Winn, *The Plug-in Drug* (New York: Viking Press, 1977); Elizabeth Crow, editor-in-chief, "Turn It Off!," *Parents Magazine*, June 1981, 4; Joan Anderson, *Breaking the TV Habit* (New York: Scribner, 1982); David Demers, *Breaking Your Child's TV Addiction* (Minneapolis: Marquette Books, 1989); Joan Anderson and Robin Wilkins, *Getting Unplugged: Taking Control of Your Family's Television, Video Game and Computer Habits* (New York: Wiley, 1998); Kimberly Young, *Caught in the Net: How to Recognize the Signs of Internet Addiction—and a Winning Strategy for Recovery* (New York: Wiley, 1998); D. N. Greenfield, *Virtual Addiction* (Oakland, CA: New Harbinger Publishers, 1999); Cheryl Pawlowski, *Glued to the Tube: The Threat of Television Addiction to Today's Family* (Napierville, IL: Sourcebooks Inc, 2000); Judith Wright, *There Must be More Than This: Finding More Life, Love and Meaning by Overcoming Your Soft Addictions* (New York: Broadway Books, 2005). See articles: Margo Trott "Better Health with a Twist of the Wrist," *Prevention* November (1991):, 41–3, 116–21; Mary Williams Walsh, "Just Say 'No' to TV Addiction, Activists Urge," *Los Angeles Times*, June 23, 1992, H4; Pam Belluck, "The Symptoms of Internet Addiction," *New York Times*, December 1, 1996, E5; Stephanie Wood, "Mommie Strategies," *Redbook*, April, 1998, 140; "Are You a Netaholic?," *Redbook*, February 1999, 48; Rebecca Buckman, "These Days On-Line Trading Can Become an Addiction," *Wall Street Journal*, February 1 1999, C1; Emily Prager, "The Day the TV Died," *Redbook*, May 1999, 88; Amy Dickinson, "Kick the TV Habit," *Time*, July 17, 2000, 81. Some enterprising programmers even marketed software to control children's video game addiction. See *Advertising Age*, "Kicking the TV Habit," 65 (1994): 50.

23 Marie Winn, *The Plug-in Drug* (New York: Viking, 1977), reprinted by Penguin, 1985, vii, 3–4, 20–1; *Unplugging the Plug-in Drug* (New York: Penguin, 1987); *The Plug-In Drug: Television, Computers and Family Life* (New York: Penguin, 2002, 25th anniversary edition); Jerome and Dorothy Singer, *Television, Imagination and Aggression* (Hillsdale, NJ: Erlbaum), 1981, 8; Anderson, 1982; Demers, 1989.

24 For examples, see J. Skow, "Games that Play People: Those Beeping Video Invaders are Dazzling, Fun—and Even Addictive," *Time*, January 18; "Video Games—Fun or Serious Threat," *US News and World Report*, February 22, 1982; Daniel Goleman, "How Viewers Grow Addicted to Watching TV," *New York Times*, October 16, 1990, C1, 8; Mary Williams Walsh, "Just Say 'No!' to TV Addiction," *Los Angeles Times*, June 23, 1992, H4; Joshua Quittner, "Are Video Games Really So Bad?," *Time*, May 10, 1999, 50–4. Books include David N. Greenfield, *Virtual Addiction* (Oakland, CA: New Harbinger, 1999); Cheryl Pawlowski, *Glued to the Tube* (Naperville, IL: Sourcebooks Inc., 2000); and Young, 2000. For a study of news magazine reports on video games use, see Dmitri Williams, "The Video Game Lightning Rod," *Information, Communication & Society* 6 2003, 523–50. See cartoon in *The New Yorker*, May 28, 2001, 107.

25 Stanton Peele, *The Meaning of Addiction: Compulsive Experience and Its Interpretation* (Lexington, MA: Lexington Books, 1985); Stanton Peele, ed., *Visions of Addiction* (Lexington, MA: Lexington Books, 1988); Ronald Akers, "Addiction the Troublesome Concept," *Journal of Drug Issues* 21 (1991): 777–93; G. D. Walters, *The Addiction Concept* (New York: Allyn Bacon, 1999).

26 On media addiction, see Robin Smith, "Television Addiction," in Jennings Bryant and Dolf Zillman, eds, *Perspectives on Media Effects* (Hillsdale, NJ: Erlbaum, 109–28, 1986; Robert McIlwraith, Robin Smith Jacobvitz, Robert Kubey, and Alison Alexander, "Television Addiction," *American Behavioral Scientist* 35 (1991): 104–21; Robert Kubey, "Television Dependence, Diagnosis and Prevention," in Tannis MacBeth, ed., *Tuning into Young Viewers: Social Science Perspectives on Television* (Thousand Oaks, CA: Sage, 1996), 221–60; Robert McIlwraith, "'I'm Addicted to Television': The Personality, Imagination and TV Watching Patterns of Self-identified TV Addicts," *Journal of Broadcasting* 42 (1998): 371–86; Robert Kubey, "Television Addiction is No Mere Metaphor," *Scientific American* 286 (2002): 74–80; George Keepers, "Pathological Preoccupation with Video Games," *Journal of American Academy of Child and Adolescent Psychiatry* 29 (1990): 49–50; S. Fisher, 'Identifying Video Game Addiction in Children," *Addictive Behavior* 19 (1994): 545–53. More skeptical reports include Mark Griffiths, "Internet Addiction: Does It Really Exist?," in J. Gackenbach, *Psychology and the Internet* (New York: Academic Press, 1998), 61–75; H. Shaffer, M. Hall, and J. Vanderbilt, "Computer Addiction: A Critical Consideration," *Journal of Orthopsychiatry* 70 (2000): 162–8; A. Hall, "Internet Addiction," *Journal of Mental Health Counseling* 23 (2001): 312–27.

27 For critiques, see Seth Finn, "Television 'Addiction?' An Evaluation of Four Competing Media-use Models," *Journalism Quarterly* 68 (1992): 422–35; K. Pedzek, "Is Watching TV Passive, Uncreative or Addictive? Debunking Some Myths," *Television & Families* 8 (1988): 41–6; Robert LaRose, Carolyn Lin, and Matthew Easton, "Unregulated Internet Usage: Addiction, Habit or Deficient Self-regulation?," *Media Psychology* 5 (2003): 225–53; Cary Horvath, "Measuring Television Addiction," *Journal of Broadcasting* September 2004, 378–98.

28 Robert Putnam, *Bowling Alone* (New York: Simon and Schuster, 2000).

## Epilogue

1 William Graebner, *Coming of Age in Buffalo* (Temple University Press 1990); James Gilbert, *A Cycle of Outrage: America's Reaction to the Juvenile Delinquent in the 1950s* (Oxford University Press, 1986). The moral panic even led to Congressional investigations, linking delinquency to working-class youth and to mass media. See U.S. Congress, Senate Committee on the Judiciary, Subcommittee to Investigate Juvenile Delinquency, *Interim Reports* (Washington, DC: USGPO, 1955–56). Even *Variety* objected, writing, "Swing never had the moral threat of rock 'n' roll which is founded on an unabashed pitch for sex." See "A Warning," *Variety*, February 23, 1955, 2. The music industry responded by manufacturing more manageable music stars such as Fabian, Frankie Avalon, and Pat Boone under their full control. See Grace Palladino, *Teenagers: An American History* (New York: Basic books, 1996), 127, 155–6; Ed Ward, *Rock of Ages: The* Rolling Stone *History of Rock & Roll* (New York: Simon and Schuster, 1986), 129, John Jackson, *Big Beat Heat: Alan Freed and the Early Years of Rock & Roll* (New York: Schirmer Books, 1991), 95–8; Jeff Greenfield, *No Peace, No Place: Excavations Along the Generational Fault* (Garden City, NY: Doubleday, 1973), 37.

2 Vanderbilt University Television News Archive on-line search of network evening news for 1968 to 2000. When a heavy metal concert in Montreal in 1992 was cut

short, several thousand rioted. News photos featured street wreckage, including a police car turned upside down (Bettman audience file). Another Montreal punk concert, in 2003, led to a street riot—overturning cars and smashing store windows—by some when it was cancelled. Jesse McKinley, "Divining the Wellspring of Rage That Incited Montreal Punk Riot," *New York Times*, October 20, 2003, E1, 5.

3 Not all incidents were due to audience agency. Poor crowd management led to crowds rushing the doors for unreserved seats and resulted in deaths and injuries in Cincinnati in 1979 and again in Salt Lake City in 1991, similar to the crowd problem at Rudolph Valentino's funeral in 1926. Paul Wertheimer, "The American Experience: Rock Concert Safety," Crowd Management Strategies Inc, 1993.

4 Paul Zielbauer, "Fans Rampage in Last Hours of Music Show," *New York Times*, July 26, 1999, B1, 8; Zielbauer, "Woodstock Festival Faces a Bad Hangover," *New York Times*, July 27, 1999, B1, 5; "Moshing and Looting," *Rolling Stone*, September 9, 1999, 55; Neil Strauss, "New Spirit of Woodstock," *New York Times*, July 26, 1999, New York and region; Zielbauer, "Inquiry Pressed into Reported Rapes at Woodstock," *New York Times*, July 30 1999, B1; Strauss, "On Night Music Died, Many to Blame for Mayhem," *New York Times*, July 27, 1999, B5; "When 'Ready To Rock' Becomes Ready to Riot," *US News and World Report*, September 6, 1999, 59; also *ABC Nightline*, July 5, 1999; "Security is the Issue for this Concert Season," *Billboard*, June 24, 2000, 1.

5 "How to Control the College Football Crowd," *New York Times*, November 30, 2002, A17; "Browns Look to Clean Up After their Fans' Mess," *New York Times*, December 18, 2001, S1, 3; John Branch, "For N.F.L., Crowd Noise Has Become a Headache," *New York Times*, September 24, 2006, 1, 29.

6 Thomas Strychacz, "American Sports Writers and 'Unruly Rooters': The Significance of Orderly Spectating," *Journal of American Studies* 28 (1994): 89. These issues were also expressed in British discourse on soccer fans. See Adam Brown, ed., *Fanatics: Power, Identity and Fandom in Football* (London: Routledge, 1998); "White Youths in Search of Mayhem," *The Guardian*, February 17, 1995, 3. On civility, see one recent example in Bob Morris, "Age of Dissonance: The Royal Me," *New York Times*, June 3, 2007.

7 Chris Anderson, *The Long Tail: Why The Future of Business is Selling Less of More* (New York: Hyperion, 2006); Jeff Leeds, "The New Tastemakers," *New York Times*, September 3, 2006, AR1, 19; David Gauntlett, ed., *Web Studies: Rewiring Media Studies for the Digital Age* (London: Arnold, 2000); Virginia Nightingale and Tim Dwyer, *New Media Worlds: The Challenges for Convergence* (Melbourne: Oxford University Press, 2007).

8 Lawrence Lessig, *The Future of Ideas: The Fate of the Commons in a connected World* (New York: Random House, 2001).

9 John Clarke, "Populism vs Pessimism: The Problematic Politics of Popular Culture," in Richard Butsch, ed., *For Fun and Profit: The Transformation of Leisure into Consumption* (Philadelphia: Temple University Press, 1990), 28-44; Stephen Kline, "Is it Time to Rethink Media Panics?," in Jens Qvortrup, ed., *Studies in Modern Childhood: Society, Agency, Culture* (London: Palgrave, 2005); but also see FlowTV.org archives, June 2005 issue.

10 Fernando Bermejo, *The Internet Audience: Constitution and Measurement* (New York: Peter Lang, 2007).

11 Erica Goode, "Struggling to Make Sense Out of Boy-Turned-Killer," *New York Times*, March 2, 2000, A25; William Glaberson, "Finding Futility in Trying to Lay Blame in Killings," *New York Times*, August 4, 2000, A1, 17; Todd Purdum, "Plenty of Vivid Adjectives But No Answers in Killings," *New York Times*, March 7, 2001, A1, 14; Marc Santora, "Student Opens Fire at a High School Near Albany," *New York Times*, February 10, 2004, B5; Kate Zernike, "Experts Debate the Sniper's Links to Popular Culture," *New York Times*, October 11, 2002, A28; reports on school shootings in the 1990s in the Vanderbilt University Television News Archive on-line.

# Index